88 PRI

"This book is exceptional on a number of levels. Well-written and logically constructed, it draws upon the experience of the authors to provide a roadmap for addressing day-to-day privacy issues at a pragmatic level. The book is directed primarily at people in business who have a responsibility for handling information, and provides direction in the form of guidelines, checklists and practical examples. Although aimed primarily at laypersons, lawyers will also find this book extremely useful as a means of advising their clients as to how best to achieve legal compliance. The book is quite unique in the approach it adopts, and should prove to be an invaluable addition to the library of anyone involved in – or even just interested in – the adoption of best practice in the handling of data in the 'information age'."

— **Gordon Hughes, Partner, Davies Collison Cave, Melbourne, author of *Data Protection in Australia*, and co-author of *Private Life in a Digital World***

"Much has been written previously for compliance officers, privacy professionals and lawyers about data protection laws in Singapore, Malaysia and the region. But this handbook is for the layperson – easy to read and practical. It fills in many gaps and answers many questions about how to comply with the law as well as the do's and don'ts in day-to-day business operations. Now that I've seen it, I wonder why something like this wasn't produced years ago. There is now no reason why anyone involved in processing personal data should say that they don't know what to do to protect the personal information of those under their care."

— **Professor Abu Bakar Muni, author of *Data Protection Law in Asia*, Professor of Law, University of Malaya, and Associate Fellow at the Malaysian Centre for Regulatory Studies (UMCoRS)**

"This book achieves a rare feat: making personal data protection practical, understandable and actionable. It is a valuable resource for marketers at all levels, and we recommend it as a reference to all our members."

— **Lisa Watson, Chairman, Direct Marketing Association of Singapore**

"In this book, Shepherdson, Hioe and Boxall do three things very well. First, they focus on the very important topic of personal data protection and data privacy, and clarify how data protection, information security and data privacy protection are interrelated. Second, they explain data protection and privacy in the context of how real-world organisations actually function and how people get their work done on a day-to-day basis. This makes it easy for any type of administrator, professional, manager or executive to understand the contents of this book and relate to it. Third, from the perspective of education, learning and cognition, this book is designed in a very clever way so that it is delightfully fast and easy to find exactly what you are looking for, and to grasp what you need to understand about whatever specific aspect of data protection and privacy you need to clarify. As such, this book can be used as a handy 'on-demand' reference at the time of need. Or, you can read it cover to cover, and then keep referring to the relevant chapters 'on-demand' as the need arises."
— **Professor Steven Miller, Dean, School of Information Systems, Singapore Management University**

"As discussed in this book, taking an operational compliance approach is the responsible and most effective approach to achieve ongoing and demonstrable compliance while minimising the chances of a breach. This book provides an excellent review of privacy by looking at the principles of privacy from the perspective of an information life cycle. This perspective provides a structure to enable truly practical guidance, and as you can ascertain from the title of the book, it delves into privacy at a granular level, providing structured guidance to privacy professionals."
— **Terry McQuay, CIPP, CIPM, President, Nymity Inc.**

"This book helps provide real-life illustrations to walk business leaders through the choices they will have to make in designing their products, services and processes whilst keeping privacy in mind. As 'being reasonable' is one of the requirements in the PDPA (Personal Data Protection Act), it is no longer just about obtaining consent, but knowing how to properly balance privacy obligations with business desires."
— **Ken Chia, Principal, Baker McKenzie.Wong & Leow**

88 PRIVACY BREACHES TO BEWARE OF

88 PRIVACY BREACHES
TO BEWARE OF
Practical Data Protection Tips from Real-Life Experiences

Kevin Shepherdson
William Hioe & Lyn Boxall

© 2016 Kevin Shepherdson and Marshall Cavendish International (Asia) Pte Ltd

Published in 2016 by Marshall Cavendish Business
An imprint of Marshall Cavendish International
1 New Industrial Road, Singapore 536196

Other Marshall Cavendish Offices:
Marshall Cavendish Corporation. 99 White Plains Road, Tarrytown NY 10591–9001, USA • Marshall Cavendish International (Thailand) Co Ltd. 253 Asoke, 12th Flr, Sukhumvit 21 Road, Klongtoey Nua, Wattana, Bangkok 10110, Thailand • Marshall Cavendish (Malaysia) Sdn Bhd, Times Subang, Lot 46, Subang Hi-Tech Industrial Park, Batu Tiga, 40000 Shah Alam, Selangor Darul Ehsan, Malaysia.

Marshall Cavendish is a trademark of Times Publishing Limited

National Library Board, Singapore Cataloguing-in-Publication Data:
Name(s): Shepherdson, Kevin Linus. | Hioe, William, author. | Boxall, Lyn, author.
Title: 88 privacy breaches to beware of : practical data protection tips from real-life experiences / Kevin Shepherdson, William Hioe & Lyn Boxall.
Description: Singapore : Marshall Cavendish Business, 2016.
Identifier(s): OCN 945629116 | ISBN 978-981-47-2198-1 (paperback)
Subject(s): LCSH: Data protection. | Business—Data processing—Security measures. | Computer security.
Classification: LCC HF5548.37 | DDC 658.478—dc23

Printed in Singapore by Fabulous Printers Pte Ltd

Contents

Section C:
Usage of Personal Data

Section D:
Data Accuracy & Integrity

Section E:
Physical & Environmental Security

Foreword

by Dr Toh See Kiat

In 1980, the OECD formulated its eight principles of data protection. In 1984, the UK came out with one of the first pieces of legislation in the world that dealt with data protection. I was in London in 1985, starting on my PhD in cyberlaw. You can imagine that it was an exciting time to begin research and study in this new legal milieu. In 1991, I obtained my PhD, the year the English Court of Appeals (in the case of *Kaye v Robertson* [1991] FSR 62) denied that there was a common law right to privacy.

The European Union came out with its data protection Directive in 1995 and this resulted in the UK reforming its law with the passing of the Data Protection Act 1998. I remember there was much excitement on this topic in Southeast Asia too as Malaysia and Singapore went neck to neck on moves to be the first SEA country to enact a data protection law. I remember that my former Parliamentary colleague, Professor Chin Tet Yung, even went as far as drafting a Data Protection Act for Singapore. Why, you may ask, did Singapore then take 32 years to introduce data protection laws when for the most part it has been running with the head of the pack in legislation to support an IT-savvy Smart Nation?

The answer is simply this: running with the head of the pack is not the same as leading the pack. It is impossible for a small nation like Singapore to lead world practice and laws. In most of our legal reforms, we have modelled our laws on the laws (and draft laws) of the US, the UK and the United Nations Commission for International Trade Law. In the area of data protection, however, there was no clear leader. The

Government decided to wait for more certainty in the world before it passed its own legislation.

In 1995, the Canadian Standards Association drafted a data privacy self-regulation regime that was so effective that the Canadian Federal Government adopted it as legislation in its Personal Information Protection and Electronic Documents Act (PIPEDA) 2000. That law was promptly accepted by the European Union as equivalent to EU law. Encouraged by that private sector initiative, Singapore drafted a Model Data Protection Code that was adopted as a self-regulatory system by businesses in Singapore.

The idea at that time was to follow the Canadian model of a private sector self-regulation system that would be business-friendly but yet robust and internationally recognised. It was particularly attractive because the Canadian model had been accepted and endorsed by the EU. We did not want a Singapore legal regime to be out of line with international best practice. Worse still, we did not want the Singapore protection regime to be rejected by the EU, a key trading partner. I sat for many years on the National Trust Council that implemented the Model Data Protection Code and associated principles of safe and trusted e-commerce. Having learned from the various data protection frameworks of the developed world, Singapore passed its own Personal Data Protection Act in 2012.

Government and businesses have realised that privacy practice is often a different creature from the law. As a global lawyer who has studied and practised in the area of privacy and data protection law in different countries for three decades now, I have often wondered when someone would write a book like this in Singapore. Dealing with the legal issues, I tell clients, is often only taking care of the final line of defence. In other words, there are many things that organisations must review to make sure they do not flout the law: the organisational culture, the time-honoured practices, the training processes, the human resource policies, etc.

For many years before Singapore had its own law, I was always urging clients to clean up their act so that a data breach would not damage their profits or reputations. This is because in a world where privacy concerns become more prominent and the demand for more stringent protections becomes standard, a data breach may be a business-killer even without legislative penalties. Where there are laws, legal compliance is a final line of defence because if you are prosecuted or sued, your data management and protection system will come under the magnifying glass. Your win or loss in court hangs ultimately on your practices and policies.

Finally, a book focusing on the operational practice, rather than the law, has been written. It has been long awaited! I am delighted that the authors have decided to share the wide experiences they have in this new area of IT practice and information governance. I wholeheartedly endorse this comprehensive and practical effort and hope it will become the standard bible for data protection practices not just in Singapore, but in Asia too!

Dr Toh See Kiat is a veteran lawyer in Data Protection, Intellectual Property Rights, Information Technology and E-commerce Law, a former Member of Parliament and former President of the Consumers Association of Singapore.

Introduction

Two good friends walked into a local tour agency to book a cruise holiday for their respective families. They were puzzled that they had to scan in their national identity cards to obtain a queue number. While waiting for their queue number to be called, they could hear distinctly a customer service officer (CSO) taking a customer's booking over the phone and confirming the customer's personal particulars in a very loud voice. They were quite sure everyone else in the waiting area could hear what the CSO had just said. When their turn came, they walked towards the assigned counter and sat opposite the CSO, who greeted them with a standard scripted message.

When the two friends asked why their national identity cards were required to obtain a queue number, the CSO replied that it was the standard company policy for record purposes. They were even more shocked to see personal data, credit card slips and cheques of previous customers strewn all over the CSO's work area. The CSO then asked them which cruise packages they were interested in. As they were not quite familiar with what the tour agency could offer, they asked the CSO to recommend some of the more popular ones.

Imagine their horror when the CSO turned her computer terminal around and showed them the records of past customers who had booked the most popular cruises! The two friends, both certified privacy professionals, whispered to each other: "This tour agency has not taken appropriate measures to handle and safeguard the privacy of their customers' personal data. We don't trust our personal data with them. Let's go and look for a more privacy-conscious agency."

Such a scenario is real and has happened. In a number of countries, the level of awareness among organisations and individuals with regard to the proper handling and protection of personal data is still low. Even in countries with data protection or privacy laws in existence for many years, we hear in the media of massive data breaches where thousands or even millions of individuals' personal records have been compromised. Where data protection or privacy laws are relatively new, the level of awareness among organisations is often even more wanting.

In either case, not only do these organisations have to face the penalties imposed by regulators and lawsuits from affected individuals, they also have to live with financial and reputational losses. These can be particularly damaging for organisations that do not have the financial resources or a deep pool of loyal customers to help them weather the storm while they rebuild trust among their stakeholders. Organisations should therefore recognise that regardless of their size or the industry sector they are in, they are all vulnerable to privacy breaches if they do not have proper data protection practices.

Faced with high-profile regulatory actions and multi-million-dollar fines and lawsuits, many organisations around the world today are forced to strengthen their data protection practices. Similarly, when they consider the adverse implications, particularly in terms of stakeholder trust, of even a limited privacy breach, many organisations choose to strengthen their data protection practices simply because it is a sensible way for them to conduct their business.

Governments are reviewing and revamping their data protection laws to address new challenges because of emerging technologies and to require organisations to treat data protection as one of their critical business functions.

For example, the European Union has responded to privacy concerns arising from today's digital revolution and the need to deal with the complexity of data by introducing its General Data Protection Regulation (GDPR), a single unifying data protection law across all its member countries.

In the Association of South-East Asian Nations (ASEAN) all the member governments have committed to legislating and implementing data protection laws in their respective countries. This is part of the establishment of the ASEAN Economic Community, an effort to integrate the region's diverse economies into a single market with free movement of goods, services, investments, skilled labour and freer flow of capital.

In short, virtually every organisation doing business in the European Union and ASEAN will sooner or later have to grapple with new or updated data protection laws. So must boards, senior management and employees generally. They must either press the reset button with regard to legal compliance or adopt a new mindset in terms of processing personal data as part of their everyday operations.

We need to move from the "What" to the "How" of data protection. Unfortunately, there are few, if any, books that go into the operational aspects of data privacy and protection, and uncover the operational risks, threats and vulnerabilities facing organisations.

Data protection and privacy must not be a mystery, especially to employees at the operational forefront of organisations. Operationally, they must not be something that only lawyers can understand. They must be "owned" by all employees of organisations.

About data protection and privacy

Data protection and privacy have different ideological roots but share many of the same sets of obligations or principles, although they may be expressed in different language or use different terms (see Glossary).

We are often asked: "What's the practical difference between data protection and privacy?"

In the U.S. the term "privacy" is used in policies, laws and regulations while in the EU and many other countries, the term "data protection" often identifies privacy-related laws and regulations. Hence, there is no difference of definition between a privacy law and a data protection law, or between a privacy notice and a data protection notice, which we often come across in the online world. From a privacy professional perspective, they are synonymous.

"Data protection" may be used to mean "information security". When there is a data breach – when there is a media report, for example, about payment card information being stolen or other customer information being stolen from a company – that is a failure to protect data. The data might be "personal data" or "personal information" about individuals or it might be confidential data such as an organisation's intellectual property.

Colloquially, a data breach occurs when someone hacks into a computer system and steals data. This is well known. Newspapers are full of stories about hacking. But a data breach also occurs when data is leaked or exposed in some other way. Classic examples include individuals leaving a file behind on public transport or in a café. Other examples include employees simply sharing data with their colleagues who do not have a right to see it and individuals speaking loudly in public places and being overheard by others.

As for privacy, it has been described broadly as the right to be left alone or freedom from interference or intrusion. Data privacy or information privacy is the right of an individual to have some control over how their personal data – data that identifies them or relates to them – or personal information about them is collected, used and disclosed, as well as how it is stored or disposed of. When it comes to data privacy or data protection laws, the term refers to rules and practices regarding the handling of personal information or personal data, such as the concepts of notice, consent, choice, purpose, security, etc.

A data breach that involves a theft of personal data or an inadvertent exposure of personal data intrudes into an individual's privacy. But an intrusion into an individual's privacy can occur without a data breach, such as where an organisation insists on collecting excessive personal data from an individual or retains their personal data for longer than is justifiable.

Hence, in this book, when we use the term "privacy breaches" we mean more than data breaches where there could be non-compliance or contravention of the data protection law.

About information security and privacy

Another question people have often asked is: "What's the difference between information security and privacy?"

Although the two concepts are different in certain aspects, there is a symbiotic relationship between them. Privacy practitioners have recognised that there can be no privacy without security.

Information security is concerned with three main elements: confidentiality, integrity and availability, or "CIA" for short. In a nutshell, it means that secure measures must be put in place to protect personal data and other confidential information from being stolen, or from being accessed or modified without proper authorisation. Users of personal data and other confidential information must trust its accuracy and currency to make timely decisions or to handle business transactions. And the right information must be available to the right person at the right time.

Designing information security systems without privacy in mind could result in treating all personal data and other confidential information in the same manner. But from the privacy perspective, some personal data and other confidential information are private, especially sensitive personal data such as health, financial, ethnic group, religious or political affiliations, or membership of trade unions. Such sensitive data, in particular, must be accessible only to people with the appropriate "need to know". Hence information security systems must be designed to allow/restrict access to users based on their job roles. They must also be designed to have different levels of security for different classes of personal data and other confidential information.

While information security is about "CIA", data privacy is about having rules that govern how personal data is collected, used, disclosed and stored. Data protection laws around the world have obligations or principles to which organisations are required to adhere. If they don't, enforcement actions can be taken, resulting in either a fine or imprisonment. When organisations fail to comply with these rules, whether they simply flout them or fail despite their best efforts to comply, we call this a privacy breach.

Therefore, while information security is about governing "unauthorised" access to information (which includes personal data), conversely, it can be said that data privacy is about governing "authorised" access to information that is personal data. However, there can be a privacy breach even when an individual is authorised to access that personal data. For example, the individual could have illegally collected the personal data or they could have legally collected it and later used it for some other unauthorised secondary purpose or they could have illegally disclosed it to a third-party. In addition, while processing it, the individual may have failed to protect the personal data, resulting in the data being exposed, leaked, lost or even stolen.

To prevent privacy breaches, organisations should put practical measures in place as they would to ensure information security. The measures should not be an afterthought. "Privacy by Design", a movement that originated in Canada, is now gaining wide acceptance and traction around the world. Privacy professionals are working closely with information security professionals and IT developers to build privacy elements into IT and information security systems upfront during the design stage.

The importance of operational compliance

Search for any obligation under a data protection law or principle under a privacy law and you'll be rewarded with an array of results about what the law means and what must be done to comply with it – from a legal perspective. But legal compliance alone is not enough.

Search for "data breach" and you'll be rewarded with an array of results about hackers cleverly infiltrating corporate IT systems and stealing personal data and other confidential information. Read behind the scenes and more often than not the root cause was the action or inaction of an employee or ex-employee, sometimes careless and sometimes malicious. While more often than not the malicious employee or ex-employee succeeds only because of negligence in their IT system's governance, it is also clear that IT system governance alone is not enough.

One of our main motivations in writing this book is to fill the gap between legal compliance (complying with the obligations and requirements of data protection laws through organisational policies) and operational compliance (embedding privacy practices in the everyday operations and processes of the organisation).

While legal compliance is obviously necessary, it is not sufficient. All employees in an organisation must know at a very practical level – at an operational level – what to do and what not to do when they handle personal data and other confidential information on a day-to-day basis.

In addition, third-parties such as suppliers, vendors, intermediaries, brokers and agents must know what to do and not do when they handle personal data or other confidential information on behalf of an organisation.

In short, everyone who has a part in handling personal data or other confidential information in the possession or under the control of an organisation must understand their individual roles, responsibilities and accountabilities – at a practical level – throughout the information life cycle.

Responsibility and accountability

As we wrote, we were reminded of the so-called Parable of Responsibility: "Everybody, Somebody, Anybody and Nobody were members of a group. There was an important job to be done and Everybody was asked to do it. Everybody was sure that Somebody would do it. Anybody would have done it, but Nobody did it. Somebody got angry because it was Everybody's job. Everybody thought Anybody would do it, but Nobody realised that Anybody wouldn't do it. It ended up that Everybody blamed Somebody, when Nobody did what Anybody could have done."[1]

Responsibility can be shared and can be assigned before or after an event. So, a lawyer can be assigned responsibility for legal compliance with the data protection/privacy law; an IT specialist can be assigned responsibility for technical systems compliance. Someone else can even be assigned responsibility for management of physical documents and other non-technical tasks. But none of this responsibility is worth anything unless individuals are accountable for their actions or inaction.

In fact, when an organisation gets into trouble under the data protection law, including as a result of a complaint by an individual, regulators will inevitably require the organisation to demonstrate accountability for compliance with it. Simply put, they will be looking

---

[1] Condensed version of Charles Osgood's "A Poem About Responsibility".

for responsibility and ownership and they will require evidence of it.

Accountability applies only after something is done or not done. If an individual is accountable for something they are also answerable ultimately for it. There needs to be ownership in order for somebody to be responsible. We have written here about what individuals need to do or not do personally or what they need to do or not do as employees of an organisation.

Organisations, on the other hand, need to document their policies and practices to guide the actions of their employees. In addition, inevitably they have to provide evidence to the regulator, such as training records or disciplinary actions. Regulators will inevitably require them to demonstrate that they have done everything practically possible to prevent any privacy breaches from happening.

For these reasons, in this book we have provided checklists of good practices for both individuals and organisations. We intend these checklists to be a good starting place for operational compliance – both individuals and organisations should look at them through the lens of the practical situation they are facing and their own specific circumstances and supplement them appropriately to meet that situation and those circumstances.

In short, everyone must be accountable for operational compliance or nothing else matters. Without this, the blame game starts when someone gets into trouble, and lots of precious time and productivity is lost.

Thrust of this book

The majority of the chapters in this book are based on our real-life experiences, either in our personal capacities or as consultants and advisers to organisations that collect, use, disclose and store personal data.

We notice in our work with clients that everyday privacy breaches, in particular, happen despite legal compliance and despite good IT system governance. They happen because of a failure in operational compliance. We notice the same thing when we read reports about regulatory action around the world – files being left on a bus or in a café, USB drives being lost in taxis and so on.

So we set out to write about operational compliance – to highlight the things that can easily go wrong operationally when an organisation seeks to comply with data protection/privacy laws. And to write it in a way that speaks to our readers, that assumes they are not lawyers or IT geeks – though we certainly welcome lawyers and IT geeks as readers. We think they'll find value too.

We have included good practices based on our experiences and observations. We do not intend to be either prescriptive or all-encompassing. Every situation is different. Organisations should evaluate how our suggested good practices should be tailored to their unique circumstances, including organisational context and culture.

This book is meant for everyone who has an interest in data protection and privacy, either as an employee of an organisation or as an individual or member of the general public.

Data protection officers, especially, will benefit from the real-life anecdotes we cite, including cases of failure to comply with data protection laws that result in regulatory action. The subsequent penalties, even where the case is settled between the organisation and the regulator, provide salutary lessons. On top of the penalties, organisations incur considerable management time and expense – the diversion of resources from "getting on with business" – as part of the regulatory investigation, even where a complaint turns out to be frivolous.

Individuals who handle personal data and other confidential information in their day-to-day operations, such as real estate agents, financial advisers, healthcare workers, salespersons, freelancers or those working in service industries, will find this book useful.

Individuals who provide or disclose their personal data to organisations will become more aware of what they should or should not do in different circumstances.

Structure of this book

We have looked at operational compliance with data protection/privacy laws through several broad categories, particularly with reference to the information life cycle of collection, usage, disclosure, storage and retention, and disposal or destruction of personal data. The principles

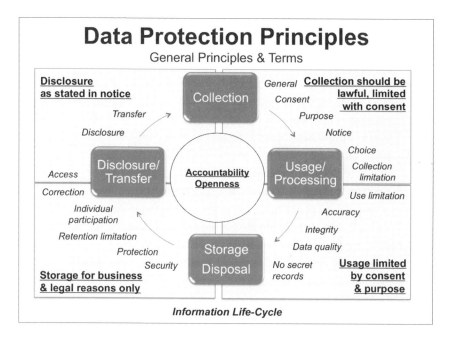

Data Protection Principles

General Principles & Terms

Information Life-Cycle

under each of these stages of the information life cycle are broad and generic enough to be applicable to most jurisdictions:

- **Section A: Governance & Information Asset Management.** These chapters (1 to 7) deal with some broad matters that apply generally to data protection and privacy.

- **Section B: Collection of Personal Data** (chapters 8 to 27). The over-riding principle is that the collection of personal data should be lawful, limited with consent. The principle of consent includes organisations notifying individuals at the time of collection of the purposes for collecting their personal data. It gives individuals the choice of consenting to organisations collecting their personal data or withholding their consent – an organisation must not coerce or force consent. The principle also gives individuals the right, having given their consent, to later withdraw it if they wish to do so. The organisation cannot change the purposes for which it will use personal data unless it gets fresh consent from the individual.

■ **Section C: Usage of Personal Data** (chapters 28 to 39). This section deals with the usage or processing of personal data, which is limited by the purpose notified to the individual and the consent the individual gives subsequently. (There are some instances where the law allows collection, use or disclosure of personal data without consent. These are beyond the scope of this book.) Elements of usage or processing of personal data include a requirement for usage to be fair.

■ **Section D: Data Accuracy & Integrity.** Organisations may store personal data about individuals, but must ensure its accuracy and integrity. The rights of an individual to have access to their personal data and to correct error and omissions, as well as the organisation's obligation regarding accuracy of personal data, are the subject of chapters 40 to 48.

■ **Section E: Physical & Environmental Security.** All personal data in the care of organisations should be protected and this includes both securing it physically and ensuring a secure environment. Physical and environmental security are covered in chapters 49 to 53.

■ **Section F: Security, Storage, Retention & Disposal of Personal Data.** Organisations must protect personal data too and must not retain it for longer than is necessary for the relevant use. We cover protection of personal data and retention – or, more accurately, the requirement for an organisation to cease to retain personal data – in chapters 54 to 75.

■ **Section G: Disclosure of Personal Data.** Finally, chapters 76 to 88 deal with disclosure of personal data. Organisations may disclose personal data only as permitted in the consent given by individuals after the organisation has notified them of the purposes for which their personal data will be disclosed and the individual has consented to those purposes.

How to use this book

We expect that some of our readers might read this book from front to back. But more often we expect our readers will want to dip into it and read the chapters of most interest to them at any particular time. We have thus written it so that the individual chapters are "free-standing" and without cross-references. We have presented some information more than once to underpin this approach and hope that those who read it from front to back will forgive us for a small amount of repetition.

Glossary

This book was written in Singapore. We have sought to use terminology that is not specific to Singapore, however, although our generic language is based on the data protection legislation in Singapore. Here are some explanations and equivalents. If your jurisdiction is not listed, words used have an equivalent meaning there.

"Data protection law" includes:

- Personal Data Protection Act 2012 – Singapore
- Personal Data Protection Act 2010 – Malaysia
- Data Privacy Act of 2012 – the Philippines
- Personal Data (Privacy) Ordinance (Cap. 486) – Hong Kong
- Privacy Act 1988 – Australia
- Privacy Act 1933 – New Zealand
- Data Protection Act 1998 – United Kingdom
- Data Protection Act 1988 – Ireland
- General Data Protection Regulation (GDPR) – European Union

"Regulator" includes:

- Personal Data Protection Commission (PDPC) – Singapore
- Personal Data Protection Department (PDPD) – Malaysia
- National Privacy Commission – the Philippines
- Office of the Privacy Commissioner for Personal Data, Hong Kong – Hong Kong
- Office of the Australian Information Commissioner – Australia
- Privacy Commissioner – New Zealand

- UK Information Commissioner's Office – United Kingdom
- Data Protection Commissioner – Ireland
- The data protection authority for the country of an organisation's main establishment and, if different, the "concerned authority" where an individual complainant resides – European Union

"Organisation" includes:
- Companies, unincorporated associations, firms and individuals conducting business (as used in Singapore and Australia)
- Data controller (as used in EU, UK and Ireland)
- Data user (as used in Hong Kong and Malaysia)
- Personal information controller (as used in the Philippines)
- Agency (as used in New Zealand)

"Personal data" is synonymous with personal information.

"Individual" is synonymous with data subject.

"Data intermediary" is synonymous with data processor.

"

Data is the pollution problem of the
information age, and protecting privacy
is the environmental challenge.

"

Bruce Schneier

SECTION A:

Governance & Information Asset Management

01 Data protection: don't forget that it is also physical

"Data protection" – when you see or hear these two words, what are the first thoughts that come to your mind? To most of us who are raised in today's Information Age and are being bombarded with multimedia-rich information content every day, we will not be too far off the mark when we say "data protection" includes:

- Secure databases with multi-layers of access controls, including passwords and multi-factor authentication
- Secure networks with firewalls and concentric rings of protection
- Data encryption
- Data loss/leakage prevention and
- Intrusion prevention and intrusion detection systems

Ironically, even though a lot of data today is in digitised or electronic forms, we still handle a massive amount of paper documents containing personal, confidential, private or sensitive information. The reasons vary. Many agreements are still in paper form, either for legal reasons or to cater to the parties' preferences. Official documents, such as land titles, marriage certificates and educational certificates, need to be in paper form with watermarks, authorised signatures and seals of the issuing authorities. Other documents, official and unofficial, such as interview or other meeting notes and assessments, are still sometimes more conveniently created and kept in paper form.

The personal data in these paper documents also have to be protected, so "data protection" must include elements that are relevant to paper documents as well – for example, keeping them under lock and key.

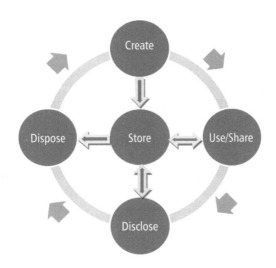

The document life cycle

For both business and regulatory compliance reasons, an organisation must protect paper documents containing personal, confidential or sensitive information against unauthorised access, use, disclosure, duplication, modification, disposal or loss.

To establish effective control measures an organisation needs to first understand the *document life cycle* – that is, what happens from the point a document is created or generated to the point it is disposed of or destroyed. This includes understanding how the document is handled at each stage, for what reason and by whom.

The document life cycle:

- provides the organisation with useful insights on the weaknesses and vulnerabilities in protecting documents in the entire "data protection" chain, and then
- enables the organisation to develop and implement appropriate preventive or mitigating controls to address these areas of weaknesses and vulnerabilities in order to protect the documents.

Journeying through the document life cycle

Here is a typical approach to determining a document life cycle:

- First, an organisation must compile a list of documents (including forms) that are required to support its various business processes.

With this *document inventory*, the organisation's objective is to get a clear view of all of its documents that are to be protected.

■ Second, the organisation must assess each document in terms of its confidentiality and sensitivity. This is done so that the appropriate level of security protection can be assigned to the document.

In other words, each document has to be classified according to a predetermined *document classification scheme*. Examples of document classification include "Confidential", "Internal Use Only" and "Public".

■ Third, it is important for an organisation to have clear visibility of which department or employees within the organisation are responsible for handling the document at each stage of the life cycle and business process.

Therefore, the organisation must construct a *document flow diagram*. This traces the movement of the document through its life cycle based on the organisation's business processes.

■ Finally, based on the document flow diagram, the organisation must perform an *onsite audit* to assess the adequacy of existing document protection measures. It must then address identified weaknesses and vulnerabilities to minimise the organisation's risk exposures.

The onsite audit should focus specifically on:

■ **Create** – where and how the documents are first created or generated, including completing paper forms
■ **Store** – where and how the documents are stored or archived
■ **Use/Share**
  ● where and how the documents are used and shared within the organisation – high-risk areas include the handing/taking over points between departments or between employees
  ● how documents in the possession of individual staff are controlled and safeguarded, including if and how individual staff can duplicate or copy them
■ **Disclose** – identifying the "outside" individuals and organisations to whom the organisation discloses documents and how this is done
■ **Dispose** – how the organisation disposes of or destroys the documents when it has no further use for them

Benefits of the document life cycle

By having a systematic process of managing the document life cycle, organisations gain better assurance and confidence that they have addressed and mitigated the risks and vulnerabilities associated with the unauthorised access, collection, use, disclosure, copying, modification and disposal of personal, confidential, private or sensitive information.

CHECKLIST OF GOOD PRACTICES

In managing their documents containing personal data and other confidential information, organisations should:

- Understand the purpose and benefits of documenting the document life cycle.
- Put in place systematic processes to:
  - produce a *document inventory* and to ensure it is kept up to date
  - implement an agreed *document classification scheme*
  - produce *document flow diagrams* and ensure they are kept up to date and
  - carry out regular *onsite audits* to address any identified vulnerabilities and weaknesses

02 Investigated by a regulator? Will it find only good… or some bad?

When we work with our clients we have a constant refrain covering two things about data protection and privacy processes:

- concentrate on your operational compliance or you will get into trouble – and concentrate on it continuously with regular audits because it is not a "set and forget" task – and
- have an effective complaints resolution process in place to minimise the risk of any complaints to the regulator – audit its effectiveness regularly too and learn from complaints received.

An adverse outcome of a regulatory investigation – a finding that the organisation has failed to comply with the data protection law – can obviously have unfavourable consequences, including a fine. But even a "clean" outcome has a downside: investigations are distractions that use up time and management resources better spent on business operations.

Here is one case where an organisation took the time to get everything right at the outset. And another case where it did not.

Case #1: Good processes pay off

An individual complained to the regulator[1] that they had received – and incurred charges related to – text messages from a subscription service after entering their mobile phone number into a website for a chance to win free flights. The individual complained that they had no knowledge of opting-in to receive text messages from the organisation.

[1] See https://www.dataprotection.ie/docs/Case-Studies-2008/939.htm, case study 7.

The regulator established that:

■ when the individual entered their mobile phone number the organisation had sent them a text message that included a PIN number and the individual then entered the PIN number into the website to verify the subscription and

■ the website indicated that the service was a subscription service and outlined the cost and frequency of the subscription element and

■ the website gave clear instructions on how to unsubscribe from the service.

Therefore the individual had not received unsolicited marketing text messages as claimed, but had legitimately received subscription service text messages after opting-in to a service on the organisation's website. The regulator was also satisfied that the organisation had put in place appropriate procedures to ensure that numbers entered on the website were validly entered. Receiving a text message and actively opting-in removed any doubt about the validity of the consent.

The regulator commented that this case study is a clear reminder that individuals need to pay greater attention to information that organisations make available to them, particularly on websites. There were no grounds for upholding the individual's complaint.

The organisation might have been complimented on taking the time to develop and implement a carefully thought-through process that complied with the requirements of the data protection law.

Case #2: Operational errors have unintended consequences

An individual provided their payment card details and email address to an organisation for the purpose of purchasing tickets for a particular concert. More than 12 months later the organisation sent them emails regarding the cancellation of another concert, for which they had not purchased a ticket.

The individual was concerned that the organisation had retained their personal data for such a long time and asked the organisation to remove their personal data from its database. At the same time, they complained to the regulator.[2] Here is what happened.

[2] See https://www.dataprotection.ie/docs/Case-Studies-2008/939.htm, case study 13.

■ **Complaint resolved:** The organisation informed the regulator that it sent "performer alert emails" to customers who had previously bought tickets. These were only sent in respect of "similar products or services" in which it thought previous customers would have an interest. In each message, the organisation gave individuals an easy and free way of opting-out from receiving future messages.

The organisation said that the emails about the cancelled concert had resulted from an operational error and that it had rectified its internal processes so that such an error would not recur. It wrote to the complainant to confirm that it had deleted all of their personal data from its records in accordance with their request.

■ **Further consequences:** Problem solved and investigation closed, right? Wrong. Regulatory investigations are generally rather thorough. They may well uncover data protection/privacy issues in addition to the subject of the complaint they are investigating.

That is exactly what happened to turn an operational email error into a much wider-ranging investigation and series of actions to be taken by the organisation. The regulator:

● was concerned about the length of time the organisation retained personal data such as payment card details and said it should be reduced from 16 months to 12 months, with the personal data being deleted if there was no activity on the individual's account during that time and

● said it would be more appropriate for individuals to opt-in to have their details retained rather than the existing practice of requiring them to uncheck a box when they purchased a ticket

In addition, the regulator was concerned that the organisation might not have appropriate procedures in place for deleting personal data when it was no longer required for the purpose for which it was collected. It therefore obtained a copy of the organisation's data retention policy. This led to the regulator highlighting issues in relation to the privacy policy statement on the organisation's website.

One issue was that the privacy policy statement referred to UK data protection legislation and made no reference to the Irish data protection legislation, whereas the organisation was registered in both England and Ireland. The regulator said that a data protection notice relevant to Ireland should be published on its website. The organisation said the omission was an oversight on its part and remedied it.

■ **Regulator's overall comments:** At the end of the investigation, the regulator said that it was satisfied that the organisation took its data protection responsibilities seriously. The regulator was "encouraged" by the cooperative manner in which the organisation addressed the issues and implemented the regulator's recommendations.

So, the outcome of the investigation might have been worse. But that was doubtless cold comfort to the organisation for a distraction that could have been avoided.

CHECKLIST OF GOOD PRACTICES

■ Organisations should:
- concentrate continuously on operational compliance with data protection laws and regularly audit it, particularly to avoid unintended consequences
- have an effective complaints resolution process

■ Individuals should pay attention to information provided to them by organisations, to make sure that their personal data is not retained beyond a reasonable period and they have an option to withdraw consent

🔒 03 Designing privacy into information systems and processes

Case A

A bank implemented a personalised service for its customers a few years ago. There was no special announcement or fanfare, and no one was the wiser.

I discovered this new service by chance when I inserted my automated teller machine (ATM) card into the bank's machine and a welcome message in big letters greeted me on the display screen: "Welcome <My name in full>".

I felt that this was an invasion of my privacy because even up to the fourth person in the queue could see my name clearly. (How did I know this despite my short-sightedness? I could see the name of the person four places in front of me when I was queueing for my turn.)

I reported my discomfort to the bank. The person-in-charge told me that names of customers appeared on the screen by default. Customers who didn't want their names displayed must inform the bank.

I suggested to the person-in-charge that, for the sake of privacy, the default should have been the other way round: no customers' names should have been displayed unless they asked the bank to display them.

Case B

Whenever consumers present their payment cards to merchants or service providers for payment of goods and services, they print a voucher in duplicate (sometimes in triplicate) for the cardholder to sign. The voucher serves as a confirmation that the consumer has agreed to the amount charged.

Sometimes, the voucher contains the full name of the cardholder, the full payment card number and the expiry date of the card. This is a lot of personal data that is clearly visible to anyone who handles the vouchers.

To protect cardholders' privacy and for security reasons (including to reduce the incidence of fraud), payment card scheme rules require merchants and service providers to mask details on payment transaction vouchers. The rules seek to achieve a balance between collecting enough information needed to process a transaction (and to trace it if there are any cardholder queries) and respecting cardholder privacy and security.

So, for example, the cardholder's name and the card number are truncated on the voucher, and the card expiry date is no longer displayed. This is certainly a positive step forward in reducing security risks while protecting individuals' personal data.

Case C

A number of smartphone apps available for download and installation from Android's Play Store and Apple iOS's App Store expect users to grant more permissions than necessary in order to use the apps. Many of these permissions intrude into the user's privacy, such as allowing the app to look at or even modify one's personal data or other confidential information stored on the device[1].

We suspect that many of these apps are outsourced by organisations to third-party software developers to write the codes. Without a clear understanding of privacy requirements, these developers could have just simply picked the permissions from the pre-defined library in Android or iOS by default.

Case D

The Westfield Group is an Australian multinational corporation that owns shopping centres in Australia, New Zealand, the United Kingdom and the United States. It implemented a ticketless parking system that aimed to make parking easier and quicker for shoppers[2]. The system

---

[1] See chapter 17, "Organisations, mobile apps and the data protection law".
[2] K&L Gates, Feb 5, 2016, "Privacy concerns over Westfield's ticketless parking system", in Lexology.

scanned the number plates of vehicles on entry into and exit from the car parks, and sent an SMS notification to registered "parkers" recording their entry time and an alert message when their free parking time was nearly up. To register for the service, users were merely required to provide a name, licence plate number and phone number (with no verification).

Privacy experts raised the alarm that any person could register false details and track another person's physical location via the SMS notifications. The system's terms and conditions failed to address any of these issues.

"Privacy by Design"

The above cases illustrate that privacy is best pre-designed into information systems and processes, and not included later as an afterthought.

Sometimes it may be difficult or too costly to retrofit privacy elements into the systems or processes once they are implemented. Software and process developers should adopt a paradigm shift to include privacy requirements in the early stages of design.

"Privacy by Design (PbD)"[3] was first developed by Dr Ann Cavoukian, the Information and Privacy Commissioner of Ontario, Canada, in the 1990s. PbD is an approach to protecting privacy by embedding it into the design specifications of technologies, business practices and physical infrastructures.

The first three foundational principles of PbD, which are relevant to this chapter, are:
- "Proactive not Reactive; Preventative not Remedial"
- "Privacy as the Default Setting" (unlike my experience in Case A)
- "Privacy Embedded into Design"

If PbD makes a lot of sense, then why are software and process developers not embracing this concept with open arms? Here are some possible reasons:

---

[3] Source: Information and Privacy Commissioner of Ontario website (www.ipc.on.ca)

- There is erroneous thinking that security built into systems and processes will take care of privacy.
- While there is no privacy without security, security on its own is not sufficient for privacy. Privacy requires, in addition, systems and processes to provide individuals with notice, choice and consent.
- PbD requires a shift in design philosophy which not many software and process developers are in the right frame of mind, or adequately trained, to do yet.
- PbD requires additional time and effort to identify and specify the privacy requirements upfront.

In a highly competitive business environment, software developers, especially, are under pressure to deliver new products and services as quickly as possible in order to be the first-to-market. And yet, a little more time built into the design at the outset will likely avoid the "pain" of having to "retrofit" privacy immediately before product launch or, worse, after receiving feedback from disgruntled users.

New privacy challenges that require privacy by design

With the increasing adoption and usage of security monitoring and surveillance systems, machine-to-machine communications and the Internet of Things (IOT), the need for PbD is all the more important.

Security monitoring and surveillance systems in the form of high-definition CCTV cameras and drones, for example, are highly intrusive. While security concerns are paramount in today's world of terrorism, the design of security monitoring and surveillance systems should consider the protection of individuals' privacy as one of the key elements.

An example of a machine-to-machine communication is in the electronic road-toll system where a vehicle's passage through certain checkpoints is automatically captured for toll charging. PbD embedded in the system should ensure that the system is restricted to computation of toll charges only and the movement of drivers is not tracked.

CHECKLIST OF GOOD PRACTICES

■ Organisations should design privacy into their information systems and processes, and not add it on as an afterthought.

■ Time and effort must be invested in identifying and specifying privacy requirements upfront.

■ Privacy must be the default setting and embedded into the design.

04 Is document classification really necessary?

One of the best practices in information security is for an organisation to classify documents into different levels of privacy and confidentiality. It can then accord an appropriate level of security measures to each classification. Typical classifications include "UNCLASSIFIED", "RESTRICTED", "CONFIDENTIAL", and even "STAFF-IN-CONFIDENCE".

Of course, an organisation must ensure that the classification is marked clearly on each document so that employees are alerted to it and know which security measures to apply.

Reasons for not marking documents with their classification

Most organisations do, at least tacitly, divide their documents into those that they consider confidential within the organisation (or confidential to, for example, HR employees) and those that may be shared with the general public.

It's the additional step of marking them with their classification that raises resistance. This is because a number of our client organisations have not implemented any classification scheme since the day the organisation was established. To do so now would be an extremely tedious and time-consuming task. We often hear from our clients statements such as the following being used to justify their non-action: "Almost all our documents are confidential. Instead of stamping the word 'CONFIDENTIAL' across all our files and documents, can't we just assume everything is confidential and inform our employees about it? Besides, classifying our files and documents invites more curiosity

– people would tend to peek into files marked 'CONFIDENTIAL' and leave unmarked files alone."

This is hardly the hallmark of a well-run organisation. Or something that would engender trust among the organisation's customers or clients if it were known publicly.

The consequences of not classifying documents

The statements made by employees, such as the one above, may sound sensible and sometimes even convincing. But accepting them could lead to the following situations:

- **The tendency to over-classify documents**

  This means treating all documents as "CONFIDENTIAL" when some of them are obviously not. This is especially confusing when documents that are meant for public consumption are, as a blanket rule, marked as "CONFIDENTIAL". And it devalues the integrity of documents that should really be classified as "CONFIDENTIAL".

- **The tendency to assume access to documents is permitted**

  Because there is no distinct delineation on who can have access to what information, all employees assume they can have access to any document in the organisation.

  Best practices adopted by most organisations ensure that highly confidential and sensitive information, such as HR and Finance documents, are restricted to a small group of employees only (based on job roles or "need to know" basis).

  Organisations should similarly restrict access to customer, client or other documents.

- **The dangers of employee turnover**

  Due to turnover, new employees may not be aware of the organisation's policies and practices, particularly if they are not sufficiently briefed about the way to treat various categories of documents.

  Classifying documents helps indicate that the organisation does have an agreed set of principles linked to information classification. Classifications that are self-explanatory are helpful.

- **And the dangers of faulty memories**

  Over time, the appropriate level of security measures meant for confidential documents could be eroded because employees tend to forget what is required.

The word "CONFIDENTIAL" on a document is a good visual reminder of the need to treat and handle confidential documents with the right level of security. When driving on public roads, visual cues in the form of traffic signs remind us not to speed, not to overtake, not to do a U-turn, even though we are supposed to know these things.

The cost-benefit analysis

When an organisation adopts document classification, agreeing on the classifications and the security measures attaching to them is a one-time set of policy decisions. It's followed by a one-time administrative effort to add the classification to existing documents. Stamping existing paper documents so that they include the correct classifications is relatively easy once organisation personnel are trained to use the correct classification. And adding a classification to any other documents they produce in future is rarely onerous once they get into the habit of doing it.

But the benefits of document classification are significant. The risks mentioned above are avoided. Employees are constantly reminded to handle confidential documents and files with the right level of information security.

Employment contracts and handbooks generally require employees to comply with the organisation's policies and practices and to maintain the confidentiality of the organisation's documents. The organisation usually has a right to apply disciplinary consequences – a verbal warning, a written warning, or termination for cause – where employees fail to comply with these requirements.

Employees caught mishandling or misusing confidential information cannot claim ignorance about the status of the documents if their classification is clearly marked on them. But if there is no document classification scheme and the status of documents isn't marked on them, the organisation may not be able to take any action against recalcitrant employees.

CHECKLIST OF GOOD PRACTICES

Organisations should adopt the following practices when handling confidential documents:

- Have a document classification scheme so that the appropriate level of confidentiality and protection can be accorded to each type of document.
- Clearly mark all documents with their classification status.
- Do not over-classify documents.
- Restrict employees' access to classified documents based on job roles or "need to know" basis.
- Train new employees on the organisation's policies and practices in handling classified documents.

05 You can delegate the task but not the responsibility

Incident #1[1]

Complaint: Hundreds of customers of a leading bank complained that they received someone else's private and confidential bank statements. The recipient's address on the envelope was correct but the name was wrong. When they opened the envelope they discovered that the bank statement was not theirs. It was meant for the customer whose name was on the envelope.

Cause: The mistakes were made by a printing company to which the bank outsourced the printing and mailing of its bank statements. It was due to a misalignment by the printing company of the name and address columns of the customer list provided by the bank.

Incident #2[2]

Complaint: Thousands of individuals complained that they could not do e-trade of shares on the company's online portal as it was down for almost six hours. Lost opportunity in e-trades for these individuals amounted to a few million dollars.

Cause: The computerised system was developed, operated and maintained by the IT division of the company. The IT division (a cost centre) was subsequently spun off as a separate company. The new IT company, now operating as a profit centre, implemented significant cost-cutting measures. There were minimal provisions for contingencies and IT service continuity.

[1] Modified from an actual incident.
[2] Ditto.

Incident #3[3]

Complaint: Thousands of customers of an organisation complained that their user IDs and passwords had been hijacked to send out spam messages without their knowledge. They discovered this only after recipients of the spam messages complained to them.

Cause: Someone hacked into the servers of the cloud service provider that hosted the organisation's web portal. Almost the entire database of user IDs and passwords of their client organisation was stolen.

Incident #4[4]

Complaint: Hundreds of members of the public complained to a real estate company that they had been contacted on their mobile phones with marketing messages. They had previously registered their phone numbers with the national Do-Not-Call (DNC) registry.

Cause: An independent agent of the company flouted the DNC policy and rules of the company and contacted the individuals.

The organisation carries the responsibility for its vendors and other third-parties

In the four incidents cited above, what is the common element? In all four, customers and members of the public complained to the organisations directly even though the faults and mistakes were caused by an outsourced company, a spun-off company, a hosting service provider or an independent agent. This goes to show that even though an organisation has delegated or outsourced its tasks to a third-party, it still has to bear responsibility if anything goes wrong.

In addition to any regulatory penalties arising from a mistake by a vendor or other third-party, the organisation's reputation and goodwill among its customer base and in its community may suffer. Damage to the reputation and goodwill of an unidentified vendor or other agent will be little or none. After all, customers and the public recognise and identify with only the organisation's name.

Therefore it is important for the organisation to minimise the likelihood and extent of risks arising from the actions or inaction of

---

[3] Modified from an actual incident.
[4] Ditto.

its vendors and other third-parties carrying out tasks or operations delegated to them. The selection of vendors and other third-parties is thus of prime importance.

Achieving a shared understanding of responsibilities and obligations

The first thing an organisation should do before it delegates or outsources tasks or operations is to draw up a list of responsibilities and obligations of both the organisation and the vendor or other third-party. This is to achieve a shared understanding of respective roles and responsibilities – that is, to avoid any misunderstanding or finger-pointing and to minimise the risk of anything going awry.

These responsibilities and obligations should be included in a written agreement between the organisation and the vendor or other third-party. Executing the agreement shows that they are agreed and accepted by both the organisation and the vendor or other third-party. Rather than relying on Court-determined damages arising from any breach of the agreement, the agreement will typically include a contractual indemnity or specify compensation due to be paid to the organisation if the vendor or other third-party breaches the agreement.

Achieving a shared understanding of operational aspects

The second thing an organisation should do when it delegates or outsources tasks or operations is to determine operational aspects of the arrangement that are relevant in the circumstances. These may include things such as the following:

- the service levels that the organisation expects of the vendor or other third-party
- key performance indicators (KPIs) to be reported by the vendor or other third-party to the organisation regularly
- the vendor's or other third-party's procedures in handling incidents when they occur and
- the vendor's or other third-party's critical operations and contingency plans to deal with any interruption to them.

Initial and continuing due diligence

As an obvious good practice, before selecting a vendor or other third-party, an organisation should audit their processes and procedures for operational capability, including their ability to comply with the data protection law.

The organisation may consider some or all of the delegated or outsourced tasks or operations to be critical to its reputation and success. If so, the organisation should insist on a feedback process under which the vendor or other third-party warns the organisation of any signs of impending incidents or faults before they occur.

Much as the organisation would like to have close and tight supervision of how the vendor or other third-party is performing, it may not have the resources to do so. Or there may be practical barriers, such as where the vendor or other third-party is located overseas.

In any case, appropriate KPIs are critical. The frequency and detail of reporting performance against them is also critical. And, it should go without saying, an organisation should review KPI reports carefully and take action in connection with any actual or threatened shortfalls. All too often, we see cases where reports are simply filed and looming problems are not identified by the organisation.

The optimal outcome

Eventually, mutual trust between an organisation and its vendors and other third-parties ensures a long-standing, good working relationship. But it is invariably built on the bedrock of:

- a good understanding by an organisation of its vendors' and other third-parties' capabilities, strengths and weaknesses through initial due diligence by the organisation
- a shared understanding of each party's responsibilities and obligations that are recorded by setting them out clearly in the agreement between the parties, and
- appropriate KPIs that are reported properly and where action is taken early to remediate any potential problems.

CHECKLIST OF GOOD PRACTICES

Organisations should adopt the following practices when they delegate or outsource their tasks to third-parties:

- Choose a trusted and reliable third-party.
- Include a list of responsibilities and obligations in the contracts, as well as the indemnity or compensation to be paid if the third-party contravenes any of the terms and conditions.
- Include expected service levels, incident handling procedures and contingency plans for critical operations in the contracts.
- Audit the third-party's processes and procedures if the tasks or operations are critical to the reputation and success of the organisation.
- Have a feedback process for the third-party to pre-warn the organisation of any impending incident or fault.
- Have key performance indicators (KPIs) for the third-party to track and report back to the organisation regularly.

06 We don't get any complaints so that's good, right? Well, maybe not.

A data protection law generally gives a regulator powers:

- to send auditors or investigators out to visit organisations and check on their compliance with the law and
- to receive complaints from individuals about a possible failure to comply with the law and then to investigate it

Where the regulator elects to do only the latter, the regime is said to be a "complaints-based regime". In fact, it is a "complaints-based enforcement model" for so long as the regulator elects not to adopt the more proactive – and resource-intensive – audit model.

It is very easy to think that no complaints to an organisation means that its clients do not have anything that they feel like complaining about to it and therefore there is little or no risk of a complaint about data protection to the regulator. But maybe "no complaints received" or, more accurately, "no complaints recorded as having been received" could mean the organisation doesn't have a complaints process that is working well. For example, individuals might be complaining to frontline employees and they are dealing with them. Maybe well; maybe not – sometimes even simply brushing them aside. Where the complaints are about data protection, that is a sure-fire recipe for the complaints to be escalated to the regulator. The only question is when this will happen.

As I read data protection case reports I often find myself thinking: "This is so petty. Didn't this individual have something better to do with their time than file a complaint with the regulator?" Reading further it becomes evident that the individual started with a problem or request, often quite a small problem or request, that may not even have concerned data protection. But they simply could not get any meaningful response from the organisation. Finally, in desperation and finding some kind of connection with data protection, they turned to the regulator to get some attention, to find someone who would listen to them.

Why go the extra mile with a complaints process?

It may sound counter-intuitive, but a well-designed complaints process gives an organisation valuable input for improving:

- the way it collects, uses or discloses personal data about its clients and
- the way it communicates with its clients.

And in at least some jurisdictions an organisation fails to comply with the data protection law unless it has a complaints process.

Elements of a well-designed complaints process

Here are some tips on designing an effective complaints process in connection with the collection, use or disclosure of personal data.

- **Make it easy for individuals to complain**

  Let individuals know how to complain to the organisation. For example, include on the organisation's website a phone number or an email and/or postal address and the job title of the employee who will help them resolve their complaint – the data protection officer (or their delegate) in those jurisdictions that require an organisation to have a data protection officer.

  Include this information in or with the organisation's privacy notice. Consider too the feasibility of letting individuals know what information the organisation will need so it can resolve their complaint.

- **Make sure employees know who handles complaints**

  Letting individuals know how to complain will not always work. Some of them will call the organisation's switchboard number, write to its head office address, send an email to an "enquiries@..." address or submit an online enquiry through "Contact Us" on its website. Or simply complain to the employee with whom they are interacting about the organisation's goods or services.

Make sure that responsibility for regularly checking any "enquiries@..." or similar email address and any online enquiry forms regularly – at least daily – is assigned and do periodic compliance audits. Make sure that employees checking these sources, answering the phone, opening the mail and dealing face-to-face with customers know who is responsible for handling complaints. And that they know to pass complaints on to this employee without delay.

It sounds obvious, right? We are amazed how often this simple step is overlooked or forgotten, including as a result of employee turnover.

■ **Acknowledge the complaint as soon as it is received**
It is good practice to:
● acknowledge a complaint in writing as soon as the organisation receives it
● ask for any information that will obviously be needed in order to investigate the complaint and
● provide information about when the organisation will respond to the complaint.
Why? To reassure the complainant that the organisation has received their complaint and is taking it seriously; to manage their expectations about when they will receive a response; and to forestall them complaining to the regulator.

Then be sure to investigate and respond to the complaint as soon as reasonably possible and, of course, within any time period specified in the data protection law.

■ **Internal complaints investigation process**
There is no "one size fits all" when it comes to devising and implementing a complaints investigation process – it depends on the size and complexity of the organisation and the points at which

it collects, uses or discloses personal data. For example, whether an organisation operates from several different locations or from a single location and whether it has a wide range of different categories of individuals that provide it with their personal data.

The first common factor in all well-designed complaints investigation processes is that responsibility is clearly assigned:

- to specific employees (usually by job title)
- to carry out specific tasks in the process.

Each employee must clearly understand what is expected of them. This is particularly important where the data protection law does not require an organisation to appoint a data protection officer to take responsibility for the organisation complying with it.

The second common factor is that evidence must be collected and retained by the organisation of each step taken in the complaints investigation process. In addition, at least where they are not obvious, the reasons for making decisions one way or another must be documented for future reference. In any regulatory investigation, the regulator will require evidence, preferably documentary evidence, about what the organisation has or has not done and the reasons why.

The third common factor is that the data protection officer – or, where there is no requirement for a data protection officer, the employee with responsibility for handling data protection complaints – must have sufficient authority within the organisation, or have sufficient senior management backing, to be able to ensure that each employee involved in the investigation process plays their role efficiently, effectively and with integrity.

■ Escalation of complaints internally

In some instances, it may be rather obvious (or at least likely) where a complaint is not resolved in favour of the complainant that "the organisation has not heard the last about this". Or that the complaint and response might, for example, "go viral" on social media.

The data protection officer or other employee responsible for handling complaints should be attuned to recognising these cases.

They should do at least two things before providing the complainant with notice of the outcome of their complaint:

- notify senior management about the complaint, the outcome of investigating it and the risk of bad publicity so that there are "no surprises" and
- ensure that a public relations response by the organisation is prepared, at least on a "just in case" basis.

■ **Informing the complainant of the outcome of their complaint**
It goes without saying that the organisation must inform the individual about the outcome of their complaint.

Typically, if the complaint is resolved in favour of the complainant there is no need to provide them with any written confirmation of that outcome unless they request it.

Otherwise, the organisation should:

- provide the complainant with written notice of the outcome, including the organisation's reasons for that outcome and
- inform them of any third-party sources they can contact if they are not satisfied with the outcome, including the regulator.

■ **Internal analysis and reporting**
The data protection officer or other employee who is responsible for handling complaints should provide a written report periodically to senior management about complaints received since the last such report and any actions taken or planned to address their underlying causes.

They should first analyse the complaints received and their outcomes to see if there is any pattern indicating action that the organisation should take to reduce the number of complaints.

For example, if there is a sudden increase in the number of complaints about the way a particular division or department of the organisation uses personal data, the underlying cause should be investigated. It may indicate that remedial training needs to be given to employees or that there is some other operational problem.

If there is an increase in the number of complaints and the increase ties back to a new form or process introduced by the organisation to, say, collect personal data and most of the complaints are resolved in favour of the organisation it may mean that communication with customers should be improved.

CHECKLIST OF GOOD PRACTICES

Organisations with a proper and well-designed complaints process should:

- make it easy for individuals to complain
- make sure that employees who may receive complaints know who handles them
- acknowledge the complaint in writing as soon as it is received by the employee who will handle it
- ensure that they have designed and implemented a complaints investigation process where each involved employee knows their role in it
- have an escalation process to notify senior management of complaints that may attract adverse publicity
- inform the complainant of the outcome of their complaint and
- have an internal analysis and reporting regime so that complaints are brought to the attention of senior management and remedial action may be taken to reduce them.

🔒 07 What if your warehouse loses personal data belonging to your organisation?

Does your organisation outsource storage of archived files to a storage warehouse vendor? What if you discover that the vendor has lost cartons belonging to your organisation? That happened to an organisation we heard about. Let's call it Company A.

Apparently, Company A's vendor – let's call it Vendor X – decided to close down. Vendor X told Company A that it was not renewing the lease for Company A's document storage. When Company A withdrew all its cartons from Vendor X to place them with a newly appointed vendor, Vendor X informed Company A that a number of cartons had been lost. The cartons contained all kinds of personal data – invoices, credit card transaction slips, insurance reports, and bank slips.

What would you do if faced with this apparent breach of the data protection law – this apparent failure to protect the personal data in the lost cartons and a possible unauthorised disclosure of it as a consequence of the loss?

Contract terms fiasco

To aggravate matters, Company A's lease agreement with Vendor X was unfavourable to Company A. Under a "limitation of liability" clause Company A had agreed that it would not hold Vendor X liable for any loss or damage exceeding $10 per carton. In addition, it would not hold Vendor X liable for any consequential loss or damage. We were surprised that Company A had agreed to these terms.

With the limitation of liability, it was no wonder that Vendor X informed Company A rather nonchalantly that the cartons were lost and offered to pay $10 per carton as compensation.

Meanwhile Company A had a serious incident on its hands – a failure to protect personal data under its control. Company A was accountable to both the data protection regulator and its customers. To make matters worse, Company A had not made an inventory of the contents of each carton and therefore did not have any idea which customers' data were lost.

To notify or not?

In some jurisdictions[1], there is a breach notification requirement – that is, it is compulsory for an organisation to notify the data protection regulator in the event of a data breach. In others[2] there is no such requirement, but the regulator typically encourages organisations to notify them in such an event – that is, there is a voluntary notification approach. It is seen as a good practice. A voluntary notification approach applied to Company A. The basic principle is to prevent further harm.

When Company A asked us whether it should report the incident to the regulator, our recommendation was "not yet". This was because Company A had not yet done a full investigation as it didn't have all the facts. What if Company A informed the regulator that there had been a data breach and then the cartons showed up later? It would be embarrassing.

We asked Company A to conduct a full investigation. We suggested it give Vendor X two weeks to investigate and confirm if the cartons were:

- completely lost (that is, stolen) or
- misplaced or
- given to the wrong customer of Vendor X or
- mistakenly trashed.

---

[1] For example, Germany, Austria, Korea, Taiwan and Mexico as well as United States (where a majority of the states have breach notification laws). The General Data Protection Regulation (GDPR) in the European Union also requires notification to the regulator within 72 hours.
[2] Including Singapore, Malaysia and Hong Kong.

With that information, Company A could decide whether the incident would be reported to both the police and the data protection regulator. As it turned out, Vendor X confirmed that the cartons were probably misplaced, prompting Company A to report the loss of personal data to the regulator.

Vendor selection and monitoring

This incident demonstrates the need for due diligence and care when an organisation outsources the management or storage of documents containing personal data. Storage warehouses may be particularly risky if not managed well, including documents being forgotten as the years go by.

Here are some tips to apply to any outsourcing contract:

■ Vet the vendor carefully prior to selection to ensure they practise proper management controls and practices, including data protection controls and practices. Continue to monitor and audit their controls and practices through the life of the contract.

■ Ensure contract language is written to cover data protection and privacy from the perspective of both regulatory requirements and the confidentiality expectations of customers.

■ Conduct a risk assessment on each shortlisted vendor. Conduct a more in-depth assessment of the likely successful vendor. A risk assessment should include consideration of the vendor's privacy and information security policies. It should also include the vendor's controls over access to personal data. In other words, an organisation should make sure that it knows and assesses where the personal information will be held along with who may have access to it.

Vendor contracts

An organisation needs to ensure that every vendor contract is tailored to the facts and circumstances of the service to be provided by the vendor to the organisation.

An organisation should never sign a standard form contract presented by a vendor without reading it, understanding its terms and the risks to the organisation resulting from them, and either negotiating any necessary amendments or consciously accepting the risk of not doing so.

The contract should usually include at least the following requirements to protect the organisation in connection with personal data under the organisation's control:

- The type of personal data the vendor will have access to at remote locations
- How the vendor must or must not use and/or disclose the personal data
- How the vendor will protect the personal data
- The vendor's responsibilities in case of a data breach
- How the data will be disposed of when the contract is terminated or, if earlier, as and when the vendor no longer needs to retain the personal data to perform its services under the contract
- The organisation's rights of audit and investigation
- As between the organisation and the vendor, each party's liability for data breach

---

CHECKLIST OF GOOD PRACTICES

Organisations should have the following practices in place when outsourcing the storage of paper documents containing personal data or other confidential information:

- Do the necessary due diligence and risk assessment of the vendor before outsourcing.
- Ensure proper contracts are in place, especially covering the vendor's responsibilities to protect the personal data.
- Audit or regularly monitor whether or not all paper documents that contain personal data are properly secured.
- If you discover a data breach in connection with your outsourced document storage and assess the risk of misuse of data as low, conduct thorough investigations before deciding whether or not to notify the relevant authorities.

"

As long as you coerce someone
to accept something, you don't really
change their attitude, you temporarily
change their subconscious behaviour.

"

Marios Evripidou

SECTION B:

Collection of Personal Data

08 Are your sales and service counters compliant with the data protection law?

I recently shopped at an electronics store and had cause for complaint under the data protection law. When I was about to make the purchase, the salesperson on duty asked:

"Can I have your full name, contact number, address and identity card number, please?"

Why would a store ever need my identity card number when all I'm doing is buying a product? I replied:

"Excuse me, why would you need my identity card number?"

"Sorry," came his reply. "We don't need it. Just the other information will do."

He gave me a scrap of paper to write the information down. I did so. I was curious to see how he would be using it. That was when I noticed that all the other sales assistants on duty were doing the same thing: they would all use the paper as a reference when keying customer details into their POS (Point of Sale) system. This was presumably to ensure that the inputs were accurate.

Watch out when you collect personal data on scraps of paper

After the sales assistant keyed my details into the POS system he handed me my product and thanked me for patronising the store. While I was happy with the purchase and the price I paid for it, I had a big issue with him and the store. He left my personal data beside the POS input device. He had forgotten about it. Anyone could see it. Not just the next salesperson, which would be bad enough, but the next customer too.

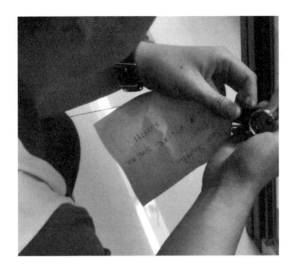

I said to him, "Excuse me, can you please get rid of my personal data?"

He looked at me, and hesitated. Obviously he was not trained in information security. At first, he wanted to crush the piece of paper and throw it away. Then he paused and tore it up instead.

Do not expose personal information of customers on your POS system

Because of this little incident, I started looking around the store.

I noticed that there was another piece of paper with a customer's personal data beside a computer nearby. And that the computer monitor was displaying the order page of another customer. The sales assistant was serving a woman a few metres away, oblivious that I was inspecting his entries. I could see her full name, contact details, address and all the products she had bought. In fact, the computer terminal was in full view of the public. Anyone could go up to the computer and peek at customers' personal data.

Do not pile invoices or receipts where they are within reach of the public

As I made payment at the cashier counter, I found another disturbing sight.

Behind the payment counters were piles of invoices and receipts of customers left out in the open. There were also files containing purchase orders, return receipts and other confidential information and personal data. The area was not restricted. Anyone could pick them up without being noticed and walk away.

I felt uncomfortable seeing my information "dumped" into a tray after I paid for my purchase. I wondered if senior management of the organisation knew that the data protection law is in force. If so, there was no evidence that its sales assistants had been trained in how to comply with it operationally. I wondered if they knew that the organisation could get into trouble if somebody complained about their personal data being disclosed to passersby.

Achieve operational compliance with the data protection law, not just legal compliance

The protection obligation or principle under the data protection law requires organisations to make reasonable security arrangements to protect the personal data that they possess or control. This is to prevent unauthorised access, collection, use, disclosure or similar risks.

In the case of my retail experience, the organisation's policies and practices were likely not compliant with this obligation or principle. Personal data was not protected. There was leakage or exposure to the public. If your organisation has retail or service counters, is it compliant with this obligation or principle?

Often when I ask organisations if they are compliant with the data protection law the answer I get is that their lawyers have done the due diligence by reviewing their documents and that training has been conducted for their staff.

However, these measures will merely get you legal compliance. But operational compliance doesn't necessarily follow. Operational compliance can only be achieved if you have implemented information security policies and practices, and embed them into the operational processes.

Training your staff about "what" the data protection law is about is different from training them "how" to comply with it. That includes enforcing your information security policies.

You should do an onsite data protection readiness audit of your entire operations. You should ensure that your information security policy is amended accordingly. You should ensure that your organisation's information security vulnerabilities are tackled.

CHECKLIST OF GOOD PRACTICES

In complying with the data protection law, organisations should do the following:

- Ensure it achieves operational compliance with the data protection law, in addition to legal compliance with it.
- Avoid using scraps of paper to record personal data so as to prevent unnecessary leakage or exposure of personal data.
- Do not expose personal data of customers on your POS or computer systems.
- Do not place invoices or receipts of customers in open places that are within reach of the public.
- Conduct periodic onsite data protection audits to monitor continuing operational compliance. Identify any deficiencies or gaps and change processes and procedures to improve operational compliance.
- Train your employees on the data protection law and your organisation's policies and practices.

🔒 **09** Common mistakes of voluntary welfare organisations

A voluntary welfare organisation (VWO) provides welfare services and/or services that benefit the community at large. Well-known examples of VWOs include worldwide organisations such as Red Cross and the Salvation Army and local examples such as charities that provide social and welfare services to the community. The services they provide mean that they frequently collect a very wide range of personal data. Often this includes sensitive health and financial information.

Here is a list of common data protection mistakes made by VWOs that I have observed.

Believing that the data protection law shouldn't apply to them

It's not uncommon for senior employees of VWOs to tell me that it's unfair for the data protection law to apply to VWOs because it uses up some of the scarce resources that should be dedicated entirely to their beneficiaries or other clients.

Except where it contains an explicit exception for charities, it is clear that the data protection law applies to all organisations, including VWOs. It is a mistake to think that it does not, even if one is convinced that it should not. It does.

Collecting an excessive amount of personal data

I've observed that VWOs are particularly prone to collecting excessive amounts of personal data in case they need it in the future.

Their data collection motives are good typically. For example, they hope that if they get a wide range of information at the "intake" stage, they will not have to bother their clients for more information in the future. Or that if they know more about their clients at the outset they will be able to provide them with valuable assistance that the clients have not requested or they will be able to refer them to an agency or other VWO that can give them additional assistance.

No matter their motives, the data protection law permits a VWO to collect only such personal data as is reasonable in the circumstances. The "circumstances" include the purposes for which the VWO notifies its clients that it is collecting the information. It is a mistake to think that "reasonable" will necessarily be given a very wide meaning just because VWOs are doing good in the community.

Not notifying clear purposes for collecting, using or disclosing personal data

Too many VWOs state their purposes for collecting, using or disclosing personal data vaguely. They tell me this gives them more flexibility. If a notification is vague it is unlikely to be a valid notification of purpose.

If a VWO is providing counselling, for example, perhaps stating the purpose as "so that we can understand your personal and family circumstances in order to prepare a counselling plan that suits your needs and to deliver it to you" is appropriate. But "so that we can assist you" or "so that we can provide services to you" is not.

Whatever service a VWO provides, notifying an individual that their personal data will be used and/or disclosed "as we see fit" or "at our discretion" is unlikely to constitute a valid notification of purpose. Again, it is a mistake to think that purposes can be notified in a vague way just because overall motives are good.

Accepting referrals from third-party sources without checking on consent

Circumstances vary, but some VWOs get referrals from a wide range of sources. They receive calls from a friend of an individual when the friend thinks the individual needs help. Or from a family member. Or a neighbour or other bystander. They receive referrals from other VWOs too. Sometimes they collect just enough personal data to be able to call the individual who is being referred to them; sometimes they collect a wide range of personal data, especially if the call comes from a family member. Often they collect sensitive personal data, including in instances where the referral is for a medical purpose.

The mistake made by many VWOs is to assume that the third-party, the source of the referral, has obtained the individual's consent to disclose their personal data. And that the third-party has written consent so they can prove that they have obtained consent.

There is an assumption by many VWOs that they do not need to worry about consent issues because they are going to help the individual who has been referred to them.

The mistake made by the VWO is to assume that, just because a third-party source says an individual needs help, the individual not only needs help but also wants help and agrees to the disclosure of their personal data so that they are provided with help.

For example, a social worker – the third-party source – believes that an individual is lonely and needs more companionship. The social worker mentions to the individual that they should attend a day activity centre for senior citizens. The individual, perfectly happy with their level of community interaction, says nothing in the hope that the social worker will stop interfering and end the conversation. The social worker provides the individual's personal data to a VWO that operates a suitable day activity centre. The individual, annoyed at being contacted by the VWO and badgered about attending their day activity centre, complains to the regulator about the unauthorised disclosure of their personal data by the social worker and the unauthorised collection of their personal data by the VWO.

Retaining personal data (more or less) indefinitely

The data protection law requires an organisation to cease to retain personal data when it is no longer necessary for a business or legal purpose. Those VWOs that put thought into how long they actually need to retain personal data and then devise and implement an appropriate data retention policy see good dividends from it, including in terms of storage space being freed up.

The mistake made by VWOs is to retain personal data after they have finished providing their services to an individual "just in case" the individual comes back for more services in the future.

Not taking internal protection of personal data seriously

I observe an interesting dichotomy among VWOs. Counsellors, for example, are bound by various ethical codes and take confidentiality of their files very seriously. They make sure that the files are under lock and key with access given to only the relevant counsellor and, usually, their manager.

But otherwise within VWOs – where they provide services other than counselling to their clients – personal data of clients is open to all staff if they feel inclined to log in to the IT system and look at files or go to unlocked cupboards and read hardcopy files. Documents and files are not marked as "Confidential". In some cases, no passwords are used in the IT system. When passwords are used they are often never changed or changed only once or twice a year.

The mistake made by VWOs is not to treat their operation as a business with protection of personal data being taken seriously. And to assume that it's fine if all staff can see all the personal data of their clients. It's not.

CHECKLIST OF GOOD PRACTICES

If your organisation is a VWO, you should take the application of the data protection law to it seriously, just like any other organisation.

- Collect only the personal data from or about your clients that you need for the particular service your client wants.
- Clearly notify clients of the purposes for collecting, using and disclosing their personal data. Be as specific as possible.
- When you receive a referral, check to make sure that the third-party source has obtained consent from the individual to disclose their personal data to you.
- Develop and implement a data retention policy that is tailored to your VWO.
- Ensure a reasonable level of protection of the personal data in your possession, such as by restricting access to a "need to know" basis.

🔒 **10** Photo and video images – including CCTV – can be personal data too

It's rather intuitive that the data protection law covers personal data about an individual that is in a written hardcopy document or in an electronic document or file – less so that the image of an identifiable individual in a photo or video is their personal data and also covered by the data protection law.

That was alarming enough in a world of film, where the expense of buying the film and, after it was used, getting it developed and printed was relatively high. Now almost every mobile phone comes with a built-in camera that can take both still shots and videos. So now photos and videos are, effectively, free of charge except in those relatively rare instances where they are printed. Huge numbers of them are taken daily; thousands of videos are uploaded to YouTube every day; millions of individuals swap photos every day.

Personal photos

The good news is that data protection laws do not extend to what individuals do for personal or domestic purposes.[1]

If my friend takes a photo of me at their child's birthday party, for example, the data protection law does not require them to get my consent to collecting my personal data – that is taking the photo – or to using or disclosing it to their friends and family by showing them the photos from the birthday party. If they want to post it on social media then, out of politeness, they might ask me if I mind, but the data protection law doesn't require them to get my consent.

[1] This is expressed differently in various data protection laws – for example, "personal or domestic".

On the other hand, if my friend wants to use the photo of me from the birthday party in a promotional brochure for their business, they would fail to comply with the data protection law if they did not first obtain my consent. This is because they would be using it for a business purpose.

Identifiable individuals only

Further goods news. The data protection law does not apply to an image if individuals are not identifiable.

My friend showed me a couple of photos taken with her smartphone at the Botanic Gardens of a group of people including a TV celebrity. The first photo was taken from a distance and it was impossible to identify anyone in it – there was simply not enough definition. So, no personal data. The outcome would have been the same if they had been facing away from the camera and unidentifiable without seeing their faces. Or if the image had been blurred or taken in inadequate lighting.

The second photo was taken from only a few feet away from the individual. Their face was clear. Not being a TV fan, I had no idea of their name in real life or of their TV persona either so that I could find out their name. But not knowing their name makes no difference. Because they were identifiable, the image in the photo was their personal data.

Photos and videos in a public place – publicly available information

An organisation may collect, use or disclose publicly available information[2] without the consent of the relevant individual. So, for example, it may take photos or make videos in a public place such as a public park or garden, in the street and inside a place that is open to the general public (such as a museum, shopping centre or theme park).

Be careful, though. Some places might be public most, but not all, of the time. For example, a restaurant is usually a public place, but if an organisation books it out for a customer event – that is, it is closed to general entry – it is not a public place for the duration of that event. The organisation will likely fail to comply with the data protection law if it does not obtain consent for the collection, use or disclosure of the images of event attendees.

---

[2] This is a general principle. There are variations under the data protection law in different jurisdictions.

And some places have both public areas and private areas. For example, a grandstand at a sporting arena may have private "boxes" in addition to its general spectator area. Images of individuals enjoying a party in a private box are not publicly available information, even though they are separated from the public space only by a glass wall or there is a clear view through windows.

Here's a good test: if any stranger might wander into view at any time, the place is probably a public place.

Nevertheless, it is good practice for an organisation to put up signs notifying individuals if the organisation is taking photos or making a video in a public place. This is so that individuals can avoid being in the photos or video if they prefer.[3]

Getting upfront express consent for photos or videos is not a good idea

Some organisations use photos or videos extensively as promotional tools, posting them to Facebook, for example, or including them in their regular newsletters to publicise their events. A common mistake they make, usually thinking they are being administratively efficient, is to get express consent from individuals at the outset of the organisation's relationship with them.

For example, we see voluntary welfare organisations, sporting clubs and other associations including a consent for collection, use and disclosure of photos and videos in their intake, membership or other similar documents. Sometimes it is optional; sometimes it is a condition of obtaining the service or joining the club or association. Here is the trouble with doing this:

- If consent is a condition of obtaining the service or joining the club or association, a regulator may consider that it is a "coerced" or "forced" consent because it is not reasonably necessary for that purpose. If so, the consent is not valid.
- In any event, the individual has the right under the data protection law to withdraw their consent at any time.

Therefore, obtaining consent upfront achieves little or nothing in terms of administrative efficiency. It means that the organisation must

---

[3] In any event, organisations should avoid using the images of strangers for commercial purposes without their consent because, in some circumstances, an individual may be able to claim compensation for commercial exploitation of their image. Or there may be other unintended consequences.

keep track of who has consented and not withdrawn their consent. And it must do so for all individuals, sometimes over a long period of time (versus addressing consent issues only when it considers using a photo or video that includes the image of an individual).

Photos and videos in non-public places

Here are some tips for organisations in connection with photos and videos in non-public places.

■ When the organisation invites individuals to an event it should notify invitees that photos and videos may be taken and specify the purposes for which they may be used/disclosed. Similarly, if the organisation has an online registration portal it could include such a notice on the portal.

■ At the registration counter or other entry point to the event, the organisation can put up a similar prominent notice.

Organisations should usually do both of these things to reduce the risk of an individual saying that they were not aware that their image might be captured. After all, some individuals may attend an event (with a friend, for example) without seeing any invitation or registration and some individuals may not be attentive when they arrive at the event.

If the individual is aware that photos may be taken or videos made and they nevertheless attend, the organisation should ordinarily be able to rely on their attendance constituting consent to the organisation collecting, using or disclosing their image for the stated purpose.

■ The individual can withdraw their consent at any time before their image becomes publicly available information as a result of it being used/disclosed by an organisation. Therefore, an organisation needs to keep good records of any withdrawals of consent.

■ Some organisations prefer to obtain express consent for use/disclosure of a photo or video even where they may rely on implied consent.

If the individual is known to them and readily contactable, obtaining express consent may be administratively more convenient than keeping track of whether or not the individual has withdrawn their consent.

If the individual may have some sensitivity about their image being used by the organisation, obtaining express consent may simply be a better way of maintaining a relationship with them (versus annoying them by using their image, perhaps in some way that they dislike personally).

My photo was taken recently without my knowledge in the foyer of a hotel – obviously a public place – chatting with a colleague before entering the nearby ballroom for a gala dinner. Throughout the evening that photo and photos of other individuals taken in the foyer and at some seminar sessions held earlier that same day were shown on a loop on several large screens on the walls of the ballroom. I was really unhappy about it and annoyed with the organisation, even though I had no valid reason for complaining.

CCTV

If an organisation has a CCTV system at its premises it may capture images of visitors. Most if not all organisations choose to rely on individuals implicitly consenting to the collection, use or disclosure of their personal data by the CCTV system.

That's why organisations need to put up a notice about the presence of CCTV cameras and, if not obvious, their purpose in a place where they are seen by individuals before they enter into the field of any cameras.

CHECKLIST OF GOOD PRACTICES

Organisations should adopt the following practices before capturing photos or videos of individuals, then using or disclosing them:

- Notify individuals you will be taking photos or making videos before relying on implicit consent, including in connection with CCTV.
- Put up warning signs in public places that you will be taking photos or making videos.
- Reconsider the photo and/or video consent upfront for administrative efficiency in light of the data protection law.

An individual who takes a photo or makes a video for a personal purpose should get consent before using/disclosing it for a commercial purpose.

🔒 11 Data protection reservations about reservations – risks for restaurants

I was passing by a restaurant the other day. Its registration stand was just outside the entrance. There was a reservation list. The woman in charge was not around. I could see the names and mobile phone numbers of individuals who had made reservations to dine at the restaurant.

The restaurant is obviously oblivious to the data protection law requiring protection of personal data – including no unauthorised access to it and no accidental disclosure of it. It's likely that it's oblivious to other requirements of the data protection law too.

Failing to protect personal data

The data protection law requires an organisation to reasonably protect personal data in its possession and to prevent unauthorised access to it.

So what happens when a reservation is made at a restaurant? The restaurant would ask for the person's name and contact details, the time of arrival and the number of diners. The required tables or seats would be reserved. When the diners arrive they would be shown to their table. The business transaction would be completed when they have dined and paid their bill. It is business as usual. Right? Wrong.

What I saw at the restaurant entrance bothered me. It showed that the restaurant does not treat its customers' personal data with care – anyone could see it. So what? Why would anyone care, you might ask?

Well, it might not matter for many of us who are just ordinary folks. But to a celebrity or VIP making a reservation at the restaurant, this could be a big concern. From the exposed data, anyone could

potentially know who the restaurant's important customers are and their contact numbers. They could do anything they like with that information.

Retaining personal data longer than necessary

In addition to reasonably protecting personal data, the data protection law requires an organisation to "cease to retain" personal data when it is no longer necessary for a legal or business purpose.

So what happens to the reservation list after the reservation dates? Does the restaurant keep it or dispose of it? If the restaurant disposes of the information, does it do so securely so that it continues to be protected? Or is it thrown into the dustbin without shredding?

Using personal data without consent

The personal data collected for a restaurant reservation cannot be used for any other purpose or disclosed without the consent of the relevant individual. If the restaurant keeps the reservation list, if it is filed away for reference, why and for how long? Does the restaurant use the personal data in the reservation list for other purposes, like marketing, without the knowledge or consent of the relevant individual? Does the restaurant give or even sell the information to a third-party and, if so, for what purposes?

Complaints to the regulator

It's clear to me that this restaurant is failing to comply with at least one of the obligations under the data protection law – the obligation to protect personal data. It may well be failing to comply with all of the obligations highlighted above!

Under a "complaints-based regime"[1] all it takes is for somebody to complain to the data protection regulator about this restaurant and the regulator will be compelled to investigate. Where the regulator has instead set up an investigation, the regulator might observe the restaurant's inappropriate data protection practices and investigate on its own initiative. In either case, fines and order for corrective action may follow.

CHECKLIST OF GOOD PRACTICES

Organisations handling personal data of individuals should do the following to protect the data:

- Do an onsite audit – walk around the premises and see where personal data might be inadvertently disclosed to third-parties. For example, contact information on reservation lists should be concealed from public view.
- Adopt effective operational practices to close operational compliance gaps identified during the audit.
- Dispose of personal data when it is no longer necessary for a legal or business purpose.
- Do not use personal data collected for one purpose (such as a restaurant reservation) for any other purpose (such as email marketing) without the consent of the relevant individual.
- Train your employees so that operations are compliant and they can recognise potential operational compliance failures and remediate them.

---

[1] A complaints-based regime is one where the regulator does not carry out audits or investigations on its own initiative but instead acts to investigate complaints made to it by individuals. Singapore's Personal Data Protection Commission takes a complaints-based approach.

12 Safeguarding privacy during data collection

Filling in forms and making entries in specially designated record books are the two most common methods used by organisations to collect personal data from individuals. There are a number of "data collection points" where such activities occur, such as:

■ when visitors, contractors or service providers fill in the visitors' record book at the security guard post of a condominium or at the reception counter of an office building

■ when buyers visit a show flat at a property launch and the salespersons help them to fill in an expression-of-interest form

■ when prospective clients meet face-to-face with financial planning advisers who help them to fill in a know-your-client form

■ when individuals submit their application forms at the service provider's counter

■ when job seekers submit their job application forms to an organisation

■ when shoppers drop lucky draw participation forms into a box or slot at a shopping mall and

■ when new patients register themselves at a doctor's clinic.

Have you seriously observed how the "data collection points" are located and designed in organisations, and how the data collection processes are executed? You may be amazed to learn that in a number of organisations there is scant attention paid to the privacy of your personal data at these "data collection points".

Visitors' record book

Visitors' record books usually have column headings indicating the information requested and horizontal ruled lines for each visitor to fill in, one row at a time. Whenever visitors add their own personal contact information to the record book, they will inevitably see the personal details of earlier visitors. This is likely an unauthorised disclosure of earlier visitors' personal data. (Some people may argue that earlier visitors implicitly consented to the data disclosure by adding their personal contact information voluntarily, while knowing that later visitors would see it. In some circumstances that might be the case, but not when they were given no real choice to opt-out.)

Organisations should protect the privacy of their visitors. For example, they could do either of the following:

■ Have individual forms for visitors to fill in, one form for each visitor.

■ Have an electronic device for visitors to provide their personal contact information. They should make sure that the screen is shielded from other visitors who are queueing behind the visitor using the device. They should also ensure that the software does not allow the current visitor to use the "back" arrow key to look at the previous entries.

Gathering information face-to-face

An organisation's representative, such as a real estate salesperson or financial planning adviser, may meet face-to-face with prospective clients. The representative asks the prospective clients questions to better understand their needs. The ideal place for such discussions is an enclosed room where no one can eavesdrop on the conversation. But at times this may not be possible, such as where an organisation seeks clients in a public or semi-public place, as in a show flat or a booth at an exhibition or trade fair. The organisation should make sure that its representative takes precautionary measures, such as the following:

■ Locate the discussion area away from the main flow of human traffic, as far as possible.

■ Ensure that the representative's notes about the prospective client cannot be easily viewed by people around. This is often overlooked, especially where the notes are taken down using a laptop computer.

Drop-in box or slot

Retailers and shopping centres often have boxes or slots for shoppers to drop in lucky draw forms with their contact information and other personal data. The organisation collecting the personal data should protect it by taking precautionary measures, such as the following:

- When retailers give shoppers lucky draw forms to fill in, they should provide a place – perhaps a separate counter or table – where the shoppers can do this out of view of other shoppers.
- The drop-in box should not have transparent sides that allow any passerby to take a peek inside and see the personal data of shoppers.
- The drop-in slot should be one-way and narrow enough so that no passerby can fish out lucky draw forms from the box.

Service counter

In today's business culture of customer friendliness, organisations design their offices to avoid putting a barrier between their employees and their customers. They may, for example, install low service counters. When prospective customers submit application forms for the organisation's services it may be fairly easy for them to view other forms that are just behind the counter. The organisation should protect such personal data by taking precautionary measures to prevent later customers from inadvertently seeing it, such as the following:

- Shield the application forms and other confidential documents from the public eye by covering them with an opaque material or putting them in a file.
- Tilt computer screens used by employees away from the line-of-sight of the public.

Registration counter

I have heard of an alarming experience of a patient's visit to a doctor's clinic from a data protection perspective. The patient arrived early for the appointment, being scheduled as the first appointment for the day. No other patients were in the waiting room. No one was sitting at the reception desk yet. But a patient's file was left unattended on the service counter next to the reception desk. The patient could have simply picked it up and read it or walked away with it.

Moral of the story

From the anecdotes I have shared, we can see that it is fairly easy for organisations to collect an individual's personal data in a range of commonplace situations. But organisations should be aware that the data protection law requires them to do so in a way that protects the personal data. They should also be aware of most individuals' desire for the organisations to respect their privacy during the data collection process.

For both of these reasons, organisations should carefully and conscientiously think about the physical or operational circumstances that apply when their employees are collecting personal data. They should require their employees to be discreet and to take precautionary measures to protect personal data when they are collecting it.

CHECKLIST OF GOOD PRACTICES

Organisations should safeguard the personal data they collect at the various "data collection points":

Visitors' record book

- Shield the personal data of earlier visitors from subsequent visitors.
- Better still, use individual paper forms or individual screens on electronic devices.

Face-to-face meetings

- Prevent eavesdropping by locating the discussion area away from the flow of human traffic.
- Shield discussion notes and computer screens to prevent unauthorised viewing.

Drop-in box or slot

- Use a non-transparent drop-in box to prevent unauthorised viewing.
- Have a narrow, one-way slot to prevent hands from going in.

Service counter

- Shield confidential documents from the public eye.
- Tilt computer screen away from the line-of-sight of the public.

Registration counter

- Have the registration counter attended at all times and do not leave personal data lying around.

13 Lucky draws – do you need to know so much about me?

There are instances where individuals take great pains to write their personal data down on paper accurately and legibly. They complete all data fields without questioning the need for the requested information. One such instance is when they complete a "lucky draw" entry form. The reason for this is very simple. They want to be absolutely sure that if they do win a prize in the draw, the organiser can contact them quickly and then easily verify their identity. They also want to be absolutely sure that they will not be disqualified from winning for failing to provide all the information requested by the organiser.

Organisations exploiting human psychology

Some organisers of lucky draws are shrewd enough to understand this psychological behaviour of humans to be able to exploit the situation. They include additional data fields in the lucky draw entry form that are not reasonably necessary for the purpose of the lucky draw. Instead, they seek the information for the purpose of future targeted marketing to individuals. For example, the organiser might include questions to gauge participants' fashion tastes and trends or their likes and dislikes of various electronic gadgets.

The unsuspecting participants feel compelled to provide the requested information for fear that they may not be eligible to win a prize if they submit an incomplete entry form.

Individuals challenging excessive collection of personal data

But things are changing. With greater awareness of their rights under the data protection law, individuals are challenging organisations on the need to provide personal data that seems to be beyond what the organisation needs for a particular purpose. Organisers of lucky draws are not immune from these challenges.

Individuals increasingly demand that organisations give them a choice whether or not to respond to the requests for information that does not seem to be relevant. In the case of lucky draws, that means individuals are demanding an approach where they are not barred from taking part in the lucky draw even if they choose not to complete the data fields that are not reasonably necessary for the purpose of the draw.

Using or disclosing personal data about lucky draw winners

The terms and conditions of a lucky draw might state that the organiser will notify winners by contacting them. Alternatively, they might state that winners' details will be published in a particular place – such as in a particular newspaper or on a particular website – on a specified date. And that winners should then contact the organisation to claim their prizes.

The organiser should consider obtaining consent from participants to contact them or publish their personal data should they win a prize in the lucky draw. The organiser might do this by seeking the individuals' express consent to their personal data being used (for contact) or disclosed (by publication) or might decide that the data protection law permits it to rely on implied or deemed consent.

Publication of winners' details

If the organiser chooses to notify lucky draw winners by publishing their details it should disclose just enough personal data for individuals to identify themselves as winners of the competition.

For example, an organisation might choose to publish only the winners' names – perhaps only their family name and initials – and the last, say, three digits of their identity card numbers. This is sufficient for individuals to either know with certainty that they are winners or, if they have a common name, to know that they should enquire with the competition organiser to find out if they are indeed a winner. Even in those cases where their name is unusual and might therefore identify them, at least the organisation has not disclosed their identity card number.

Data protection lessons

From the above illustration we can see two principles of the data protection law at play:

- Do not over-collect personal data beyond the primary purpose for which the personal data is to be used – that is, in the case of lucky draws, to notify winners by contacting them or notifying them by publication and then to verify their identities when they come forward to claim their prizes.
- One expert has opined that the mere intent of the organisers to collect market-related data beyond the primary purpose of the lucky draw, even though data subjects are given a choice to opt-out, may constitute a failure to comply with the data protection law.
- Do not over-disclose personal data beyond the primary purpose – that is, in the case of lucky draws, to notify the winners.

CHECKLIST OF GOOD PRACTICES

Organisers of lucky draws should adopt the following practices:

- Do not require individuals to provide more personal data than is reasonably necessary to participate in the draw.
- Allow the participants to opt-out of providing additional personal data for purposes beyond the lucky draw (for example, marketing purposes).
- Disclose just enough personal data of the winners to notify them and verify their identities.

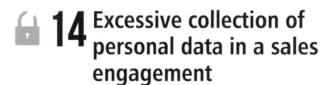

14 Excessive collection of personal data in a sales engagement

"Hello, I would like to get an insurance quotation," an individual asked an insurance company.

"Sure. Before we proceed, can you please provide us with your date and place of birth and your mother's maiden name for security purposes?"

"But I am only seeking a quotation and I don't have any insurance policy with your company. Do you need all that information?"

"It is a requirement under the data protection law for us to ask such questions as a security measure."

Extent of collection of personal data

What are your thoughts on this phone conversation? It's imaginary, but it is based on a complaint lodged with the Irish Privacy Commission[1].

Under the data protection law, an organisation is not permitted to collect personal data that is not reasonably necessary for the purpose for which it is being collected. Here, the individual complained that the insurance company was asking for an excessive amount of personal data when she contacted them by telephone seeking a quote for pet insurance.

The regulator's view

The regulator:

■ informed the insurance company that there was no requirement

---

[1] The Office of the Data Protection Commissioner, Ireland, https://www.dataprotection.ie/, 2011 - Case study 7: Allianz requesting excessive personal information at quotation stage.

under the data protection law for it to collect date of birth, mother's maiden name and place of birth data when a person phones for a quotation – especially for pet insurance!

- said that any personal data collected is limited to what is adequate, relevant and not excessive in relation to the purpose or purposes for which it is collected and
- said that telling an individual that the collection of such information was a requirement under the data protection law was both false and misleading and a misrepresentation of the requirements of the data protection law.

The outcome
The regulator required the insurance company to:
- cease using its ID verification screen at quotation stage and
- undertake not to seek information in the future at the quotation stage regarding a caller's date and place of birth and mother's maiden name.

The data protection law constrains sales organisations
Sales organisations have an understandable desire to collect as much personal data as possible from any and all individuals with whom they come into contact. Personal data about potential prospects is in many ways the life-blood of their business.

But, as the case study above demonstrates, because of the data protection law, organisations should consider the stages throughout the sales-cycle at which it is reasonably necessary to collect personal data. In particular, they should take care not to collect too much personal data too early in the sales-cycle.

In our consulting work, we have noticed excessive collection of personal data too early in the sales-cycle – namely, at the prospecting or quotation stage – by property agents and financial advisers, for example.

Excessive zeal by property agents
At property roadshows and seminars, property agents typically ask prospects to complete a "sales interest" or similar form. It often

requests excessive information such as the individual's identity card number, information relating to properties they own, their previous property transactions and even their financial status.

If the purpose of the "sales interest" form is to provide the property agent with a record of individuals who are open to contact from them after the roadshow or seminar, of course individuals' names and contact details are required. Their identity card numbers are certainly not required.

Whether collecting information about their existing property portfolio is reasonably necessary is questionable, though some high-level information might be sought legitimately if an appropriate purpose for collecting it is notified by the organisation to the individual (by stating it in the "sales interest" form). If so, organisations should consider the least privacy-intrusive way of collecting it.

For example, instead of seeking details of properties owned by the individual as a way of gauging their wealth or their future purchasing interests, the organisation might be able to get relevant information by simply asking individuals to specify the property price ranges in which they might be interested:

Please tick the property price range(s) about which you would like us to contact you:
❑ *under $500,000*
❑ *$500,000 to $5 million*
❑ *over $5 million*

Excessive zeal by financial advisers

In many jurisdictions, financial advisers are required to have their clients complete a "Know Your Client (KYC)" form before they provide them with financial advice. The KYC process is directed at ensuring that the adviser understands their clients' needs and provides financial advice that is appropriate to them.

However, the first inquiry individuals make to financial advisers is often quite preliminary, such as a question about what financial products are within the scope of the adviser's business. Similar to seeking an insurance quote, the individual is making a preliminary enquiry to find out whether or not to enter into a more detailed conversation with the organisation.

But many financial advisers ask individuals to complete a KYC form before they will respond to any enquiry, even if the individual is clearly just at the exploratory stage of learning what financial products the adviser may be able to sell to the individual. The adviser may genuinely believe that the KYC form must be completed before they are permitted to respond to even a basic and preliminary enquiry.

From the perspective of the data protection law, it makes no difference if the financial adviser has genuinely misunderstood the KYC process or if their aim is to collect as much personal data from every prospect as possible. In either case, the financial adviser will fail to comply with the data protection law if they collect more personal data than is reasonably required at any stage of their sales process. In addition, of course, they may be irritating their prospect and not contributing to the rapport they should be building to help win the sale.

The tension between data protection and building a sales database

It is true that many requests for a quote or for preliminary information and expressions of interest in talking to a sales agent may just be individuals shopping around for the best price and value or otherwise for the best deal. Meanwhile, sales organisations are keen to create databases to generate leads, including to follow up later to offer them other deals that might interest them. And, sometimes, it is undeniably convenient – for both an organisation and their new client – for the organisation to have already collected personal data about that client when a contact results in a sale for the organisation.

But the data protection law seeks to balance the right of individuals to protect their personal data and the need for organisations to collect it for reasonable purposes. Collecting personal data from individuals that is excessive in regard to the stage of the sales-cycle at which it is collected is not permitted by the data protection law.

Organisations should therefore adapt their sales approach and techniques accordingly.

Bridging the tension between data protection and sales needs

You might decide to seek consent to collect and use personal data earlier in the sales-cycle than would otherwise be possible under the data protection law. However, the balance between, say, building a database and irritating potential customers comes very much into focus. Here's another imaginary conversation, this time with a financial adviser:

"Hello, I would like to find out if you are able to offer life insurance products," an individual asks a financial adviser.

"No, we don't at the moment, though we might do so from next year onwards. We do offer investment products issued by some very prominent local banks. Would you like us to provide you with some information about them?"

"No, I'm really not interested in investment products right now and I want to get life insurance quite soon."

"OK, I understand. Would you like us to add you to our mailing list so that we can send you email updates about our product offerings from time to time? You'll be able to unsubscribe from it at any time if you no longer want to receive our updates."

Similarly, if you want to use personal data collected at any stage in the sales-cycle for sales purposes other than the original purpose intended by the prospect, you can do so if you first get the individual's consent. You should notify them if you intend to do so, state the purposes clearly and get their consent to that purpose. Nobody likes surprises, especially if it involves their personal data and they feel that an organisation uses it unfairly or without their knowledge.

Instead of looking at the data protection law as a barrier to sales, understand it and use it so that you turn it into a competitive edge vis-à-vis your competitors. Position yourself as a trusted adviser – and that includes getting individuals to trust you when it comes to their personal data!

A quick comment on disposing of personal data

The more personal data you have in your possession, the more responsibilities you have under the data protection law because it requires you to protect it. The law also requires you to "cease to retain" it when it's no longer necessary for a legal or business purpose. You should dispose of it securely, such as by shredding, so that you protect it during disposal. These requirements extend to all the notes you scribbled about your leads – their appointment dates, concerns, preferences and requirements.

CHECKLIST OF GOOD PRACTICES

Organisations collecting personal data of prospects, customers and other individuals should adopt the following practices:

- Do not collect excessive amounts of personal data in the early stage of the sales-cycle.
- Only collect personal data beyond contact details at the time when it is necessary, such as when you close the sale and are required to complete any relevant sales agreement.
- Do not use the data protection law as an excuse for collecting personal data, even when doing so is not false or misleading or a misrepresentation.
- Engender trust by explaining to individuals why you are collecting their personal data and how you will use and/or disclose it.
- Get the prospect's consent if you want to use their personal data for other sales or marketing purposes. Written consent is best because it can be proven. Verbal consent that is confirmed in writing may also be able to be proven, depending on the circumstances.
- Protect personal data in your possession and dispose of it securely when it is no longer necessary for a legal or business purpose.

15 Excessive collection of personal data in an online membership form

Many organisations tend to collect excessive information as part of a registration or initial sign-up process. While collecting basic information such as the individual's name and email address would be sufficient for the purpose for which they are collecting and will be using the personal data, they collect additional information for statistical purposes.

Do you often encounter websites that ask intrusive questions and even require excessive information when you want to join their membership or community? What happens when you refuse to provide the information because it is too personal or irrelevant? Does the site prevent you from completing the registration process?

One individual complained to the regulator when this happened to him. An online travel portal did not allow him to complete the online membership registration process because he refused to provide personal data that he felt was excessive for the purpose of registration on the site[1]. It was mandatory for registrants to provide as part of the registration process:

- Occupation
- Education level
- Marital status
- Personal monthly income
- Family monthly income
- Number of family members

[1] PCPD case notes: Ref No.: 2011C06. https://www.pcpd.org.hk

The privacy policy for the portal did not state the purpose for collecting the personal data. The organisation told the regulator that the collection was for statistical purposes only.

The regulator ruled that:

■ individuals have the right to decide whether or not to provide personal data that is required for the statistical purposes of an organisation and

■ if an individual refuses to provide personal data that is sought for statistical purposes the organisation should not for that reason deny them access to the goods and/or services sought by them.

As a result, the organisation added the statistical purpose to its privacy policy. It also amended its web page, making it optional for individuals to provide the personal data that it sought for statistical purposes.

The data protection law and the online environment

The data protection law applies online to the same extent that it applies in a "bricks and mortar" environment. They apply to online collection of personal data to the same extent as they apply when individuals complete paper forms or provide personal data verbally. They apply to organisations that have an online presence or that are online businesses.

Collecting personal data for statistical/marketing purposes

"Statistical purposes" is frequently a perfectly legitimate purpose for an organisation to collect personal data.

The purpose for collecting personal data sought by an organisation's marketing department might be described as "statistical purposes" or it might be described as "marketing purposes". It is behavioural, demographic and psychographic information, which can be invaluable for advertising and targeted marketing campaigns. It may result in more effective marketing by the organisation, which saves the organisation money. It also saves the individual from being bothered by marketing messages that are not of interest to them.

Personal data described as being "for statistical purposes" might equally be sought by an organisation's planning or finance department – demographic information can be invaluable for an organisation planning expansion of its number of business outlets or planning how to deliver its services in the future. The organisation benefits by optimal use of its resources. Individuals benefit from the organisation being able to plan around expected capacity constraints or being able to provide their goods and services in convenient ways and from convenient locations.

Notification of purpose is key

Under the data protection law, organisations that want to collect personal data for statistical purposes, including for marketing purposes, should notify individuals of that purpose.

As a matter of good practice, this should be done at the point of collection – the website in the above example could have included a question mark icon next to each relevant data field and give individuals a "click through" to the organisation's privacy policy or statement. In any event, the purpose should be disclosed clearly in its privacy policy or statement.

Optional requests for personal data is also key

Forcing individuals to provide additional personal data as mandatory fields in a registration process creates customer resistance. As in the above example, it can result in complaints to the regulator. But it also results in many potential customers not completing the registration process because they refuse to satisfy excessive requests for personal data. And having many customers who complete it grudgingly so that they can complete a registration is far from the best way of starting a customer relationship.

In addition, of course, the regulator has made it clear that fields requesting personal data for statistical purposes should be marked as optional – the individual should be given a choice whether or not to provide information that an organisation requests for statistical purposes.

Optional requests may still be excessive requests

Marking a data field as "optional" is not a magic bullet. Making fields optional doesn't mean that an organisation may collect any information without regard to purpose and relevance. Even where provision of personal data is optional there is a balance to be struck under the data protection law between the right of individuals to protect their personal data and the need for organisations to collect, use or disclose it. Otherwise, marking data fields as "optional" can easily be abused, not least because studies show that individuals are more likely than not to provide personal data that is marked as "optional".

An organisation that wants to collect personal data for statistical purposes needs to be able to justify its requests in terms of relevance from the organisation's business perspective. For example, it's unlikely that it would be reasonable for an e-commerce site selling women's shoes to know the names of all family members and their birthdates. But it might be reasonable for an e-commerce site selling computer games to know the names of family members interested in computer games and their birthdates if it would provide them with a free link on their birthday to a game that might be age-appropriate for them.

Tips about expressing the purpose for collecting personal data

Organisations should take due care when specifying the purpose(s) for which they will collect, use or disclose personal data, including where it is part of a membership scheme.

We have seen purposes expressed as "valid business or marketing reasons" or as "in the way we see fit at our discretion". This is unlikely to be considered valid notification of purpose under the data protection law – it does not really indicate to individuals how the organisation may collect, use or disclose their personal data.

In any event, you should not assume that your organisation has the right to do what it wants with personal information. Especially where a notification of purpose is too generic. The purpose should express the outcome – for example, to send newsletters, invitation to events or provide special offers.

If the organisation intends to disclose or sell the personal data to a third-party, individuals need to be informed and be given a choice to opt-out or to withdraw their consent.

Adding individuals to your database

Since we are on the topic of memberships, not everyone wants to be included in a membership system or be part of an online marketing database. For example, in our consulting work we have seen cases where organisations automatically add individuals to their email database when they make online queries.

An organisation must get consent from the individual before using personal data provided for the purpose of responding to an online query for the different purpose of marketing to them using the organisation's email database.

Protecting personal data in electronic form – encryption

If an organisation collects personal data online, the data should be transmitted securely from the online form to the organisation's database. This is because the data protection law places an obligation on an organisation to take reasonable measures to protect personal data, including personal data in electronic form.

An organisation's database should usually be encrypted to protect it. Where personal data is sensitive, such as financial information, the need to encrypt it is even more important on the basis that encryption would more likely be a reasonable measure to take in order to protect the personal data.

As part of taking reasonable security measures to protect personal data, it is often reasonable for an organisation to do a security assessment of its website (such as a vulnerability assessment or a penetration test) from time to time.

Protecting personal data in electronic form – passwords and other access controls

Any database maintained by an organisation should be password-protected so that access to it is restricted to employees who "need to know" – that is, they need to have access to it in order to do their jobs. Stated another way, organisations need to ensure that only authorised users can access personal data.

We have seen many organisations that have no access and security controls in place. Any employee in, say, the marketing department has access to any file maintained by the organisation. They can find a file containing personal data that the organisation collected for a non-marketing purpose, download it and use the personal data for marketing purposes. They can even send files to unauthorised third-parties as email attachments.

This can be both a failure to comply with the data protection law and a vulnerability in the organisation's general business practices – for example, there is nothing to prevent disgruntled employees from sharing information in the database with a competitor or from using it to set up their own business in competition with the organisation.

We see similar problems arising in organisations that provide services, such as secretariat services, to other organisations. They hold files containing the personal data of members of each organisation to which they provide services. If files are not carefully protected, an employee could use personal data of members of one organisation for the purposes of another organisation. (This is similar to a call centre engaged by several organisations and receiving their client lists as call lists. Without access controls, employees might use a call list received from one client to make calls for another client.)

The multiplier effect of excessive personal data

Collecting excessive personal data exacerbates the issues and vulnerabilities discussed here. Organisations have responsibilities in connection with the personal data that they hold – the more data they hold, the larger the responsibilities. Not forgetting that the possibilities and impact of a data breach are also much higher.

CHECKLIST OF GOOD PRACTICES

When collecting the personal data of individuals for business purposes, organisations should adopt the following practices:

- Notify individuals of the purposes for which you collect, use or disclose personal data and obtain their consent.
- Do not collect excessive personal data.
- Include the purposes for collecting, using or disclosing personal data in your privacy notice.
- State clearly which data fields are optional if you collect personal data for statistical purposes.
- Ensure that optional data requests are not excessive and that they are reasonably related to your business.
- Perform regular security assessments of your website. Ensure that personal data is transmitted securely from your website or online portal to your organisation's database. Ensure that the databases are encrypted.
- Ensure that access to your organisation's databases is restricted to employees who have a "need to know" in order to do their jobs.

🔒 16 Is your public WiFi service collecting excessive personal data?

World-4-Kids[1] offers fun and entertainment for children – they can pretend to be in a particular occupation, such as a teacher, police officer, fire-fighter, doctor or pilot and experience what life would be like in that occupation. It has various "stations" where the children can participate in activities. For example, at the petrol station they can play as attendants to fill up the motor vehicles of other children bringing their vehicles in for a refill. Each station is sponsored by a well-known commercial brand.

I recently visited World-4-Kids with my two children. While they were excited about visiting a make-believe world where they could role-play various occupations, I was looking forward to seeing how World-4-Kids would handle their personal data.

Personal data nicely secured and used for the right reasons

Lo and behold, I was rather impressed by how World-4-Kids handled personal data. World-4-Kids collected the usual personal details when we purchased tickets online, namely the ages and names of the customers. World-4-Kids did not ask for any passport or identity card number when I purchased the tickets. It did not ask for any additional information when we arrived at World-4-Kids either.

We were each given a security wrist band that resembled a wrist watch. Our personal data was transferred to it. As we visited each station World-4-Kids employees scanned our wrist band into a

---

[1] This is a pseudonym for an actual organisation in a jurisdiction that has a data protection law.

dedicated workstation to keep track of what stations each child visited. No personal data was physically exchanged, reducing any risk of information leakage or accidental disclosure.

My son chose to be a fire-fighter so we headed off to the in-house fire station where there was already a queue. I was told that the wait would take more than an hour. I agreed to it as this was a highlight for my son – he would get to ride in a mini fire engine (complete with loud sirens) and he would have a chance to put out "fires".

I was not sure whether to leave my son in the dedicated queueing area. It was supervised by World-4-Kids employees so there was really no need to be physically there to accompany him. Nevertheless, I was concerned about leaving him alone. I was impressed when World-4-Kids employees assured me that there was no need to worry because he was wearing his wrist band. It was not easy to dislodge it. Therefore, he would not be able to leave World-4-Kids without triggering off alerts. Hmm, personal data used for the right security reasons, I thought.

World-4-Kids' WiFi service

So my experience of World-4-Kids as far as personal data was concerned was a good one. Until I tried accessing their public WiFi service.

I was surprised that I had to input personal data such as my email address, mobile number and my date of birth just to use it. Whatever for?

World-4-Kids' WiFi service was managed by a third-party service provider. It was disconcerting to learn that the third-party could disclose my personal data to:

■ World-4-Kids and

■ the sponsors of World-4-Kids – that is, to the sponsor of each station.

To be fair to the WiFi service provider, the bulk of the policy was very transparent with regard to how it collects, uses and discloses personal data. The policy stated that:

We may also use your data, or permit selected third parties to use your data, to provide you with information about goods and services that may be of interest to you.

We will only contact you by electronic means (e-mail or SMS) with information about goods and services.

Where We permit selected third parties to use your data, We (or they) will only contact you by electronic means.

But, the WiFi service provider also made the point that:

If you do not want us to use your data in this way, or to pass your details on to third parties for marketing purposes then you should not use our wifi Service.

They unfairly tied the use of their WiFi service by individuals visiting World-4-Kids to receiving marketing messages from them and from other third-parties. There was no choice to opt-out of receiving them. Any consent I gave them would not likely be valid under the data protection law, but that was cold comfort – my personal data would still have been used for the WiFi provider's marketing purposes and disclosed by them to other third-parties.

Closing remarks

Both World-4-Kids and its selected WiFi service provider still have a long way to go in terms of personal data protection.

Seriously, how many of us actually bother to read the fine print in a privacy policy? Well, with the data protection law firmly in place, we should read it. Then we can decide not to use services that require us to provide our personal data unnecessarily and who opt to use and disclose it for marketing purposes. Or we can file a complaint with the regulator. Either way we have a role in improving practices about the collection, use and disclosure of our personal data.

CHECKLIST OF GOOD PRACTICES

Organisations working with service providers of WiFi services (or any other services) to their customers should ensure that their service providers:

- comply with the requirements of the data protection law
- do not collect excessive data from customers
- do not disclose any personal data collected from customers to any third-party except as approved by them and stated accordingly in the privacy policy, and
- do not use any personal data collected from customers for any purpose not stated in the privacy policy.

Individuals should:

- always read the privacy policy of the WiFi service they are accessing and
- refrain from using WiFi services to conduct sensitive transactions like online banking or e-commerce purchases.

17 Organisations, mobile apps and the data protection law

Do you download mobile applications on your smartphone and tablet? Beware of mobile applications that are functionally equivalent to handing your device – and all the personal data in it – to a stranger.

Does your organisation make mobile applications available to its customers? Do these apps collect personal data when they are downloaded? If so, is this explained in your privacy policy? Beware that some developers may include that download functionality without checking whether you want it or not. And you will be responsible for any failure to comply with the data protection law.

Handing your smartphone or tablet to a stranger

Would you hand over your smartphone or tablet to a total stranger and allow them full access to the personal data in that device – to look at it and even to change it? Of course you wouldn't. But do you know that every time you download an application from Android's Play Store or Apple's App Store onto your mobile device this might happen?

By clicking on the "I accept" button you may have given the application permission to look at or even change some or all of the personal data and other information on your device. You are not offered the option to choose what to allow – you can only click "I accept" and the application will download. Or you can click "Do not accept" or something similar and be unable to proceed with downloading the application.

Global regulatory survey

Some 26 privacy regulators in 19 countries conducted their second Global Privacy Enforcement Network (GPEN) Privacy Sweep in May 2014[1] to assess the transparency of the data protection/privacy practices of 1,211 popular mobile applications. The survey looked at:

- the types of permissions applications were seeking
- whether those permissions exceeded what would be expected by the sweepers based on the application's functionality and
- most importantly, how the application explained to individuals why it wanted the personal information and what it planned to do with it.

We decided to do the same survey in Singapore in August–September 2015[2]. We looked at 100 of the most popular local applications.

The Singapore survey

The findings of the survey that we conducted in Singapore, as compared with the global survey, were as follows:

- 75% of the applications surveyed globally requested more than one permission, but 89% did so in Singapore.
- 31% of applications surveyed globally had excessive permissions based on the surveyor's understanding of its functionality, while this was almost double for Singapore, at 58%.
- 59% of applications surveyed globally raised concerns regarding pre-installation privacy communications – privacy information provided was not adequate because it did not tell the sweeper how information would be collected, used or disclosed. In our Singapore survey, the figure was 65%.

Some applications provided, in effect, an online brochure for real estate agents and financial advisers. But they required an individual to give a wide range of permissions to enable them to access personal data on the device to which they would be downloaded. Other applications provided information on transport services (for example, train or bus routes) but they required access to the phone, device ID, application

[1] Results of the 2014 Global Privacy Enforcement Network Sweep, https://www.priv.gc.ca/media/nr-c/2014/bg_140910_e.asp
[2] Results of the top 100 mobile app survey conducted in Singapore by Straits Interactive, http://www.straitsinteractive. com/research-findings/summary-findings-from-singapores-first-privacy-survey-covering-mobile-applications/

history and the phone identity. One application gave a list of public holidays in Singapore but required access to location and photos/media/files of all its users.

The survey found that many applications access the location of the device[3], including where location is not related to the functionality provided by the application. For example, an application provided to a user to enable them to locate the nearest ATM or the nearest bus stop clearly needs to know the location of the user. But an application providing a list of public holidays in Singapore does not.

Other applications required access to photos and videos on the device, and even access to the built-in camera, where the access was not related to the application's functionality. While these access requirements may make sense for a mobile app that is a photo editor, for example, it is excessive for applications providing mainstream news or applications for booking movie tickets online, which was the case for a few applications surveyed.

We believe that the main reason an application requires so many permissions is because, typically, it is actually passing the user's phone number, address book, and location to an advertising network's servers so they can track the user and serve what they consider to be relevant advertisements to the user. Or that application developers expect that organisations for which they develop applications will want such functionality and build it into their applications unless they are instructed not to do so.

Implications for organisations providing applications in Singapore

The results of the survey have significant implications for organisations in Singapore providing mobile apps. The implications relate to excessive permissions and inadequate notifications of the purposes for which organisations will collect, use or disclose the relevant personal data.

First and inevitably, we believe that asking for excessive permissions will prompt complaints to the regulator. It seems to us likely that investigations will show that organisations seeking excessive

[3] Even the need for location data may bring regulatory risks. In 2014, Uber, which is akin to a smart taxi service, discovered that a security breach had exposed the data of 50,000 drivers across the US. It was subsequently fined $20,000 over the breach, which also included a settlement focusing on rider privacy involving the potential abuse of real-time locations of riders in an Uber vehicle.

permissions will be found to have failed to comply with the data protection law.

Failures like these can result in the regulator giving organisations such directions as it sees fit in the circumstances to ensure compliance with the data protection law. They can also result in the regulator ordering the organisation to pay a financial penalty. The publicity surrounding a complaint and regulatory action can also damage the reputation of the organisation.

It remains to be seen whether there will be any significant difference in the eyes of the law between an organisation setting out to develop an application seeking excessive permissions, and an over-zealous developer building in the excessive permissions.

Secondly, and to aggravate matters, we found in our survey that most organisations providing mobile applications do not inform their users about how their personal data will be collected, used or disclosed. At best, they have a "standard" privacy policy informing users about what personal data they collect in their "non-application" business and how the organisation will use or disclose it. But they totally omit mentioning the personal data collected via their mobile applications. It is as if employees responsible for their privacy policy and notice are not aware that the organisation promotes mobile applications that collect personal data.

Summary findings for mobile applications privacy practices

The following table shows the findings of the second Global Privacy Enforcement Network (GPEN) Privacy Sweep. Some 26 privacy enforcement authorities in 19 countries participated in the 2014 Sweep. Over the course of a week, participants downloaded 1,211 popular mobile apps in a bid to assess the transparency of their privacy practices. The Office of the Privacy Commissioner (OPC) of Canada focused on 151 apps that were either made-in-Canada or were downloaded frequently by Canadians. The first two columns show the permissions requested by the 1,211 global apps and 151 OPC apps respectively. The third column shows the permissions requested by 103 mobile apps developed in Singapore (SG) from a similar study performed by Straits Interactive.

	Global apps	OPC apps	SG apps
Total number of apps examined	1211	151	103
Apps requesting 1 or more permissions	75%	70%	89%
Permission requested			
Location	32%	22%	70%
Contacts	9%	10%	7%
Calendar	2%	2%	8%
Microphone	5%	7%	4%
Camera	10%	8%	29%
Device ID	16%	13%	52%
Access to other accounts	15%	23%	49%
SMS	4%	6%	12%
Call log	7%	11%	2%
Privacy communications			
Apps with concerns regarding pre-installation rivacy communications	59%	42%	65%
Apps with excessive permissions based on sweeper's understanding of app's functionality	31%	28%	58%
Apps with privacy communications not well tailored to small screen	43%	31%	Not assessed
Overall privacy marks			
0 = No privacy information, other than permissions	30%	11%	18%
1 = Privacy information not adequate; sweeper does not know how information will be collected, used and disclosed	24%	15%	55%
2 = Privacy information somewhat explains the app's collection, use and disclosure of personal information; however, sweeper still had questions about certain permissions	31%	46%	17%
3 = Privacy information clearly explains how app collects/uses/discloses personal information; sweeper is confident in his/her knowledge of app's practices	15%	28%	10%

Concerns over security practices

To drill down further into the security and privacy loopholes, we worked with Appknox, a company that does privacy and security scans, to do a code analysis of the 103 SG apps. This covered basic coding practices, data flow and metrics that include OWASP or Open Web Application Security Project configurations. The top three security risks we discovered in Android applications were:

69% – **Remote code execution through Javascript interface:** This gives privilege to hackers to execute or run any code and perform unexpected results or actions on behalf of the user remotely without even touching the device physically.

61% – **Misconfiguration in Secure Sockets Layer (SSL):** SSL is the standard security technology for establishing an encrypted link between a web server and a browser. This link ensures that all data passed between the web server and browsers remain private and integral. A misconfiguration in the SSL can lead to attacks which compromise user details. It simply means any hacker can intercept the Internet connection. This can lead to "man in the middle" attacks.

52% – **Poor encryption:** This can be misused to get access to users' personal data by hackers. Easily decrypted information is like keeping users' keys in the open for any thief to steal their data.

The table below summarises the high-risk vulnerabilities uncovered:

High-risk vulnerabilities uncovered	SG apps
Misconfiguration in SSL – Broken Trust Mgr for SSL (High Risk)	61%
Weakness in SSL – Broken Host Name Verifier for SSL	45%
Weakness in SSL – Host Name Verifier Allow All Host Names	31%
Remote code execution through Javascript interface	69%
Insufficient Transport Layer protection (Transport Layer Security (TLS) is a protocol that ensures privacy between communicating applications and their users on the Internet. When a server and client communicate, TLS ensures that no third-party may eavesdrop or tamper with any message.)	28%
Derived Crypto keys	52%
Application Log (medium risk)	45%

CHECKLIST OF GOOD PRACTICES – FOR USERS

Individuals downloading mobile applications should be careful and adopt the following practices:

- Do not download applications that are "nice to have" or merely popular. Some applications may make your device vulnerable to hackers.

- Be aware what permissions you are granting when you download a mobile application. Decide whether or not they are excessive in relation to the app's features and functionality.

- If the application is free, you are likely "the product". Your personal data may be "harvested" and sold to advertisers.

- Read the privacy policy and understand how your personal data will be used. Be suspicious when no or too little information is provided.

- Only download applications offered by organisations that you trust. Ignore applications written by individuals. Read reviews to determine the credibility of the vendor. Take note of any complaints involving privacy and security.

- If you use your device for work purposes, make sure you follow your organisation's security policies. Take extra care of your device if you are in a management position, particularly if you have confidential information of your employer on your device. Take special care too if you have personal data, particularly sensitive personal data, on your device.

- Do not let your children use your device to download and play games. Applications that contain harmful add-ons, including malware, may be aimed at them and they may unwittingly download them onto your device.

CHECKLIST OF GOOD PRACTICES – FOR ORGANISATIONS/DEVELOPERS

Organisations and developers should take privacy and data protection considerations seriously when designing and deploying mobile applications. There are standards and obligations imposed by regulators and trade associations worldwide with which an application developer or platform designer is required to comply. See, for example, the tool at https://iapp.org/news/a/the-all-new-iapp-mobile-app-privacy-tool/.

- Ensure that applications are built in accordance with "privacy by design" principles – that is, privacy considerations and concerns should be addressed at the design stage and not as an afterthought.

- If you contract a designer to build an application for your organisation, ensure that you understand the permissions that the application will seek and why they are reasonably necessary for the purpose of the application.

- Provide a privacy policy that covers the mobile applications and ensure there is transparency and choice for users.

- Scan the application proactively for privacy and security breaches in the same way as online services and applications.

- Even if your organisation does not deploy its own mobile applications, you should address privacy and security vulnerabilities introduced by employees granted permission to use mobile applications on their own devices. You should ensure your organisation has an appropriate Bring-Your-Own-Device (BYOD) policy and that employees are trained accordingly.

ADDITIONAL CHECKLIST OF GOOD PRACTICES FOR DEVELOPERS

If your organisation is a developer of mobile applications you should adopt the following practices in designing and deploying mobile applications:

- Do not collect excessive personal data via your mobile applications.

- Your privacy policy and privacy notice should cover the collection, use and disclosure of personal data by your mobile applications.

- Provide transparency and choice to users of your mobile applications.

- Comply with, or follow, data privacy guidelines, standards or obligations as required in your jurisdiction and in jurisdictions in which your mobile applications are made available.

- Scan your mobile applications for potential privacy and security vulnerabilities.

18 Over-collection of personal data: "This is our company policy" is no longer acceptable

A few years ago, my wife and I walked into a well-known spa company in Singapore to redeem a voucher for a free massage for two. At the service counter, the staff member on duty asked us to fill in a registration form. We obediently wrote in our personal contact details in the first section of the form. When it came to the second section we were hesitant to provide the information requested. This was because there was a whole series of questions about our medical conditions. We felt that the disclosure of such sensitive information had no bearing on the massage.

To our surprise, the receptionist insisted that we could not leave any section of the form blank, nor indicate "not applicable"; otherwise we would not be given the massage. We asked why the spa company would want full knowledge of our medical conditions when such information was not requested by any one of the other spa companies where we had massages before. Without hesitation, the receptionist said smugly, "This is our company policy." When we argued that this company policy was not in line with industry practice and it was an invasion of personal privacy, the receptionist repeated, "This is our company policy."

In order to resolve the stalemate, we requested to speak to the supervisor, who again chanted the same mantra: "This is our company policy." Flabbergasted, we asked to speak to someone higher up the organisation hierarchy who could throw further light on what this company policy was all about. Imagine our chagrin when a senior manager said this to us: "I'm sorry there is nothing I can do as this is our company policy." We gave up! We stormed out of the spa and did not redeem our free voucher. Our parting words to them were: "Your company has just lost two potential customers."

Companies have to be open with their data protection policies

Under the data protection law, organisations collecting personal data can no longer say to their customers that "This is our company policy". The data protection law requires organisations to be open and transparent. The law requires them to share their data protection policy with their customers – and with any other individuals who request it – as and when requested. They have to notify and explain to their customers the purpose of collecting, using and disclosing their personal data, and to obtain their consent first, before they can collect the personal data. (They must not provide false or misleading information with respect to the collection, use or disclosure of personal data either.) Furthermore, organisations are not permitted to "coerce" or "force" consent from their potential customers as a condition for providing the service.

CHECKLIST OF GOOD PRACTICES

When collecting personal data from customers, organisations should abide by the following:

- Do not collect more personal data than is necessary to provide a product or service to the customer.
- Do not "coerce" or "force" consent from potential customers as a condition for providing a product or service.
- Be open about your data protection policies. Hiding under the mantra of "This is our company policy" is not acceptable.

🔒 19 The trouble with overzealous sales and marketing techniques

If you are a salesperson, you know that every year your sales target or quota goes up. It's inevitable. There are already enough pressures trying to meet your sales goals and you look for new ways to generate sales leads.

Any method of generating sales leads that does not comply with the data protection law will backfire on you and your organisation. This includes "techniques" to illegally, secretly or unfairly acquire personal data.

A method that does not comply with the data protection law might even work for a short while. But it will inevitably get you and your organisation into trouble. Someone will complain to the regulator and the regulator will investigate you and your organisation. An investigation will drain your time, energy and resources when they could be used better in concentrating your efforts on meeting your sales goals.

And if the regulator finds that your organisation did, as a result of your actions, fail to comply with the data protection law, the regulator may give such directions as it sees fit so that the organisation does comply with the law. The regulator may also impose a financial penalty on the organisation. Oh, and at this point your job security will likely be tenuous.

Do not acquire personal data illegally or secretly
In our experience, acquiring personal data illegally or secretly is probably the most common method of sourcing leads that gets sales

people into trouble under the data protection law. They look for "creative" ways to acquire customer lists or leads. Many organisations and even individuals have faced regulatory action – in some jurisdictions, criminal or civil prosecution – for illegally or secretly collecting personal data.

An estate agent and a director of SAI Property Investments Limited[1] were found guilty of committing such an offence under the UK's Data Protection Act. They were found to have unlawfully obtained details about their tenants from a rogue customer service adviser at Slough Borough Council. The Council was also fined for supplying them with information relating to individuals receiving a Housing and Council Tax Benefit.

In another example, a man unlawfully obtained personal data of online bingo players[2]. The data set contained individuals' names, addresses, email addresses, telephone numbers and user names. It was sold to him in 2008 while he was working for an Israeli poker company. He later sold it on an industrial scale for approximately £25,000, compromising the privacy of more than 65,000 online customers. He was fined for doing so.

Do not access customer databases illegally

Everything Everywhere (EE) is a telecommunications company. A director of three marketing and telecommunications companies was fined[3] after illegally accessing one of EE's customer databases. He did this by impersonating a member of EE's security team in calls and emails he made to EE. On one of them he was successful and got the passwords and log-in details of 1,066 of EE's customers. Apparently, he then logged in to the customer accounts and found out when they were due for a mobile phone upgrade. Then he targeted them with services offered by his own telecommunications companies.

The Information Commissioner said: "Fines like this are no deterrent. Our personal details are worth serious money to rogue operators. If we

[1] http://swarb.co.uk/sandhu-prosecution-ico-30-mar-2012/
[2] http://www.out-law.com/en/articles/2011/november/man-fined-after-selling-unlawfully-obtained-personal-data-of-online-bingo-players/
[3] http://www.itv.com/news/calendar/update/2014-11-11/mobile-phone-network-director-fined-for-data-offences/

don't want people to steal our personal details or buy and sell them as they like, then we need to show them how serious we are taking this. And that means the prospect of prison for the most serious cases."

Do not acquire personal data through unfair or deceptive means

Two individuals came up with a supposedly innovative way to acquire a qualified sales list[4]. They would sell the lists to claims management companies looking for compensation cases to in turn pass on to lawyers who would pay commission to the claims management company.

To promote compensation claims for personal injury or payment protection, the two individuals spammed text messages such as the following message without identifying the source of the message. In addition, despite appearances to the contrary, they did not offer an effective way for recipients to opt-out:

> *CLAIM TODAY, you may be entitled to £3500 for the accident you had. To CLAIM free reply CLAIM to this message. To opt out text STOP.*

Most recipients ignored the messages. A few responded by enquiring about a claim that could be sold to a claims management company. Many tried to opt-out, but by doing so they confirmed their telephone number as being "active", making it more valuable to "list brokers". The two individuals made a substantial profit from the sale of personal data. Although it was overturned on appeal, the regulator imposed a £440,000 fine.

Collating customer data from all sources within the company

In our advisory engagement with clients we have seen that sales and marketing employees within an organisation sometimes collate personal data about potential customers from all sources within the organisation.

For example, sales and marketing employees might download information about individuals from the organisation's customer relationship management (CRM) system. And if it's not included in the

---

[4] http://www.bbc.com/news/technology-20528301, Spam text message pair are fined £440,000. 28, Nov, 2012.

CRM system, they also download other information such as contact information generated by corporate customer enquiries and customer support databases. They seek to mine these databases with the intention of running marketing campaigns, including by sending newsletters to individuals. If the organisation is holding a marketing event, they will use email addresses to send out invitations to individuals.

If the individuals receiving newsletters and invitations to events have not consented to their personal data being used for these marketing purposes the organisation is likely failing to comply with the data protection law. When we point this out we usually hear, "Yes, but it's OK because our email system lets recipients opt-out of receiving further emails and invitations from us".

The trouble is that enabling recipients to opt-out of receiving further emails and invitations does not in some way retroactively "fix" any failure by the organisation to comply with the data protection law when they were sent out.

CHECKLIST OF GOOD PRACTICES

Organisations that acquire personal data to build and collate customer lists should adopt the following practices:

- Do not acquire personal data illegally or secretly without individuals' knowledge.
- Do not access customer databases without authorisation or illegally. This includes tricking someone into providing access information, as well as using technological means to hack into databases.
- Do not acquire personal data by providing false or misleading information or by using deceptive or misleading practices.
- Do not take personal data that is collected for one purpose and use it for another purpose without the consent of the relevant individual. Providing the individual with an opt-out option does not overcome the need for consent at the outset.

🔒 20 The trouble with poaching ex-customers

In our consulting work, we often see that sales people are under a misconception: they think that they "own the customer". Or to state the misconception in the language of the data protection law, they think that they are free to do whatever they like with personal data about their customers, including their ex-customers. They forget that individuals have the right to control the ways in which their personal data is used or disclosed.

This misconception gives rise to sales people "poaching ex-customers" – moving to a new organisation and marketing to "their customers" at their previous organisation. If they do this without the consent of the individuals concerned, the sales people and their new organisation will generally fail to comply with the data protection law.

The following case studies demonstrate how this has caused trouble in the past.

Client personal data used by ex-employee to market new employer's offerings

A salesman moved from one organisation ("Organisation A") to another organisation ("Organisation B"). Using Organisation B's letterhead, the salesman sent a marketing letter to one of his customers at Organisation A. The salesman had recorded the customer's contact details in his personal diary during the course of his business relationship with them when he worked at Organisation A. The letter stated that he had moved to a different employer, Organisation B, and was promoting offerings from Organisation B.

The customer complained to the regulator on the basis that neither the salesman nor Organisation B had obtained consent to use the customer's personal data to send marketing communications.[1]

The regulator:

■ instructed Organisation B to destroy the customer's personal data
■ concluded that Organisation A was at fault for failing to ensure security measures were in place to protect the personal data in its care and
■ recommended that the data protection provisions in the employee contract of Organisation A be amended to include specific reference to the use of personal data to prevent any ambiguity. The previous contract referred to the use of business data.

The regulator wrote in its report that:

there appears to be a misconception by some employees that the customers are their customers rather than that of the data controller, that is, the employer. Data controllers must be aware that where they process data which has been brought in to the organisation by a new employee from their previous employment, without the consent of the individuals, they are in breach of the Data Protection Act.

Client personal data retained by ex-employee

A life insurance agent left his agency ("Organisation A") and joined a different company ("Organisation B"). He then called one of "his clients" at Organisation A and asked her if she would like to transfer her life insurance policies from Organisation A to Organisation B or, as an alternative, if she would like to take out new policies with Organisation B.

When the client met with the agent to discuss the proposed changes she did not have the documents relating to her existing policies with Organisation A readily at hand. "No problem," said the agent. He opened his laptop computer and brought up details of her existing policy.

The client was horrified that confidential personal data relating to her life insurance was still available to an ex-employee of Organisation

[1] Data Protection Commissioner, Ireland, Case 14. https://www.dataprotection.ie/docs/Case-Studies-2012/1354. htm#14

A. She was even more unhappy that this could happen when the ex-employee now worked for a competitor.

The client confronted Organisation A about the incident. However, she was not satisfied that Organisation A treated the breach of confidentiality with the seriousness it deserved. Consequently, she escalated the matter to the regulator, which investigated it.[2]

Organisation A told the regulator that:

- its field representatives were allowed access to client information on laptop computers
- its data protection policies stated that if field representatives left their employment with Organisation A they must return their laptop computer and all company records and documents to their immediate supervisor and
- the former employee had violated Organisation A's policy and did not return the laptop.

It was this violation of policy that had given rise to the complaint. As a result, the regulator required Organisation A to put new procedures in place so that client data would be erased automatically from all laptop computers every six weeks and would be erased automatically whenever a field representative ceased to be employed by Organisation A.

A final word

As you can see from the above examples, clients or customers may not appreciate being contacted by ex-sales people. They also get upset knowing that their personal data is being retained when a salesperson leaves an organisation.

If you do have a close relationship with a customer, inform them that you are leaving the company and get unambiguous consent from them before continuing to use their personal data.

But, in addition, ensure that you do not breach the obligation of confidentiality you have to your ex-employer or, if you are working as an agent, your ex-principal. And ensure that you comply with the data protection law.

---

[2] Data Protection Commissioner, Ireland, Case Study 2/99, https://www.dataprotection.ie/docs/Case-Study-2-99-Life-Insurance-Company/137.htm

CHECKLIST OF GOOD PRACTICES – SALESPERSONS

Individual salespersons who have left their previous organisation and have joined a new organisation should adhere to the following:

■ Do not take customers' personal data with you unless authorised to do so.

■ Observe the employee/agent exit requirements when leaving an organisation.

■ Do not contact any of your clients from your previous organisation for any purposes, including to market to them, unless you have their consent to do so.

■ Even if you have their consent, check that a contact is not in violation of any confidentiality obligation you have to your previous organisation.

CHECKLIST OF GOOD PRACTICES – MANAGERS AND EMPLOYERS

Managers and employers should adopt the following practices when their employees or salespersons leave their organisation, or when new employees join the organisation:

■ Require your employees and agents to sign a confidentiality obligation. Have a clear written policy that is consistent with those confidentiality obligations.

■ Require them to return all the organisation's property when they leave.

■ Require them to return all the organisation's documents and not make and/or keep any copy of them (including a copy on any personal computer that they may have used to access the organisation's personal data remotely).

■ Wherever possible, have technical controls to prevent ex-employees and agents from remotely accessing the organisation's confidential information or personal data. If this is not feasible, put in place technical controls to keep track of any remote access, and particularly any downloads.

■ Do not use (or disclose) personal data brought into your organisation by new employees unless you are satisfied that:

   ● the relevant individuals have given their consent to your organisation using (or disclosing) it for the stated purpose and

   ● the new employees are not in breach of any confidentiality or similar obligation to their previous organisation (who might be able to sue your organisation for inducing breach of that obligation).

■ Ensure that all new employees (and agents), especially salespersons, are trained in their obligations under the data protection law and your organisation's data protection policies and practices.

🔒 21 Review your employment application form before it's too late

All of us – companies and individuals – are creatures of habit. Or is it simply laziness? I see many job application forms that collect a wide range of personal data without considering the data protection law. And it's a business issue too. If a job candidate with a lot of job options gets an impression from a job application form that an organisation is out-of-date they will give preference to other opportunities.

Out-of-date information requests

The worst example I've seen of an out-of-date data field in a job application form recently was a request for a pager number. A pager? What's a pager? I'm sure they were all discarded about 20 years ago when mobile phones started being used widely.

Almost as bad have been a handful of requests I've seen for shorthand speeds and typing speeds – that is, "words per minute". And, now that we're well into the 21st century, does an organisation need to ask about "word processing skills" or "familiarity with" Word, Excel and PowerPoint (versus assuming that candidates can use modern technology just as an organisation assumes that they can use a telephone)?

Fair employment practices – selection only on the basis of merit and job requirements

Some jurisdictions have legislated fair employment practices. Some have guidelines that are enforceable by the relevant authorities to a greater or lesser extent. Some have no formal requirements at all.

In any event, it is now generally accepted business practice to recruit and select employees on the basis of merit, such as skills, experience or ability and the applicant's ability to perform the job, regardless of age, race, gender, religion, marital status and family responsibilities, or disability. Selection criteria should be related to the job requirements to ensure that applicants/employees are fairly and objectively assessed on their suitability.

Reasons to update job application forms

Revising job application forms to get rid of out-of-date information requests makes good business sense. Revising them to get rid of data requests that do not relate to the applicant's merit and the requirements of the job similarly makes good business sense.

In any event, job application forms should comply with the data protection law.

Excessive collection of personal data

The data protection law does not permit an organisation to collect personal data beyond what is reasonably necessary in the circumstances.

In the case of a job application form, this means that an organisation should collect only the information it needs to decide whether to invite the applicant for an interview and to otherwise decide whether or not to hire them.

Answering questions about why an organisation collects personal data

An organisation should have a clear understanding of the reasons for collecting each piece of personal data in a job application form.

This is because the organisation must nominate a person who is able to answer questions about the collection, use or disclosure of personal data. Of course that person needs to have the necessary clear understanding so that they can respond to these questions.

Getting express consent to collect and use personal data in a job application form

An organisation may decide to obtain express consent from job applicants. The organisation would include in its job application form notification of its purpose for collecting and using the personal data and ask the job applicant to sign to give evidence of their consent.

Any express consent given by the job applicant to the organisation collecting personal data beyond what is required for that purpose is likely not valid. In addition, where an organisation collects personal data beyond what it is reasonably necessary it will have failed to comply with the data protection law.

Relying on implicit consent to collect and use personal data in job application forms

In some jurisdictions, organisations may rely on a job applicant implicitly consenting to the collection and use of their personal data for the purposes of a job application. This is because consent can be implied where:

- an individual voluntarily provides the personal data to the organisation for the particular purpose and
- it is reasonable that they would do so.

If personal data is not reasonably necessary for the purpose of deciding whether to invite the applicant for an interview and to otherwise decide whether or not to hire them, it could never be reasonable for an individual to voluntarily provide it. Therefore any rules in the data protection law about implicit consent – sometimes referred to as deemed consent – are not likely to apply.

Some tips on what personal data an organisation cannot usually collect

An organisation should review its job application form and delete requests for information that is not reasonably necessary to enable the organisation to decide whether or not to invite the applicant for an interview and to otherwise decide whether or not to hire them.

Additional information that the organisation needs to collect from the individual it decides to hire can be collected from the individual before, when or immediately after they start work with the organisation.

Here are examples of requests for information that I often see in job application forms that are generally not necessary:

- Identity card or passport number – if identity needs to be confirmed at the interview stage the interviewer should ask to sight the applicant's identity card or passport and can write in their interview notes that they have confirmed the applicant's identity.

- Date of birth/age, race, gender, religion, marital status, languages/ dialects spoken and family responsibilities – although these are not general selection criteria there might be specific circumstances where some of this information is relevant and, of course, age can usually be estimated by looking at the applicant's educational qualifications and the year they were obtained.

- Photograph of the job applicant – of course, if they are hired a photograph might be collected later for a security access badge or for the organisation's intranet or other employee purpose.

- Nationality, place of birth, foreign passport number – it is often sufficient to ask a question such as "Are you entitled to work in <country name>?" or "Do you need to obtain any visa or other authorisation in order to work in <country name>?" at the interview stage.

Similarly, I see questions such as "Have you ever suffered any physical or mental illness?" A more relevant question might be "Are you under any physical or mental disability that might adversely affect your ability to do the job for which you are applying?" I also often see "Do you own a driver's licence?" where a driver's licence isn't relevant to the job vacancy.

Collecting and using personal data about third-parties generally

While there are some exceptions to the rule, an organisation is not permitted to collect and use personal data from an individual about a third-party without the consent of the third-party. In a typical recruitment scenario, none of the exceptions applies.

Where the job applicant says that a third-party has given consent to the job applicant disclosing the third-party's personal data, the organisation should do "appropriate due diligence" to check or confirm that the third-party consented to the organisation collecting and using the personal data for the relevant purpose.

Personal data about character and professional referees

Most organisations require the name and contact details of at least two individuals who will provide a character and/or professional reference about a job applicant.

Because a referee's personal data might be provided by a job applicant, an organisation should conduct "appropriate due diligence" to assure itself that the referee consented to the job applicant disclosing their personal data to the organisation for the purpose of the organisation getting a character or professional reference about the job applicant.

One way this can be done is to include words confirming the referees' consent in the job application and getting it signed by the job applicant. This is usually included in the part of the job application form where the referees' details are set out.

Personal data about third-parties

I frequently see job application forms that ask for details of the applicant's family members – spouse and children if the applicant is married and parents if the applicant is not married. The details sought vary, but often include full name, date of birth and occupation. Occasionally identity card number too.

A parent can consent to the collection, use and disclosure of personal data about their children, but:

- collecting personal data about an applicant's children is generally beyond what is reasonable to make a decision about whether or not to hire the applicant and
- collecting personal data about other family members is not permitted without their consent and, at the shortlisting and interview stage of recruiting, there is usually no available exception to the consent requirement.

Job application forms often ask for at least the name and contact details of an applicant's next-of-kin or an emergency contact. Again, this is not reasonably required for making a hiring decision and, in any event, at the shortlisting and interview stage of recruitment there is no available exception to the need for consent.

Where an individual is hired, an organisation can collect, use and disclose personal data about an employee's family members without consent if it is reasonably necessary for providing services to the employee. This likely includes services such as calculating employee leave entitlements and/or providing health or other insurance benefits to the employee and their family. An organisation can collect the personal data of an emergency contact (who might or might not be a next-of-kin) for emergency purposes.

A two-stage process

With the advent of the data protection law, the hiring process has transformed from:

- a one-stage process – a job application form that has:
  - all the information required to make a shortlisting/hiring decision and
  - almost all of the information required by the organisation if it hires the individual – the usual exception is that the job application form doesn't include details of the individual's bank account for direct credit of their salary

to:

- a two-stage process, which involves:
  - a job application form that has only the information required to make a short listing/hiring decision and
  - an employee data form that is filled up only by successful candidates and that includes all of the information required by the organisation to manage their employment relationship (including things such as tax office submissions, retirement benefits, direct credit of salary, calculation of leave benefits, provision of health and other insurance benefits).

CHECKLIST OF GOOD PRACTICES

Hiring managers and human resource personnel of organisations should adopt the following practices in collecting, using or disclosing the personal data of job applicants:

■ For business reasons, your organisation should review the job application form to make sure that it is up to date and reflects good employment practices.

■ For compliance with the data protection law, your organisation should review the job application form and delete requests for:

● personal data that is not reasonably necessary for recruitment and

● personal data about third-parties (except referees)

and adjust any questions that are over-broad or simply not relevant.

■ Consider designing and implementing a two-stage process for collecting personal data from job applicants whom the organisation hires.

■ Decide whether to add provision for express consent to the job application form or whether it will rely on implicit/deemed consent.

■ Consider amending the job application form so that the job applicant confirms in writing that they have consent from their referees for you to contact them for a reference.

22 Shhhh… Speak softly for privacy's sake

Many of us at one time or another would have been to a public library. One of the things we would have noticed are signs displayed prominently in big letters that spell the word "SILENCE". This is to remind library users to keep quiet, or at least speak softly, so as not to disturb others who are there to concentrate on serious reading or studying. Many a time we would have been ticked off by a stern-looking librarian when our verbal communication volume crossed a certain threshold.

Where communications containing personal data and sensitive information can be overheard

Without the seven-letter word "SILENCE" to remind people at other public places, I'm often amazed at how much private information is being disclosed within earshot of others around them, especially at restaurants and food courts. Not that I like to eavesdrop on other people's conversations, but I can't help it when people speak loudly and their sound waves travel into my eardrums. "Do you know so-and-so is having an affair with… ?", "Have you heard so-and-so's son is suffering from… ?" are the usual type of gossip I often pick up.

Doctors' clinics are another place where private information is routinely disclosed – to the doctors in the privacy of their consulting room and to the receptionists or nurses in the clinic's reception area and waiting room. And this is without a "SILENCE" sign to remind them to speak softly. On visits to some doctors' clinics, I never fail to be amazed by receptionists and nurses who must think that all patients are hard of hearing. They speak so loudly that everyone in the clinic can hear distinctly:

The doctor will see you next week for your <name of medical condition>.

or

Your total bill for today's visit is $xxx.

I had an interesting encounter at a doctor's clinic once. As I was a first-time patient to this clinic, the receptionist asked me for my national identification number, name, home address, telephone number, blood type and drug allergies. All the while the receptionist was talking very loudly. She repeated everything I said. Everyone in the clinic's waiting room heard everything about my personal and medical details. The clinic should have taken measures to protect my privacy as it has an obligation to do so under the data protection law. For example, the receptionist should have been required to speak more discreetly with a lower voice or told not to repeat my personal data. Or the clinic could have changed its data collection process so that I was simply asked to write down my personal data.

Think before you speak... especially if you speak loudly
We are increasingly aware of the need to protect personal data about individuals from being viewed or accessed by other individuals who do not have a genuine "need to know". But this is not enough.

It is equally important to take care about the volume of our conversations, both face-to-face and on the phone. And organisations too must ensure that their employees are aware of the need to observe the volume of their conversations on behalf of the organisation. In both cases, individuals must make sure that the personal data and private information of individuals being discussed are not inadvertently overheard by people around them.

This is always important. But it is especially important when individuals are discussing sensitive personal data, such as identity card numbers and medical or financial information. And it's just as important not to be overheard during a phone conversation as it is to avoid being overheard during a face-to-face conversation.

For privacy's sake, speak softly!

CHECKLIST OF GOOD PRACTICES

Organisations should adopt the following practices when communicating personal data or sensitive information:

- Speak softly and discreetly on the phone and in face-to-face conversation, lest you are overheard by people around you who are not supposed to know.
- Train and remind employees on how to communicate softly and discreetly at all times.

🔒 23 The trouble with third-party sources… of personal data

An organisation may collect personal data about an individual from the individual themselves or from someone else – that is, from a third-party source.

Examples of third-party sources of personal data

Third-party sources differ depending on what business or other activities are carried out by an organisation, but here are some examples:

- **Database resellers**

  If you Google "selling marketing lists", for example, you'll get a host of search results listing businesses advertising marketing lists, email addresses and other databases for sale. I looked at one sample list. I saw that for individuals I could get their name together with their gender, date of birth, email address, physical address and telephone number. I was invited to ask for a database according to my requirements. What a boon for marketers! (We'll get to the trouble with this shortly.)

- **Customer referrals**

  An individual might allow an existing customer of a business to give consent to the business collecting their personal data. For example, it is a common practice among multi-level marketing firms for the salesperson to ask for three referrals from each customer.

- **Intra-group transfers**

  Where there is a company group structure, one company in the group might have a valid reason for disclosing personal data to another company in the group.

Let's say SG Retail Sales Ltd collects personal data from individuals who shop in its store, but all the social media marketing for the group is done by its subsidiary, SG Marketing Pte Ltd. SG Retail Sales Ltd collects the personal data directly from the individual. It discloses the personal data to SG Marketing Pte Ltd, which therefore collects it from a third-party source.

■ **Sales leads**

It is common business practice for salespersons to give each other "leads". "Let me know", a person selling mortgage loans might say to a real estate agent friend, "whenever you think you'll sign up a sale of a house and the purchaser will need finance and I'll give them a call".

■ **Non-commercial referrals**

Third-party sources of personal data aren't necessarily commercially focused. For example, doctors routinely refer their patients to other doctors and to hospitals; hospitals routinely refer their patients for step-down care and other services; welfare organisations that are unable to assist a client routinely refer them to agencies and other voluntary welfare organisations that may be able to assist them.

So what is the trouble?

As a matter of plain logic, whenever a collecting organisation collects personal data from a third-party, the third-party is disclosing that personal data. The data protection law applies to both of them.

For example, Kevin is a financial adviser and wants to collect personal data from William, who is a real estate agent, about a potential home purchaser, Lyn, so that Kevin can offer home financing to Lyn. William wants to disclose personal data about Lyn to Kevin so that Lyn can get home financing for the house purchase to go ahead.

Kevin is not permitted to collect the personal data without Lyn's consent and William is not allowed to disclose personal data about Lyn without Lyn's consent[1].

The trouble is that the data protection law doesn't allow Kevin, the financial adviser, to get off scot-free where William, the real estate

[1] There are some exceptions to the need for consent. But they usually do not apply to the third-party source examples mentioned in this chapter.

agent, discloses Lyn's personal data without consent to him. In that case, both William and Kevin can be liable for failure to comply with the data protection law.

(William could suggest to Lyn that Kevin would be a good person to call about home financing. Lyn is deemed to have given her consent by calling Kevin herself. But here we are worried about the case where Kevin wants to be able to call Lyn about the home financing.)

Personal or domestic circumstances

The data protection law does not apply to an individual acting in a personal or domestic capacity.

"Give me your friend Jane's phone number and I'll call her and see if she wants to come to John's birthday dinner with us next week" is OK. This is because both the discloser and the collector of Jane's personal data are acting in a personal or domestic capacity.

"Give me Jane's phone number and I'll call her and see if I can sell some life insurance to her" is not OK. This is because the collector of Jane's personal data wants it for a business purpose.

Business contact information

In some countries, the data protection law does not apply to "business contact information"[2]. The information on an individual's business name card is usually all "business contact information" – their name, position title, business telephone number and business fax number, for example. But not if they provide it solely for a personal purpose.

"Let me know", a person selling mortgage loans might say to a real estate agent friend, "the purchaser's name and office phone number whenever you think you'll sign up a sale of an office building for them to use for their business and the business will need finance and I'll give them a call". This is OK. It's business contact information and the call will be made for business purposes.

By contrast, "Let me know the purchaser's name and office phone number whenever you think you'll sign up a sale of a house and the purchaser will need finance and I'll give them a call" is not OK. This is because financing a home purchase is a personal purpose.

---

[2] For example, in Canada and Singapore.

What the collecting organisation must do

Let's illustrate what the collecting organisation must do by using the above example. (By the way, an individual can be "an organisation", just as a company or other entity can be "an organisation" in certain jurisdictions.)

■ **Notification:** Before Kevin, the financial adviser, collects personal data from William, the real estate agent, Kevin must notify William of the purposes for which he will be collecting, using or disclosing the personal data (namely, to contact Lyn about home financing). This is so that William can be satisfied about the things listed below.

■ **Appropriate due diligence:** Before collecting personal data from William, Kevin should make enquiries until he is satisfied about the things listed below and document these enquiries so that he has evidence on file about them.

The things that both William and Kevin should satisfy themselves about are that:

■ Lyn has consented, expressly or implicitly, to her personal data – for example name, contact details, and information that William knows about Lyn's financial circumstances – being disclosed by William and collected (and used) by Kevin for the purpose of Kevin calling Lyn about home financing or

■ the disclosure by William and the collection (and use) by Kevin can be done without consent or the circumstances are such that the data protection law doesn't apply (such as in the case of business contact information mentioned above).

Evidence of what was done

An additional key factor is that both William and Kevin should keep records about what they have done to satisfy themselves about the consent. It is not enough, for example, for Kevin to simply trust that William has done the right thing. After all, Lyn might not recall having given consent to William and then complain to the regulator when Kevin makes contact. In any investigation by the regulator they will need evidence that they both did the right thing.

Let's say, for example, that Lyn gave verbal consent to William for the referral to Kevin. In that case, William could confirm in writing (such as by an email) to Lyn that they had discussed the referral during such and such meeting and that Lyn had consented to it. Kevin could ask William to confirm in writing (again, such as by an email) that Lyn's consent had been given to William to make the referral.

Ensuring accuracy when collecting data from a third-party source

The data protection law requires an organisation to make a reasonable effort to ensure that the personal data it collects is accurate and complete if the personal data is likely to be disclosed by the organisation to another organisation.

So, before collecting personal data from William, Kevin needs to decide what to do to satisfy the accuracy obligation. William's reliability is one thing for Kevin to take into account – is William usually quite painstaking in getting things right or is William inclined to take a broadbrush approach? Kevin should consider whether to require William to confirm that William has verified the accuracy and completeness of Lyn's personal data, particularly the information about Lyn's financial circumstances because Kevin might be making a decision based on it. And Kevin should consider the need to conduct further independent verification, including, in this example, checking with Lyn about the financial information.

The trouble is that the accuracy obligation also applies to Kevin. It is no excuse for Kevin to say, "But I got this personal data about Lyn from William and I trusted William to give me good data".

CHECKLIST OF GOOD PRACTICES

Organisations that collect personal data from third-party sources should adopt the following practices:

- Take care if you collect personal data from third-party sources, including database resellers or if you get sales leads from customers or contacts.
- Take care if your organisation is a member of a group of companies and personal data is transferred between them.
- Non-commercial third-party sources require care too.
- Make sure the third-party source has consent from individuals concerned to disclose the personal data to you for the relevant purpose.
- Check that personal data collected from third-party sources is accurate.

24 Personal data and warranty cards: tips for the customer care team

Does your organisation invite retail purchasers of your products to send you their personal data so that you can register their products and validate them for the warranties you offer on them?

If so, the data protection law affects the way you collect, use and disclose the personal data of these registered users/retail purchasers. Your customer care team needs to take the data protection law into consideration.

Warranty cards

Does your organisation have warranty cards that require retail purchasers of your products to complete them and mail them to you to validate the warranty? These are usually bundled with the organisation's products so that when the retailer sells the product the warranty card is inside the box or other packaging. Often these are warranty cards where the address of the organisation is on one side and the retail purchaser completes the reverse side with their registration and purchase details. If so, beware.

Requiring retail purchasers to send the warranty cards "as is" (with an area for a postage stamp) might invite complaints to the regulator about a failure to comply with the data protection law. The reason is that the retail purchaser's details are fully exposed in the mail – they are disclosed to anyone who happens to see the warranty card when it is posted to your organisation.

It is easy to argue that any retail purchaser who completes the warranty card, adds a postage stamp to it and posts it implicitly consents

to the disclosure of their personal data in the postal system. But it is also easy to argue that a retail purchaser thought they had no choice but to do this if they wanted the benefit of the warranty and that your organisation should have been proactive in adopting alternative ways for them to register their warranty without unnecessarily disclosing their personal data.

An electronic alternative to warranty cards
Now that most retail purchasers have access to the Internet many organisations provide a way for these purchasers to register their warranties online. An organisation should consider providing an online registration option and encouraging retail purchasers to use it.

Where your organisation provides a warranty card as an alternative to online registration, it should instruct retail purchasers who choose not to use the online system to return the warranty card in a sealed envelope. As an additional customer service and encouragement to retail purchasers not to put unprotected information in the mail, your organisation could include a "postage paid" envelope with the warranty card where most of your retail sales are domestic.

Recording personal data and other information in warranty cards
When an organisation has a warranty card, the retail purchaser completes it and mails it. The physical card arrives at the organisation's mail box. What happens to the warranty card after the organisation receives it? Most likely, the information on the warranty card needs to be keyed into the organisation's customer relationship management

system or otherwise digitised. If so, several important considerations then arise under the data protection law.

Accuracy of personal data

Do the organisation's employees key the information into the customer relationship management system? If so, the organisation should have processes and controls in place to make sure that the personal data in the warranty card is complete and that it is keyed in accurately, which is a requirement under the data protection law.

Selecting a vendor and entering into an agreement with the vendor

Instead of employees keying information into its customer relationship management system, does the organisation outsource the data input to a third-party vendor? If so, does the organisation carry out due diligence to assure itself that the vendor is capable of complying with the data protection law?

Does the organisation ensure that there is a written agreement between the organisation and the vendor that clearly sets out the responsibilities, obligations and liabilities of the vendor so that the organisation has legal protection to the extent possible in case of a failure by the vendor to comply with the data protection law?

Protecting personal data in warranty cards

Are the warranty cards piled up somewhere until someone has time to process them in-house? Or are they piled up until there is a batch ready to be sent to the third-party vendor for the data input to be done?

The organisation has an obligation under the data protection law to protect personal data in its possession. Therefore, in either case, the organisation should ensure that the warranty cards are stored securely while awaiting data input, such as being kept under lock and key. Access should be restricted to selected employees who have a need to handle the warranty cards for the purpose of doing their jobs.

The organisation should also protect personal data collected in warranty cards after it has been recorded electronically. It must take reasonable security arrangements and establish controls to protect it from unauthorised access, collection, use, disclosure or similar risks.

Retention of personal data in warranty cards

After the information in a warranty card is keyed into the organisation's customer relationship management system or digitised by its third-party vendor, what happens to the hardcopy of the warranty cards?

The obligation to protect the personal data in them continues. In addition, the data protection law does not permit an organisation to retain personal data when it is no longer necessary for a legal or business purpose. Therefore the organisation should develop and implement a policy for securely disposing of the personal data in the hardcopy of the warranty cards.

The organisation should also develop and implement a policy for securely deleting personal data collected in warranty cards from its electronic records when it is no longer necessary for a legal or business purpose.

Ongoing access to personal data collected in warranty cards

After information from warranty cards is keyed into the organisation's customer relationship management system or digitised by a third-party, which employees have access to it? For what purpose? The organisation should have detailed policies and procedures setting out which employees have access to the personal data and the purposes for which they are permitted to use or disclose it.

Responding promptly to any customer inquiry

Individuals have a right under the data protection law to access to their personal data in the possession of an organisation or under its control.[1]

Manufacturers and distributors who provide product warranties can expect retail purchasers to become more familiar with these rights over time. And they can expect individuals to test them by calling the organisation's customer service line to request access to their personal data and information about how the organisation has used it.

There is a time limit within which organisations must respond to any such request. It varies depending on the jurisdiction. An organisation should make sure that it understands the requirements applicable to it and that it trains its employees to respond properly to requests.

---

[1] In some jurisdictions they also have a right to information about how the organisation may have used their personal data.

Using personal data collected in warranty cards for marketing purposes

Where a retail purchaser completes a warranty card (or an online warranty registration) it is likely that they implicitly consent to the organisation collecting, using and disclosing their personal data for the purpose of registering the warranty and meeting their product support commitments under the warranty.

If the organisation wants to use personal data in a warranty card or registration for any other purpose – such as for marketing and promoting its products – it must first obtain express consent from the retail purchaser. Any such express consent can be included in the warranty card or online registration portal or the organisation could seek it at a later time. It should be optional (so that the retail purchaser may obtain the benefit of the warranty without agreeing that the organisation may use their personal data for marketing and promotion purposes). And the organisation should establish a process that enables it to respond whenever a retail purchaser withdraws their consent to the organisation using their personal data for marketing and promotion purposes.

Marketing and promotion purposes include contacting retail purchasers and sending them product advertising and promotional materials, including where an existing product is reaching the end of its warranty period. It also likely includes aggregating the warranty cards submitted by any particular individual to determine their purchase history and using data mining techniques to target individuals the organisation has determined are likely to spend more on its products through, for example, up-selling to them and offering them incentives to purchase more of the organisation's products.

Generally applicable to all organisations that collect personal data from their customers

Whatever kind of organisation you are in, as long as you collect, use or disclose personal data of your customers, you have to comply with the data protection law. All the above processes that are applicable to organisations collecting and processing personal data through warranty cards are equally applicable to your organisation, whether it is in the form of paper or electronic documents.

CHECKLIST OF GOOD PRACTICES

Organisations that collect personal data of their customers (for example, through warranty cards) should:

- Protect the personal data during transit. For example, warranty cards should not be mailed through the postal system without an envelope. Use a sealed envelope or provide an electronic alternative.

- Have written policies and processes to ensure that the personal data is complete and recorded accurately in the customer relationship management system (or some other database).

- Vet the third-party vendor hired to process personal data (for example, keying warranty card information into an electronic system) to make sure that it is capable of complying with the data protection law. Have a written agreement with the vendor that clearly sets out rights, obligations and liabilities.

- Take reasonable steps to protect the personal data, whether it is in paper form (for example, warranty cards) or when it is entered into an electronic database system.

- Devise and implement data retention policies in connection with both the hardcopy of documents containing personal data (for example, in warranty cards) and the electronic version.

- Have written policies and practices about access to personal data and the purposes for which it may be used or disclosed. All personnel should be trained in them.

- Be prepared to receive and respond to requests for access to personal data that your organisation holds. Respond to requests within the statutory time limit for doing so. Document these processes and train personnel in them.

- Make sure you do not use personal data collected for one purpose (for example, in warranty cards) for any purpose for which you do not have implicit or express consent.

25 Watch out – your security post may not be secure

Do you have a security post or guardhouse in your organisation? Have you done an audit of whether security measures are in place to protect personal data at your security post or guardhouse?

We always ask our clients if they have a security post or guardhouse. If so, it's the first place we tell them to start when they conduct an audit for potential data breaches. Sometimes they staff their security post or guardhouse themselves; sometimes they outsource it to a third-party vendor, such as a security company. In either case, they are often horrified by what they find. And in either case, the organisation is liable for any failure to comply with the data protection law, even in those cases where the third-party vendor is also liable.

Here are a few examples of unauthorised disclosure of personal data, including disclosures without consent and failures to protect personal data in the possession or under the control of the organisation.

Unclaimed identify cards displayed at security post

One of our clients did an audit of their security post – "audit" in this case means that they went to the security post and looked around to see if there was any personal data in public view. They were horrified to see two identity cards in full public view.

The security guard said that the identity cards had been collected from visitors to the organisation, but the visitors had forgotten to pick them up from the security post after their visit. The logic for displaying the identity cards was that the security guard was hoping that someone who knew the relevant individuals would see the identity cards and would tell them that they were at the security post.

So here we had an unauthorised disclosure of personal data by the organisation, whether they manned the security post or had outsourced it to a vendor. The audit also raised two related points:

- why they needed to display the identity cards to find their owners given that they had collected contact numbers from all visitors and
- why there was a need to collect the identity cards rather than writing down visitors' identity number (if collecting their identity numbers was reasonable, which depends on the circumstances).

Collection of ID card number of visitors by security guard

An organisation instructed the security guard at its commercial building to ask visitors to the building to complete a visitor's record card, which included giving their identity card number.

An individual entered the building to attend a party and completed the visitor's record card. Later when the individual left the building, the security guard gave him a pile of visitors' record cards and told the individual to search for his own card and to fill in the departure time.

The individual could obviously read the personal data of other visitors to the building – and other visitors could read the individual's personal data – so the individual complained to the regulator[1] about what the security guard had done. He also complained that:

- the visitor's record card did not include a statement required by the data protection law
- there was no information about how long the organisation retained personal data and
- there was no information about the security measures regarding access to and disposal of the record cards.

The regulator found that the property management company for the building did have proper procedures in place where proper visitors' record cards were used and no third-party could access the personal information of other visitors. However, the stock of record cards had run out. The security guard had photocopied only part of a record card

---

[1] Office of the Privacy Commissioner for Hong Kong, Case No.:2003C11, https://www.pcpd.org.hk

and had used these copies. Hence the security guard was not following the proper procedures.

As a result, the security guard apologised for the inconvenience caused to the complainant. The complainant's card was destroyed. The organisation revised its internal memo guidelines for its employees and reminded them of its requirement for strict compliance with its proper procedures for visitors.

Hence, the regulator considered the matter to be resolved effectively through mediation and decided that further investigation of the case was unnecessary.

Security guards who talk too much

Try asking security guards of a condominium how much they know about certain residents or tenants and you will be surprised, especially if you have come to know the security guard over time. Then you will likely get whatever "juicy details" they happen to know about owners and tenants. Some of the "juicy details" are likely to be an unauthorised disclosure of personal data.

Sometimes people talk too much even when you don't know them. In an audit for data breaches we did for a client I asked a security guard about a tenant to find out if personal data would be disclosed. The security guard willingly gossiped and disclosed personal data about the tenant to me. The security guard evidently assumed that I was the owner of the relevant condo unit asking about my own tenant. Even if I had been the owner, the security guard likely was not entitled to disclose the tenant's personal data to me without the tenant's consent.

"Social engineering", in the context of information security, is the art of manipulating people so they give us personal data. I didn't set out to do any social engineering when I asked the security guard about a tenant. Some individuals deliberately embark on social engineering and they are very successful. Many individuals, obviously including the security guard, are easily susceptible to social engineering and can be tricked into releasing personal data that they are not authorised to.

Where there is an unauthorised disclosure of personal data, it makes no difference if the disclosure results from social engineering or other trickery.

Visitors' sign-in books displayed openly

Visitors' sign-in books are common at the security posts of commercial buildings and organisations. Visitors are asked to fill in their details upon entry in the book. When they do so, they see the personal data of individuals who signed in on the same page before them. And sometimes they can even flick back to earlier pages to see who signed in on previous days.

Outside a voluntary welfare organisation, I noticed a volunteer browsing the pages of the visitors' sign-in book. They must have spent five minutes looking at it.

One of our property clients caught a property agent taking photos of the registration information in a showroom. Visitors' sign-in books are a goldmine to sales people, especially if they contain contact details.

In any of these types of circumstances, the organisation that "owns" the visitors' sign-in book is likely liable for any failure to comply with the data protection law by reason of the unauthorised disclosure of personal data.

And here's another tip: the organisation should also take care about what it does with "old" visitors' registers. It should have a policy about how it will store them securely under lock and key, how long it will retain them and how it will dispose of the personal data in them securely.

Unmanned guard posts

In many of our onsite audits of organisations for compliance with the data protection law we have seen unattended guard posts and security desks. Sometimes this is simply because the security guard is away for a few minutes or has moved a few metres away while assisting another visitor. Other times it is because the post or desk is attended only after office hours.

An organisation should take care to ensure that whenever a guard post or security desk is unattended, a passerby or other individual is not able to browse through the visitors' register, incident logs or other documents that may contain personal data. And that they are not able to look into unlocked cabinets or drawers.

CCTV surveillance in full public view

Many organisations have CCTV surveillance systems. Where the organisation has a security post or guardhouse, it is usually monitored by a security guard.

When we did an audit at a shopping centre, we discovered that members of the public could view the same live footage as the security guard. The monitors were positioned such that they could be viewed by anyone passing by the security post. And what was particularly disconcerting was that the security guard did not stop us or any curious onlookers from viewing the monitors.

An organisation should take care to ensure that CCTV monitors can be viewed only by individuals who have a need to see it in order to do their jobs. This clearly does not include members of the public.

CHECKLIST OF GOOD PRACTICES

Organisations should adopt the following measures to help ensure that the collection, usage and disclosure of personal data of visitors are protected:

- Inform visitors of the purposes for collecting their personal data. This is usually done best by displaying a notice at the building entrance, security post or guardhouse.
- Do not permit visitors to see the personal data of visitors preceding them. A security guard could write down their personal data, rather than asking them to do it themselves. Or each visitor could be asked to complete a separate form for their own personal data.
- Ensure that visitors' personal data is kept under lock and key and is securely destroyed when it is no longer necessary for a business or legal purpose.
- Ensure that security guards are trained, including to be able to explain to visitors why the organisation needs to collect their personal data and how long the organisation will retain it. They should also be trained not to disclose any personal data during a conversation with any individual other than organisation personnel with a "need to know" to carry out their jobs.
- Secure all personal data, such as identity card numbers and CCTV monitors, away from public view.

26 No, giving a purpose for collecting excessive personal data may not avoid trouble

Many organisations new to data protection laws are putting their data protection policies in place and ensuring that they share their purposes for collecting personal data with individuals. However, just stating these purposes does not necessarily mean that the organisation has the right to collect, as these two scenarios below will demonstrate. There is a need to justify with proof as well.

Purpose of collecting personal data because of a presumption

A management company of a car park in a commercial building decided to record identity card numbers of drivers who entered and exited the car park. This did not go well with a driver who lodged a complaint with the regulator.[1]

The management company claimed that there had been many incidents of theft in the car park and the commercial building. So it adopted a policy of recording identity card numbers for the purpose of preventing crime and assisting police in detecting crime. The management company said that recording identity card numbers complied with guidelines issued by the police.

But here's the problem: the management company was not able to provide evidence to support the alleged numbers of thefts in the car park. Nor could it show that collecting identity card numbers had reduced the number of crimes. And the regulator found that the guidelines issued by the police applied to visitors to a building but not to individuals using a car park.

[1] Office of the Privacy Commissioner for Hong Kong, Case No.:2005C05, https://www.pcpd.org.hk

As a result, the regulator concluded that the management company's purpose for collecting the identity card numbers was unreasonable and therefore constituted an excessive collection of personal data. The regulator required the management company to cease collecting identity card numbers and to destroy all the identity card numbers that it had already collected.

Collecting personal data to offer privileges or benefits that never existed

A theme park operator in Hong Kong required an individual's full date of birth when applying for an annual pass. An applicant, applying for themselves and their two children, complained to the regulator about this requirement.

The theme park operator said it needed adult pass applicants to provide their date of birth in order to enjoy the benefit of bringing a guest to the theme park free of charge during their month of birth.

The regulator said there was no need to collect an applicant's month of birth to ascertain whether they were entitled to redeem free tickets as a pass holder. They could instead physically inspect the pass holder's identity card to determine eligibility.

To aggravate matters, the theme park operator did not actually have concrete plans to offer privileges or benefits to adult pass holders associated with their date of birth. Nor would any such "free guest offer", if and when developed, be available to children with annual passes.

As a result, the theme park operator agreed with the regulator to:

- cease collecting date of birth data from adult pass applicants unless and until it had the necessary concrete plans
- cease collecting the date of birth of child pass applicants
- modify its application forms accordingly and
- ensure all relevant staff were trained to comply with the requirements of the data protection law.

Guidelines for organisations

While the data protection law requires organisations to give notice to individuals stating the purpose for the collection, use and disclosure of personal information, if your stated purposes are unfair or excessive, you could still be in breach.

As can be seen from the above case studies, trying to justify a purpose for collecting personal information based on a presumption, imagined scenario or even a future need may not be acceptable and will likely be considered excessive. Collect only the information you need to fulfil your intended purposes, when there is a real and practical need to do so.

CHECKLIST OF GOOD PRACTICES

Organisations should adopt the following practices when collecting and processing personal data of individuals:

- Do not collect and process personal data for purposes that are based on a mere presumption or assumption. Be prepared to justify your purposes with evidence if the need arises.
- Refrain from collecting personal data for offering privileges or benefits that do not exist.
- Ensure that your stated purposes are fair and not excessive.
- Collect only the information you need to fulfil your intended purposes.

27 Signing visitors into your premises – what does that do to your privacy programme?

We all know that it's very common for organisations to get every visitor to their office to sign-in so that it has a record of them. What's sometimes less clear is why signing in is important – or even necessary for some sensible reason. And what's often overlooked is getting visitors to sign-in in a way that is sensitive to their privacy. Building managers, including management companies at condominiums, do the same thing.

Let's look at what these arrangements can do to your privacy programme if the sign-in process isn't thought through carefully.

Why the privacy of visitors matters

Case study #1

A multinational corporation based in Singapore had a sign-in book. It required each visitor to write down their name, organisation, phone number, the person they were visiting and the purpose of the visit. Kevin signed in at 10:30 a.m. He wrote that he was visiting David Lim for an interview. David Lim was the local HR manager.

William, a work colleague of Kevin's, signed in at 3:00 p.m. William was also there for a job interview with David Lim. While William was signing in the receptionist took a phone call. William idly glanced through the sign in page for the day. William saw that Kevin had come in during the morning for an interview with David Lim. William concluded that he and Kevin were competing for the same job.

Now, if he'd been so inclined, William could have told his and

Kevin's boss that Kevin was being interviewed for another job. And he could have dropped subtle hints to David Lim about Kevin.

Case study #2

In another instance of recruitment, an internal candidate applied for an advertised role. While pretending to have a friendly chat with the receptionist, the internal candidate looked at the sign-in book each day to find out who had come in to see the HR manager that day.

The internal candidate noted down their names and then tried to figure out ways to undermine them during the interview process.

Case study #3

A social club requires members to sign-in their guests. They need to write their name, their membership number, the guest's name and the club facility (for example, the restaurant, bar or sporting facility) that they will be using.

Imagine Mary Lee's surprise one morning when she signed her friend in for tennis, but noticed that her husband had signed a woman in the previous evening for dinner in the restaurant. He'd told her that he had not touched down from Jakarta until around midnight.

As these examples show, the privacy of visitors matters because it is not possible to predict the damage that might be done where there is a breach of their privacy.

In addition, after the sign-in process, the data protection law requires organisations to protect the personal data collected and not retain it for longer than is reasonably necessary.

An organisation needs to find a way to balance its legitimate need for security at its business premises with the privacy interests of visitors.

Does an organisation need to collect personal data from visitors?

Sometimes an organisation needs to collect personal data from visitors. But not always. In case study #1, Kevin could simply have said to the receptionist, "Hello. I'm Kevin and I'm here to see David Lim. He's expecting me at 10:30." The receptionist would then let David Lim know his visitor had arrived. David Lim would come to the reception area to escort Kevin to the meeting room or he would ask the receptionist to do so. There is no need to collect any personal data in a sign in book.

In the case of individuals who register for a training or other event, why does the organisation need to confirm who has arrived and who has not arrived? Sometimes there are good reasons; sometimes there's no apparent reason and it's done as a matter of habit.

I am always quite mystified about what an organisation achieves when I am handed a couple of pages listing all delegates at an event and I am asked to initial or sign against my name to verify my attendance. I could pretend to be anyone and initial against their name; anyone could pretend to be me and initial against my name. And often I see the phone numbers and email addresses, and sometimes even the identity card numbers, of all other event participants.

The key is to think about what personal data, if any, needs to be collected from visitors and for what purpose. We need to get out of a "just in case we need it" or "this is what we always do" mentality.

How to collect personal data from visitors

If there is a need to collect personal data, there are several ways it can be done that minimise any intrusion on privacy:

■ To keep a record of attendees at business meetings, the receptionist could simply ask each individual for their name card with their business contact information.

■ To check off the arrival of individuals who have registered to attend a training or other event, the receptionist could simply check them off against a list of registered participants or delegates, by putting a tick next to their name so no one else sees the entire list.

■ Where there is not a large number of visitors to the premises, the receptionist could ask the individual for the information that the organisation needs and write it down. The visitor will not see the personal data of earlier visitors.

■ Where there is a large number of visitors to the premises who need to be identified with certainty for some good reason, the organisation might invest in a barcode scanner and simply scan the identity cards of visitors.

■ Where it is too burdensome for a receptionist to ask for personal data and write it down for each visitor, an organisation could ask each visitor to fill up a separate slip of paper with the necessary information. Or to enter it into an electronic device, such as an iPad. In any case, the organisation should ensure that other individuals cannot look over the visitor's shoulder and see the personal data.

The key here is to figure out what works best for the organisation from a practical perspective while also protecting the privacy of visitors. We need to get out of an "everyone else does it this way" mentality too. Even if it is true that "everyone else does it this way", that does not make it right. And it does not mean that their privacy is not important or should not be protected.

Protection and retention of personal data

An organisation is obliged to protect personal data in its possession or under its control. It is permitted to retain personal data only for so long as it is necessary for a legal or business purpose.

But what typically happens to sign-in books? Whenever a new book is started, the old book goes into some cupboard or drawer. It's out of sight and out of mind, and often not secured under lock and key. It is kept, if not forever, then until the organisation does a clean up, such as when it next moves premises or does some spring cleaning for some other reason.

The same applies when an organisation uses sign-in slips or captures personal data electronically or keeps registration or other lists.

The key here is for an organisation to:

■ decide how long it needs to retain personal data in its sign-in records, which is of course very closely related to the reason for collecting that personal data

■ devise and implement a retention policy that ensures the sign in records aren't retained for longer than necessary and

■ ensure that the sign in records are protected from loss or theft for the time that the organisation does need to retain the personal data in them – and that they are protected from the idle gaze of employees who have no need to see them (as in case study #2) or from other visitors (as in case studies #1 and #3).

CHECKLIST OF GOOD PRACTICES

Organisations that have a process for signing in visitors to their premises should adopt the following practices:

- Make sure that you have a reasonable purpose for collecting and retaining the records of visitors.

- Do not collect more personal data than is reasonably necessary for the relevant purpose.

- Consider collecting less sensitive personal data if the purpose is served (for example, an office telephone number rather than an identity card number).

- Ensure that the visitors' records are adequately protected.

- Have a data retention policy for your visitors' records and carry out regular audits to ensure compliance with it.

"

It ain't what you don't know that
gets you into trouble. It's what you
know for sure that just ain't so.

"

Mark Twain

SECTION C:

Usage of Personal Data

🔒 28 Anonymising personal data – but is the individual really not identifiable?

At an unidentified beach resort somewhere, two friends are lazing by the beach and debating the affairs of the world. The conversation soon turns to the concept of anonymity…

A: Why do people want to be anonymous?

B: So that others will not know their true identities.

A: Whatever for?

B: So they can hide under a cloak of secrecy to say and do things that society or the government might not approve of them saying or doing.

A: Such as?

B: You may have heard of the "Anonymous" group of "hacktivists" who hack into government, religious and corporate websites, defacing them or posting vitriolic anti-establishment or protest content. By doing so, they hope to expose cover-ups, scandals or corruption in government and corporations in the name of justice or in their fight for the rights of the disadvantaged. None of the members of the "Anonymous" group ever uses any name. If they appear in public, such as when they make a public statement about their position on some issue, they wear a mask so that they can't be identified.

Or you may have read comments posted by individuals on social media platforms using a pseudonym – a fictitious name or an alias, for example – rather than their real names. They feel more liberated to air their views freely without fear of being tracked down by the authorities, lobby groups or other people who oppose their views.

A: Are you saying that being anonymous is different from using a pseudonym?

B: Yes. When an individual is anonymous they can't be identified by name. So if they do two or more different things there's no way of knowing that the same individual did them.

When someone uses a pseudonym they are using a false name. They still can't be identified by name. But if the same person does two or more different things under the same pseudonym it's known that the same individual did those things.

A: So, using a pseudonym is, strictly speaking, not anonymity but pseudonymity. But they are both ways in which an individual can hide their identity.

B: You are absolutely right. If I were to place the two concepts on a scale, I would say that pseudonymity is less strong in concealing the true identity of an individual as compared to anonymity.

A: So far, you have cited examples of the negative side of anonymity. Are there positive examples too?

B: Plenty. Say a rich person wants to donate a large sum of money to a certain charity. They don't want their true identity to be known in case there is publicity. It may infringe on their personal privacy, for example, because they are suddenly newsworthy and stories are written with details about their life or because they receive a spate of letters and phone calls seeking donations. Or simply because other people, including their friends, congratulate them about their generosity when they would prefer not to talk about their donation. So they donate the money anonymously, so that not even the recipient charity knows their identity.

In research, there are many instances where the researcher anonymises the raw data of the sampled individuals so that they become non-identifiable. This is intended to ensure that sensitive personal data of individuals, such as health and medical data, are not disclosed. After all, in most research studies, the researcher is interested in trends, patterns and profiles derived from aggregated data. The identity of the individuals in the research sample doesn't matter.

A: If, as you say, researchers are interested in aggregated data only, then why don't they just leave out the unique identifiers of the individuals, such as their full name, home address and identity card number when they collect the personal data?

B: Ah, that's a good question. And the answer depends at least partly on the type of research and also on whether the personal data was collected solely for the research or whether it was collected for some other purposes and then later used for research.

For most research projects the researcher needs to have some unique identifiers of the individuals surveyed for two reasons. First, for the research to be accepted as valid the researcher may for practical reasons need to be able to verify that the data comes from real people. Secondly, when researchers are analysing and compiling their survey results they may need to clarify with the individuals concerned any ambiguity or discrepancy in their survey responses.

For some research projects the researcher doesn't need to have any unique identifiers for the individuals surveyed. This happens most often when the research is merely observational. For example, in a survey of public transport usage the researcher may simply need to observe and count the number of individuals, divided into categories of men, women and children, boarding certain buses and trains at specific times of the day and night.

A: OK. That's interesting. What did you mean when you mentioned that an organisation might collect personal data for a particular purpose and then later use it for research?

B: Well, say for example, that a voluntary welfare organisation, a charity, provides counselling and support in connection with an addiction, such as gambling addiction. For that purpose, it collects a wide range of personal data from individuals about themselves and their families and family circumstances.

Under the data protection law, the organisation must dispose of this personal data when it is no longer necessary for a legal or business purpose. Or the organisation may anonymise it and then can continue to keep it. The organisation might want to use it for research purposes or for similar purposes such as planning future service delivery or assessing the effectiveness of the organisation's counselling services.

To anonymise it effectively, the organisation must remove and dispose of all the personal data that might identify an individual and then it may keep the remainder. The organisation might assign a unique identifier to individuals for convenience when it refers to them. But for the data to be anonymised for the purposes of the data protection law the organisation must not keep the "key" to re-identifying any individuals.

A: You've lost me. What do you mean?

B: Well, John Lim of such and such address may be identified as "Man #1" and David Lee of some other address may be identified as "Man #2" and so on. Imagine a spreadsheet with the real names and addresses in two columns and "Man #1", "Man #2" in another column. To anonymise this personal data, the organisation must get rid of the two columns of names and addresses, retaining no copy, so that it is not possible to work out the identity of "Man #1", "Man #2", etc.

And this is just a fairly simple example that I've given. Depending on the circumstances, there may be more personal data that will need to be taken away so that re-identification is not possible, such as the individual's mobile phone number and their identity card number. This can all be really tricky. I'm just giving you an idea of the way it works. To avoid unpleasant surprises, such as not complying with the data protection law, anonymisation of personal data collected for a specific purpose usually needs some expert assistance.

A: Right. I get it. But how can one be sure that once the data is anonymised, there is no means to re-identify it and link it back to the original individuals?

B: Well, most research organisations are governed by strict policies and codes of practice. These require them to remove the unique identifiers from the datasets once the research study is completed. They have to overcome any "just in case" thoughts of researchers who want to keep the unique identifiers just in case they might need them in the future.

And of course there is also the data protection law. If an individual finds out that an organisation has kept the means of identifying them for longer than the organisation needs their personal data for business or legal purposes they can complain to the regulator. The penalties for an organisation failing to comply with the data protection law can be stiff.

A: So much for research organisations. As an individual, how can I be sure that my anonymity is protected if I choose to be anonymous on certain occasions or under certain circumstances? For example, what if I want to remain anonymous when I contribute to an online forum that is discussing controversial and sensitive issues?

B: Well, usually you need to use some identifier on online forums, so you'll use a false name or alias that you think doesn't identify you. It'll be a case of pseudonymity, rather than anonymity.

Unfortunately, even if you can't be identified by your pseudonym it is impossible to be absolutely sure that your personal identity will never be found out, especially in today's highly connected and networked world. This is because your mobile devices and other gadgets are sure giveaways of your location.

What I'm talking about here are mobile phone networks that can pinpoint your location through the signals emitting from your mobile phone. If you use public WiFi networks they also keep track of your location. Then there is the GPS (Global Positioning System) function in your phone or tablet. Some devices and gadgets (such as payment cards) use NFC (Near Field Communication) or RFID (Radio Frequency Identification).

If any of these methods show that you are usually in the same location from, say, 10:00 p.m. every day to 7:30 a.m. the following day, your home address is known. Ah, you say, but it's a condo so no one can know which of several individuals is me. Easy. Someone who wanted more information could sit outside the condo and wait until they see your mobile phone moving. Then they'll have you car registration number. They could follow you to your office and then know where you work. They could come into your office and ask the receptionist for your name or they could find it out through car registration records.

A: This is getting scary. Maybe I should be careful and turn off the location-identifying functions on my devices where possible and get rid of those devices and gadgets where I can't turn it off.

B: That sounds pretty inconvenient to me. And it won't necessarily keep your identity hidden. This is because when you surf the Internet, visit websites, communicate via emails or do online shopping, you leave behind loads of digital trails like your IP address, cookies downloaded on your computer, and the websites you have visited.

Service providers can use this information to match against their databases to identify you easily. I recall a police investigation where telephone companies – mobile phone carriers – were ordered by the Court to reveal the identities of a suspected group of drug traffickers who used their mobile phones to communicate with one another. And in several countries in 2015 the Courts ordered Internet Service Providers (ISPs) to reveal the identities of individuals who had allegedly downloaded illegal copies of a movie called Dallas Buyers Club.

In a publication of the International Association of Privacy Professionals (IAPP) it was reported that knowing just three pieces of information about an individual – namely the birth date, zip/post code and gender – can identify the individual with a high degree of certainty by matching them against public records.

A: Wow, that's scary! We can't go around ignorantly thinking that anonymity or pseudonymity will protect us from being identified. We have to be very careful in what we say or do from now on. Hey, why don't we blog about what we have discussed today, to share with a larger audience? Should we do it anonymously, pseudonymously or with our true identities?

B: Haha! That depends on the content and the audience.

The two friends then enjoy the beautiful sunset, while sipping the exotic fruit punch. Another fruitful day!

CHECKLIST OF GOOD PRACTICES

Organisations and individuals should be aware of how to deal with anonymised data:

- Personally identifiable information can be anonymised by removing the unique identifiers, through aggregation or generalisation, or by replacing the actual data values with other values.
- Do not assume that anonymity is safe. People can be re-identified through a few pieces of information about them and matched against public records.
- The Internet and portable smart devices make it easier to track the location and usage patterns of individuals, and service providers can link these back to their databases for re-identification.

🔒 29 Beware of secondary usage of personal data

I applied to the local utilities company to open an account for my apartment that had just been vacated by the previous tenant and was to be marketed to a new tenant. The application process was a cinch. All I needed to do was to visit the website of the utilities company and fill in the application form online. So I keyed in all the information I expected would be sought, such as my name, identity card number, address of the apartment, the billing address, my email address and my phone number. So far so good.

Then there was a field that asked for my ethnic group, which I was quite reluctant to provide. In my mind I was thinking: why would the opening of a utilities account require a knowledge of my ethnic group? But since time was running short – I had to have the power and water turned on in a few days' time – I submitted the form with the field for ethnic group duly completed.

The next day, I sent an email to the utilities company asking them to clarify why they need to know my ethnic group for the purpose of opening a utilities account. The reply from the utilities company came back after a week with a terse one-liner to say that the information was required by their principal for analysis and reporting purposes. Apparently the utilities company was collecting the data on ethnic group on behalf of another organisation and they did not know much of the details.

Not satisfied with this answer, I wrote directly to the principal for enlightenment. Two weeks later, someone from the principal replied to say that the data on ethnic group was relevant to their study of electricity consumption. This got me even more intrigued as I could not understand the cause-effect relationship between ethnic group and electricity consumption. I had learned in school that electricity consumption is affected by the number and type of electrical appliances, and how long they are being switched on. I wouldn't have minded so much if the principal had asked for the floor area of my apartment, the number of air-conditioning units or the number of occupants.

Beware of secondary usage of personal data

The reason I am sharing this experience of mine is that as individuals providing our personal data to organisations, we should at least be notified of the purpose for the collection, usage and disclosure of our personal data. The utilities company should not have collected personal data beyond what was required for the primary purpose of opening an account. Worse still, the utilities company was collecting and disclosing personal data to a third-party for another secondary purpose without express consent from the customers. It would still be unacceptable even if the principal of the utilities company could assure consumers that their personal data would be anonymised for research purposes.

Sales or marketing as a secondary use of personal data

Collecting personal data for a primary purpose and then using or disclosing it for a secondary unrelated purpose is not uncommon. For example, it is very tempting for the sales or marketing department in an organisation to conveniently get personal data that has been collected by another department for a particular (primary) purpose and use the data for their prospecting purposes. Organisations must guard against such a practice and require their employees not to do so, in order to ensure that the organisation does not fail to comply with the data protection law.

CHECKLIST OF GOOD PRACTICES

Organisations collecting personal data of customers should adopt the following practices:

- Notify customers of the purpose of collecting, using and disclosing their personal data.
- Do not collect more personal data than is required for the primary purpose or use it for a secondary unstated or unrelated purpose.
- Do not use personal data that is collected for a non-marketing purpose to prospect for new customers.

🔒 **30** How securely is the information baton passed in your organisation?

One of my favourite track and field events in athletics is the 4x100 metre relay. It's always a beautiful sight to behold as teams of four runners race round the 400-metre track, each sprinting like a gazelle for 100 metres before the next runner in line takes over.

What is more amazing to watch is the slick coordination and precision with which each runner passes the baton to the succeeding runner. The "passer" waits for the right moment to release the baton. The "receiver" waits for the right moment to grasp it tightly and securely before taking off for the next leg of the race.

How I wish personal data and other confidential information could be passed between employees within organisations with the same slickness – without dropping the "information baton". ("Information" here refers to both personal data and other confidential information.)

In our consulting work, one of the most common shortcomings we see in organisations is the lack of proper processes for employees, particularly in different departments, handing/taking over documents containing personal data or other confidential information. More often than not, the "passer" of the information baton does not check to make sure that the "receiver" has got it securely in their grasp.

In other words, the organisation does not have a policy and documented practice for the "passer" to get an acknowledgement from the "receiver" that they have received the personal data or other confidential information. The common mindset is: "I've already done my part. It is up to the other person in the downstream process to take over from there."

But what if the personal data or other confidential data gets lost, misplaced or delivered wrongly along the way? An organisation should ensure that it complies with the data protection law whenever the information baton includes personal data. And of course for sensible business reasons an organisation certainly does not want to lose, misplace or deliver wrongly any confidential information, even if does not include any personal data.

Here are some tips for passing information batons within an organisation securely.

Type A baton: Documents moving within a department or work group

Personal data and other confidential information may be in hardcopy form and need to be passed between individuals in the same department or work group. Their desks are usually close to one another.

This is easy. Individuals simply hand hardcopy documents to others in the department or work group. There is face-to-face interaction between the "passer" and the "receiver", so the information baton is passed securely to the right person.

When the "receiver" is not at their desk, the "passer" can either deliver the document later or leave a note on the "receiver's" desk to have them collect the document from the "passer".

Type B baton: Documents moving from one department or work group to another department or work group

Personal data and other confidential information may be in hardcopy and need to be passed from one department or work group to another. Their desks are often not close to one another. Often, an inter-departmental "mail run" is used. Sometimes an organisation maintains a system where employees each have a secure "pigeonhole" for exchanging documents and other items.

In any event, organisations should have policies and documented practices in place about confidential documents in hardcopy that are not hand-delivered by the "passer" to the "receiver".

The policies and practices should require employees to put confidential documents into a sealed envelope with "Confidential" stamped on both sides of it. Employees should also make sure that:

- they do not use one of those brown envelopes that are designed for reuse – tying the string around the stud does not make it into a sealed envelope; and putting a piece of sticky tape across the flap (which gets done a lot of times during the "life" of these envelopes) does not make it into a sealed envelope either
- if personal data or other confidential information can be read through the envelope, they should use a thicker envelope or insert an additional sheet of paper to shield the information.

Of course, the front of the envelope should also have the name of the addressee and will sometimes show their department's name and even their office location. This is because appropriate steps should be taken from both a data protection perspective and a business perspective to ensure that the envelope is not lost, misplaced or wrongly delivered. Or not delivered at all and, perhaps, simply thrown into a rubbish bin by employees who do not know where and how to deliver it.

The policies and practices should also require the "passer" to put a packing list in the envelope listing the documents in it. This is for the "receiver" to verify the number and type of documents in it. The "passer" should also be required to put an acknowledgement slip in the envelope for the "receiver" to sign and return to the "passer".

And of course the policies and practices should require the "passer" to make sure that they receive the acknowledgement slip and file it appropriately. This is so that it can be retrieved readily if there are any queries in the future about the way in which the relevant personal data was handled within the organisation.

Type C baton: Documents moving outside the organisation

Personal data and other confidential information may be in hardcopy form and need to be passed to a "receiver" who is outside the organisation, but in the same country. It could be another entity within the same group of companies. It could be a vendor retained to process the personal data in some way. Or it could be some other separate organisation to which the personal data may be disclosed legitimately.

In some cases, the "receiver" is an entity within the same customer group or the organisation has a close relationship with frequent interaction with the "receiver". Passing the personal data or other confidential information from the "passer" to the "receiver" might, in practice, be done in exactly the same way as when it moves between departments and work groups within the same organisation.

Otherwise, documents containing personal data or other confidential information will likely be passed by the "passer" to the "receiver" by a courier service or the national postal service. Either mode of delivery service should include registration, on-route tracking and acknowledgement of receipt of the package by the rightful "receiver".

If using a courier service, the organisation should carry out appropriate due diligence to satisfy itself that it selects a reputable and reliable courier service that will guarantee a safe and secure delivery of the confidential documents from the "passer" to the "receiver". If using a national postal service, the organisation should consider whether doing so is appropriate versus engaging a courier service, particularly where the personal data or other confidential information is sensitive and/or the postal system might not be particularly secure and/or reliable.

In either case, policies and practices adopted by the organisation should require employees to mark the envelope and/or courier package as "Confidential". Personal data or other confidential information should be put into an inner envelope that is placed inside the outer envelope that will be mailed or inside the courier package. The inner envelope should be addressed to a specific named individual. It should be marked "To be opened only by <name of that specific person>". After all, there is little point in going to the trouble of protecting personal data or other confidential information in transit only to have it opened by any virtually unidentifiable individual whose job it is to open all incoming mail at the "receiver" organisation.

Of course, the "passer" should be required to take care in specifying the name and address of the "receiver" completely and accurately. The policies and practices should also require the packing list and acknowledgement described above, at least where the personal data or other confidential information is sensitive for some reason. And require the "passer" to make sure that they receive the acknowledgement slip and file it appropriately.

Type D baton: Documents moving outside the country

Personal data and other confidential information may be in hardcopy form and need to be passed to a "receiver" in another country. The considerations set out above for documents moving to another organisation in the same country apply.

In addition, whenever the information "baton" includes personal data the "passer" is required to satisfy any requirements of the data protection law relating to transfer of personal data outside of the country. These are often complicated – too complicated and varied to be described here – and sometimes include specific rules about consent for transfer of personal data outside the country.

For example, the "passer" organisation might be required to ensure that the "receiver" is located in a country where the laws governing personal data protection are of a standard that is comparable to that of their country's laws. Or, the "passer" organisation might have to get the "receiver" organisation to sign a legally binding agreement to take specific steps to protect the personal data.

Is the administrative burden too heavy?

It may seem that the above processes and practices introduce inconvenient and perhaps inefficient administrative burdens to organisations.

But in general circumstances, these are necessary to give a reasonable assurance of compliance with the data protection law. In specific circumstances, an organisation may need to do even more to support compliance with the data protection law, such as where the organisation is handling highly sensitive personal data. As the old adage says, "It's better to be safe than sorry".

When any confidential document containing organisation-critical information (such as personal data, commercially sensitive information or intellectual property) goes missing, is misplaced or is delivered to the wrong party, it may bring about grave damage to the organisation. If it becomes known publicly, it can undermine stakeholders' trust in the organisation too.

An after-note on information in the electronic domain

The passing of the information "baton" in the electronic domain poses an even higher risk than in the case of hardcopy documents. This is because the transmission of confidential emails or e-file attachments transcends any organisational or geographical boundary. A proper handing-over and taking-over procedure is even more necessary in the electronic domain.

CHECKLIST OF GOOD PRACTICES

Organisations should have documented policies and practices for passing personal data and other confidential information internally and externally.

Passing Type A information baton

■ Hand over confidential documents personally.

Passing Type B information baton

■ Use inter-departmental mail run or place confidential document in the individual's secure pigeonhole.

■ Put document together with packing list and acknowledgement slip in sealed envelopes stamped "Confidential".

Passing Type C information baton

■ Use a reliable courier service or the national postal service with procedures for registration, on-route tracking and acknowledgement of receipt.

Passing Type D information baton

■ Ensure the recipient's country has a comparable data protection law as the sender's country.

■ Otherwise, get the recipient to sign a contract that requires the recipient to safeguard the transferred information.

---

31 Importance of controlling document access and duplication

When we were kids our parents used to drum into us the need to share our toys and goodies with our siblings, and also with our cousins when they came to visit. We grew up with the acceptable norm that "sharing is good".

This sharing behaviour carried on during our first few years in school. But when we progressed on to upper primary school and beyond we became more selfish with our sharing. We became wary about sharing what we knew with our classmates, due to competition in examinations.

Then when we started our working life we were cautioned not to share too much about what we were doing, such as the organisation's vision and strategies, and details of our projects, due to external competition and even industrial espionage.

Many organisations, especially those handling highly confidential and sensitive information, are paranoid about safeguarding their proprietary information because leakage may result in significant adverse business outcomes. In addition, where confidential information is personal data, organisations should ensure that they comply with the data protection law. If they fail to do so the regulator may require them to comply with its directions or may fine them. Regulatory action is generally likely to bring with it a risk of adverse publicity and a consequent lack of trust, giving rise to another adverse business outcome.

With the ubiquity and accessibility of affordable photocopiers, scanners and digital cameras, how can organisations prevent their employees – either disgruntled and unscrupulous or simply lazy and careless – from making unauthorised copies of confidential paper documents, including cases where it contains personal data?

Below we offer a few practical tips which organisations can adopt to minimise their employees getting access to confidential documents, including documents containing personal data, and making unauthorised copies of such documents.

Getting the "structure" right first

First and foremost, it is important to note that an organisation should adopt policies and documented practices about how their employees may and may not handle confidential paper documents.

In any information security regime, the human being is often the weakest link in the entire chain. That is why clearly spelt out policies, rules, processes and procedures for handling and duplicating confidential documents are of great importance. Everyone in the organisation must "play by the rules" – they can do so only if they know what they may do and what they must not do.

Employment contracts and/or employee handbooks should require employees to comply with theses policies and practices. There should be disciplinary consequences for failure to do so, including warnings and training, up to and including dismissal.

Access to documents

The organisation's policies and practices should cover access by their employees to confidential paper documents.

This will cover points such as who – defined by job role or title – can have access to what type(s) of information. Defining permissions by job title means that it may remain stable over time, though the organisation should review them regularly to ensure that they remain relevant. After all, job roles do evolve over time and requirements for access to confidential information may change.

If an organisation chooses to define right-of-access by reference to named individuals (instead of being defined by job roles or titles), the organisation should review their permission whenever the individual's job role changes.

Transferring documents

The organisation's policies and practices should cover the processes and procedures for transferring confidential paper documents internally within the organisation and to third-parties outside the organisation.

The individual handing confidential documents over to another individual is usually responsible for safeguarding the confidentiality of the information, including personal data, included in the document. However, the responsibility should be documented clearly so that employees understand it. It is too late after something has gone wrong for employees to say, quite genuinely, "But I didn't know that I was supposed to...".

Copying and sharing documents

The organisation's policies and practices should cover when employees may make copies of a confidential document or of personal data and when they may share it with other employees within the organisation. Sometimes this may include a requirement for employees handing a document over to other colleagues to remind them that they must not make copies of the document or to share it with anyone else. And it may include retrieving copies of documents after they have served their purpose.

In some organisations, for example, employees in the Human Resource (HR) Department make enough copies of a potential employee's job application form and résumé so that there is one copy for each member of the interview panel. The copies are put into sealed envelopes and sent to the intended recipients through the organisation's internal mail system. At the end of the job interview, the HR employees retrieve all copies of the documents that they sent to the members of the interview panel and seek assurance that the panel members did not make any copies of them.

Permission for copying documents

The organisation's policies and practices should not permit its employees to make copies of confidential documents without the explicit permission of the documents' originator (or of some other specified individual).

Using copiers and scanners

The organisation's policies and practices should state that only staff with legitimate staff access passes may use the organisation's photocopiers and scanners. Preferably, use should be controlled and tracked by requiring employees to input access codes which are assigned to them and which they are not permitted to share with other employees. These codes should, in any event, be changed by the organisation periodically.

Records of usage of photocopiers and scanners should be reviewed by employees to whom that responsibility is assigned. They should ask employees to account for any usage that seems unusual or inappropriate given their job role.

CCTV monitoring

The organisation should consider whether, as an additional safeguard, CCTV cameras should be installed at strategic locations within their office to deter any malicious insider from stealing or taking digital images of confidential documents. (Of course, access to the office should be controlled so that any outsiders cannot enter and steal or take digital images of confidential documents.)

CHECKLIST OF GOOD PRACTICES

To control the unauthorised duplication of paper documents containing personal data and other confidential information, organisations should put in place the following measures:

- Explicit policies and rules on how confidential paper documents are to be handled by employees within the organisation.
- Processes and procedures on how confidential paper documents are to be transferred from one party to the next.
- All employees should be briefed to not make copies of confidential documents without the explicit permission of the documents' originator.
- Only employees with legitimate staff access passes can make use of the organisation's photocopiers and scanners using access codes.
- As an additional safeguard, CCTV cameras can be installed at strategic locations to deter any malicious insider from stealing or taking digital images of confidential documents.

🔒 32 Bad things happening with documents and personal data

Have you lost, misplaced or accidentally exposed any physical documents containing personal data – especially those with sensitive information?

Personal data has been lost, misplaced or accidentally exposed in the UK and the regulator has prosecuted individuals and organisations. These cases may provide warnings about what may happen under other data protection laws in similar circumstances.

Case #1: Sensitive documents left behind in a plastic shopping bag on a train

A local government authority incurred a monetary penalty after a social worker left sensitive documents in a plastic shopping bag on a train. The social worker had intended to take them home to work on them.

The files, which were later recovered from the rail company's lost property office, included doctors' and police reports and allegations of sexual abuse and neglect.

Case #2: Documents with personal data stored in transparent bags

The regulator required an estate agency to sign an undertaking to comply with the data protection law after it continued to leave papers containing personal data on the street despite a previous warning.

The papers, meant for disposal, were stored in transparent bags and the personal data on them was clearly visible to anyone who walked past.

Case #3: Folder containing personal data left in a café

A legal aid worker lost a folder by leaving it in a café. The folder contained confidential client information.

The regulator required the legal aid agency to sign an undertaking to comply with the data protection law.

Case #4: Recycled paper with personal data

The regulator fined a local government authority £250,000 after former employees' pension records were found in an over-filled paper recycle bank in a supermarket car park.

Tips to help you avoid doing bad things

Here are some tips about how you can avoid doing bad things, including when you are busy or just absent-minded and forgetful.

Mark files or folders "Confidential"

If you are constantly on the move and handling personal data of clients is part of your job, ensure that your confidential documents are placed in a non-transparent folder or envelope with a "Confidential" stamp on it.

"Why warn people that you are carrying a sensitive document?", you may ask.

An organisation should have confidentiality policies governing which of its employees are permitted to see various categories of documents, including those marked as "Confidential". And complying with these policies should be part of the organisation's employment contract so that all employees are legally obliged to comply with them. Therefore, in an office environment, anyone who looks at a confidential document that they are not authorised to see breaches the policy and therefore their employment contract with the organisation. It's only fair that files be stamped as "Confidential" so that individuals do not inadvertently look at them.

If you lose a confidential folder in a public place, the confidential warning – hopefully – will be noticed by a good Samaritan who, equating confidentiality with importance, might return it to your office… without looking at it and without reporting your organisation to the regulator for failing to comply with the data protection law. Now imagine if there were no "Confidential" notice.

Secure any file or bag containing personal data

When you are handling personal data of clients, you might think you have a choice between carrying loose sheets of paper around in transparent folders or plastic bags, and securing them in a closed bag or sealed envelope. But in reality, you do not. You need to guard against misplacing or losing personal data.

I always carry my umbrella, my notebook, my train timetable and my files and documents, including my confidential files and documents in a closed – zipped up – backpack. I take something out of it when I need to look at it or use it and then put it back again. I would surely lose something by absent-mindedly leaving it behind if I had to carry several things separately. And my bad luck would mean that it would inevitably be something important, such as a confidential file.

When you are constantly on the move, work out what strategy works for you to guard against leaving confidential information behind on the train or losing it in a café.

Do not expose personal data by recycling paper

When we do onsite data protection audits for our clients, one of the most common findings is personal data on paper that has been set aside for recycling. Sometimes the paper will have been put into a recycling bin that will be taken away by another organisation; sometimes it will be put into a recycling tray for internal use. It is common for organisations to place a recycling tray next to the printer or photocopier, for example, so that the reverse side of any unused printed pages or copies can be used. But employees fail to notice that the paper may have personal data on the side that has been printed on.

While saving the environment is an important initiative, protecting personal data is a legal obligation under the data protection law. There are other ways of reducing paper usage while not exposing the organisation to data protection compliance risks.

For example, the printer or copier can be set to "duplex" mode so that it always prints or copies on both sides of the paper when a document is more than one page long. And documents can be printed, say, two pages on each side, which is often perfectly workable for checking and reviewing draft documents.

Dispose of unwanted documents containing personal data securely
You should always shred any document that includes personal data. Or get it shredded for you by an appropriate vendor.

Never throw any document that includes personal data into the wastepaper basket. Never throw it into a recycle bin that gets taken away by another organisation unless you have done appropriate due diligence and confirmed that the other organisation will, in fact, shred it securely. (Did you know that some so-called paper recycling organisations that say they shred paper and then recycle it actually sell at least some of it? And that it ends up being used in all sorts of ways where personal data may be exposed?)

When you print documents that include personal data or photocopy them, make sure that you do not leave discarded or imperfect prints behind at the printer or copier for whatever reason, including so that the paper can be recycled internally.

Beware when you move house
We see that individuals who are constantly on the move as part of their job – for example, where they are sales agents and other independent contractors – end up with files and documents stored at home. If that describes you, beware when you move house.

People tend to get careless when getting rid of old stuff – they throw it into a bin or get someone to take it away and don't care what happens to it. But the old stuff that you get rid of so carelessly could happen to be your old transaction records containing other people's personal data. You should always shred it or get it shredded for you by an appropriate vendor.

Beware when submitting or archiving personal information

Whether you are in a hurry to meet a submission deadline or handing over documents to another person, your should take steps to put proper security measures in place.

Never leave a document containing personal data on someone's desk or even in an exposed tray for incoming documents. You never know who might walk past and see it. They may be other employees, but that does not mean that they are authorised to see it. At least put the personal data in a sealed envelope marked to the attention of the individual you want to receive it.

If you have to submit documents to your agency or company and the medium for doing so is not secure, inform their management that the data protection law requires organisations to take reasonable measures to protect personal data in their possession or under their control. The submission box should be secure and it should not be possible for unauthorised employees to retrieve documents.

CHECKLIST OF GOOD PRACTICES

Organisations and individuals handling documents containing personal data or other confidential information should do the following:

- Ensure that all physical files and folders containing personal data are clearly marked as "Confidential".
- Put in place policies and practices that require any files or bags containing personal data, particularly where it is sensitive, to be secured so that the personal data is not disclosed when the files or bags are in transit or taken into meetings.
- Ensure that no personal data is exposed due to any paper recycling and that documents are disposed of securely, such as by secure shredding.
- If you are constantly on the move as part of your job, do not dispose of personal data carelessly, leave it exposed when delivered to someone else or submit it to an organisation in an insecure manner.

🔒 33 Paper documents – the Achilles heel for organisations

The newspapers frequently report newly discovered data breaches that sound like an organisation is the victim of a dastardly crime perpetrated by mysterious hackers. Sometimes the reports note that these data breaches are being investigated by the regulator and sometimes they tell us that the regulator plans to take action against the organisation. We do not often hear subsequently that the incident would not have happened except for the actions or inaction of employees – that it was not so much a dastardly crime perpetrated by mysterious hackers, but a case that is more attributable to careless or malicious employees within the organisation. But, nevertheless, "cyber-security" is getting a lot of attention, and causing a lot of alarm, at all levels of business and government.

In any event, while these cyber-related incidents get media attention, they are not the only incidents organisations should be guarding against. Paper documents may be the Achilles heel for many organisations – the weakness in spite of overall strength that can actually or potentially lead to data breaches. Just as electronic databases may be compromised, paper documents can also get organisations into trouble due to the actions or inaction of careless employees within the organisation.

Let's check out some statistics to understand what's going on

The Ponemon Institute asked 584 IT professional how data breaches occur. In the study titled "Aftermath of a Data Breach", published in

January 2012, 66% of respondents cited employees and other insiders as posing the greatest threat to an organisation's sensitive data.

Specific to the loss of paper records, one study of 1,500 data breaches in 2013 and 2014 found that it was one of two most common sources of breaches, accounting for 24% of total breaches[1].

A data breach may have severely adverse business implications. A regulator may also determine that it constitutes a failure to comply with the data protection law, namely the obligation or principle that requires an organisation to protect the personal data in its possession or under its control.

In the year before writing, we did more than 50 onsite data protection audits of organisations in Singapore and Malaysia. Most of these audit clients were small or medium enterprises (SMEs). The biggest risks we identified related to paper documents containing personal data. The top five areas we identified (outside the IT infrastructure) in organisations we audited were:

[1] https://www.beazley.com/news/news/bbr_1500_breaches.html

■ 73% had confidential information/personal data lying exposed on desks to which other employees had easy access – that is, the desks were not in enclosed offices

■ 68% had uncollected printed documents and/or original documents left on, at or around the photocopier

■ 50% had unlocked or exposed screens on computers/mobile devices and/or unlocked cabinets or locked cabinets with the keys left in the keyholes

■ 33% had papers and/or documents with confidential data thrown into wastepaper baskets or recycle bins

As you can see, the risk of paper documents tends to be overlooked at an alarmingly high rate. These findings were made within organisations that were conscious enough about data protection to have asked us to audit them for operational compliance with the data protection law or who had sent employees to our hands-on data protection officer's course. We can only guess that results at other organisations would be even more alarming.

Tips for finding and fixing data protection risks in paper documents

The gaps in operational data protection compliance we mentioned above are easily addressed with recommended information security measures that are rather obvious.

Our audit methodology included a data inventory assessment and an analysis of the flow of personal data within the organisation. This was followed by an actual site inspection of where personal data was collected, processed and stored. The risks mentioned above were identified simply by observation.

So, what's our tip? An organisation should do regular onsite audits to identify its operational data protection compliance risks. An audit can be done by suitably trained employees or by suitably qualified and experienced external consultants. For many organisations, paper document-related risks are a time-bomb waiting to explode!

CHECKLIST OF GOOD PRACTICES

Organisations and individuals handling paper documents containing
personal data or other confidential information should do the following:

- Understand that while IT-related risks of data breaches might be significant,
  paper document-related risks should not be overlooked.

- Conduct an onsite audit of your organisation's operational compliance with
  the data protection law, or hire a suitably qualified and experienced external
  consultant to do an initial identification of the paper document-related data
  protection risks.

- Respond to risks identified in the onsite audit by adopting policies and
  documented practices to eliminate or minimise the risk. Organisations should
  ensure that all employees are trained and will implement those policies and
  practices properly.

- Develop a schedule for further periodic onsite audits to ensure compliance
  with existing policies and practices and identify any additional gaps that
  should be closed.

🔒 34 The perils of file exchange and sharing

Do you or your organisation use cloud storage services such as Dropbox and Google Drive, which are hugely popular among many property agents, insurance agents and other mobile workers? Or do you often share personal data through email with other employees in your organisation or third-parties?

If so, you need to be alert to at least the following three sets of requirements:

■ **Information security policy**

You need to know whether what you are doing is permitted by your organisation's information security policy. Or, in the case of individuals under an agency contract with an organisation, whether it is permitted by your agency agreement with that organisation.

If that information security policy is silent about using these types of cloud storage services, we suggest it should be amended either to permit it (and to include any protocols that employees are required to follow) or to forbid it.

While forbidding it is likely an unpopular and probably inconvenient outcome, it is better than not raising questions about it now and finding out later when there is a problem that you are blamed for it. And that unpleasant consequences may attach to that blame.

■ **Data protection law**

You need to know whether what you are doing is permitted by the data protection law, which requires personal data in the possession or under the control of an organisation to be protected by that organisation.

■ **Sectoral regulations**

You need to know whether what you are doing is permitted by any sectoral regulations that apply to the organisation. (For example, the central bank in your jurisdiction may have made regulations that apply to your organisation's use of cloud storage services.)

The perils of file exchange and file sharing

Most users of file sharing services or those sharing files via email are not aware that they are creating potential data protection issues and compromising security for their organisations if they only use the default functions and basic features within the service. This creates governance, risk and compliance issues for the organisation. As mentioned above, it can lead to trouble and blame for you.

In one survey in the US[1], approximately 61% of respondents confessed they often or frequently:

■ sent unencrypted emails

■ did not delete confidential documents or files as required by applicable organisational policies

■ accidentally forwarded files or documents to individuals not authorised to see them

■ used personal file sharing/sync-and-share apps in the workplace.

Major risks for organisations include the following:

■ Hackers being able to gain access to your file sync-and-share system and then taking control of it. They might then have access to an unprecedented amount of your organisation's information, including personal data. Access might extend to your organisation's client's information, including personal data, too.

■ Employees sharing documents or files containing personal data by email with other employees who are not authorised to see it and/or with third-parties who are not authorised to see it.

Then it becomes even more precarious, especially if your documents are unprotected and can easily be accessed. How many

---

[1] Ponemon Institute "Breaking Bad: The Risk of Insecure File Sharing", Oct 2014.

times have we heard of employees who carelessly shared confidential documents with others who are not authorised to view that information?

In one instance reported in the papers in Singapore in 2015, a teacher accidentally sent out the personal data of 1,900 pupils to parents. A spreadsheet attached to an email to parents contained the names and birth certificate numbers of every pupil in the school, along with the names, phone numbers and email addresses of their parents.

Tips to minimise the perils of file exchange and file sharing

Here is a list of tips for achieving reasonable protection when exchanging or sharing files online, although more may be necessary in particular circumstances, for example if the personal data shared is sensitive.

Use two-factor or multi-factor authentication when logging into your cloud service

Dropbox[2] and Google Drive[3], for example, both offer several optional security functions. One of them is two-factor authentication, which includes using one-time-password tokens. With two-step verification enabled, you will have to enter both your usual password and a security code that is sent to your mobile phone whenever you sign in to the Dropbox website or add a new device to your account

The outcome of two-factor authentication is that even if someone knows your Dropbox or Google Drive password, they will not be able to log in to your account unless they can also obtain the time-sensitive code from your phone.

Password-protect or encrypt the document

Whenever you share a Microsoft Office document or PDF document that includes personal data or other confidential information, you should password-protect it. The relevant applications allow you to save the documents with a password.

[2] Instructions for Dropbox users: https://www.dropbox.com/help/363
[3] Instructions for GoogleDrive users: https://support.google.com/accounts/answer/185839?hl=en

A strong password should prevent a hacker or other unauthorised individual from opening your document.

But of course you must protect your strong password too. Call the recipient to tell them the password or send it to them in an SMS. If there is no alternative but to email the password to the recipient, send it in an email separate from the email to which you have attached the document. And avoid sending the two separate emails within seconds of each other and with the same subject heading.

Sometimes you may need to share an image of a document, such as a passport or driver's licence, which is obviously sensitive personal data. Image files cannot easily be encrypted or protected with passwords. Therefore you should embed the image file in a Word document first and then password-protect the Word document.

Advanced users should explore using dedicated encryption tools to encrypt their documents or folders[4].

Verify the recipient's email address for accuracy – and be stingy when you "cc"

Although getting email addresses correct sounds very straightforward, many individuals still send files to the wrong recipients carelessly. The auto-find/select feature in many email programs that automatically selects a name based on whichever letter or partial name you type can lead to errors. If you often send emails containing personal data, eliminate this risk by turning the feature off. Otherwise, always be very careful, especially when you are in a hurry.

Be very stingy about who you include in any "cc" to an email where it, or an attachment to it, includes personal data. If several individuals need to see the message in the email, but not all of them need to see, or are authorised to see, the personal data in an attachment, send the email without the attachment. Then send a separate email with the attachment only to those individuals who need to see the personal data and are authorised to see it. This should reduce the risk of data exposure or leakage as well as enabling you to comply with your organisation's policy about who has access to personal data.

---

[4] Visit the Lifehacker website for tips: http://lifehacker.com/five-best-file-encryption-tools-5677725.

A further quick note on emails – protecting the personal data of recipients too

Sometimes you need to send emails to multiple individuals, including where there is an attachment that contains personal data.

Take some time to think about whether or not it is appropriate for each recipient to see each of the other recipients' email addresses. And whether or not it is appropriate for each of them to know who else will see the personal data in the attachment to the email.

If in any doubt include all the recipients under blind copy/"bcc" so that no recipient can see the email addresses of other recipients or see who else will view the personal data in the attachment to the email.

Check or verify who and what links you are sharing

When you share documents using Dropbox, Google Drive or other file sharing services, you send a link to the individual or individuals with whom you want to share them. Because you see only one link, it is easy to forget that you have a particular document that is shared with multiple individuals. It is also easy to forget that they can forward the link to just about anyone.

Always be aware of what files you are sharing and verify who has access to them. Be careful about the permissions you give to the recipient, such as the ability to edit or add new files.

You should regularly review shared access rights to your documents and folders. You should retire the links that are no longer being used or no longer required. Dropbox, for example, allows you to see which files you have shared and with whom – you can easily decide what files or folders should or should not continue to be accessible and to whom. The same logic applies if you are syncing multiple devices or sharing folders with others. Unlink devices you are no longer using.

Delete emails containing personal information that are no longer needed

Make it a point to delete emails that contain confidential data. This includes any attachments you may have downloaded. If you use your mobile device to share documents, practise the same care – whether you WhatsApp or snap a photograph of somebody's identity card, driver's licence or other document.

CHECKLIST OF GOOD PRACTICES

Organisations and individuals sharing and exchanging files containing personal data and other confidential information should take the following precautionary measures:

- Make sure that you and your organisation are permitted to use cloud storage services.

- Use cloud storage services and share documents and files only in accordance with protocols set out in your organisation's information security policy.

- Use protection measures such as two-factor authentication, password protection and/or encryption.

- Ensure that email addresses are correct and be stingy about who gets a copy of the email. Think about whether copies should be sent using the "bcc" function rather than the "cc" function.

- Keep your shared documents and links up to date. Do regular housekeeping and delete emails containing personal data when you no longer need them.

🔒 35 Publicly available data – is it really free to use?

The data protection law invariably requires an organisation to obtain consent from individuals before collecting, using or disclosing their personal data. However, there are exceptions to the consent requirement.

A typical exception relates to "publicly available information" or "publicly available data". To illustrate, here is a list of some types of publicly available information:

■ Government and public sector agency records – for example, land title records, company registration records (including details of directors and shareholders) and bankruptcy records.

■ Information about listed public companies that they disclose to the public in the company's Annual Report and in their stock exchange filings. For example, they might disclose the remuneration of their directors and/or senior executives.

■ Videos and photos taken of individuals in places that are open to the public, even if it is necessary to buy a ticket or book a seat, for example.

Note: Videos and photos taken of individuals at private functions held in public places where entry is by invitation only (such as a private room in a restaurant or a restaurant that is booked out for a private function) are not publicly available information. Nor are videos made and photos taken from a public place looking into a place that is not open to the public (for example, looking from the street through the window of a house).

■ Personal contact information of individuals who advertise in the newspapers or on the Internet to offer products or services for sale or to source for products or services to purchase.

■ Personal details of individuals posted on social media platforms that are not restricted to select groups of people.

Is an organisation free to collect, use or disclose publicly available information?

The question one might ask is: "If consent of the individuals concerned is not required in the above scenarios, does it mean that anyone can have unfettered use of such publicly available data?"

The answer matters, particularly from a sales and marketing perspective. If the answer is "Yes", rich sources of personal data are a marketer's bonanza. Unfortunately, the answer is usually "It depends".

So access to publicly available data does not automatically give an organisation or an individual the right to use or disclose such data in any way they like. It seems to be better to err on the conservative side rather than to have a complaint or even a lawsuit against the organisation.

Some reasons why "It depends" follow. There may be additional reasons in specific circumstances or concerning specific information. This is an area for consideration on a case-by-case basis.

Licensing or right-of-use considerations

The organisation that publishes personal data may restrict its use. For example, where personal data is made available by a government or public sector agency it may impose specific licensing or right-of-use conditions. These may include restricting use of purchased data to the individual or entity that purchases it and prohibiting any re-sale of the personal data to a third-party.

Before using or disclosing any personal data that is publicly available information, an organisation or individual must be sure to check for applicable terms and conditions and make sure to comply with them.

Intent of the individual who made their personal data available publicly

An organisation has to be cognisant of the intent of the individuals who make their personal data publicly available. Individuals who advertise in the newspapers to look for a vehicle with certain specifications might tolerate someone offering them another vehicle with slightly different specifications in response to their advertisement.

But they would most likely not tolerate someone trying to sell them a spa package or financial advice. Even though the data protection law may permit the organisation to collect and use their personal data without consent for sales and marketing purposes, it will be futile and possibly counter-productive from a business perspective if the individual feels that the organisation should not have done so.

The law of unintended consequences

Care is always needed if images of individuals are used without their knowledge and consent. There may be unexpected and unintended consequences and the organisation using the images might be responsible for them.

The use needs to be reasonable in the sense of being personally acceptable to individuals if it is to win or retain their goodwill. For example, a group of people whose photo is taken at a public place would most likely be annoyed if they discover that their photo is being used to promote a weight management programme or a hair implant programme.

CHECKLIST OF GOOD PRACTICES

- Organisations should understand that they will not usually have the right to use or disclose publicly available information indiscriminately.
- The use or disclosure of publicly available data should take into consideration:
  - licensing or right-of-use requirements
  - the intent of the data originator
  - the law of unintended consequences

🔒 36 Secrets and dangers of using a digital copier

How much do you know about photocopiers or what are known as multi-functional devices? Here's something I learned that is very important from the perspective of operational compliance with the data protection law.

These machines used to use a process called analogue copying. An internal mirror copied the image of a document onto a drum and then, using static electricity, particles of toner created the image that was on the drum. Then around 2002, digital copiers came onto the market. At first they were expensive compared with analogue copiers, but of course technology got cheaper and so did digital copiers. A digital copier scans a document and saves it into its memory – it contains a hard disk – and then a laser is used to print the saved image.

The copier has since evolved into a multi-functional device (MFD), providing centralised document management, distribution and production within an office setting. Besides the photocopy function, a typical MFD now acts as a combination of some or all of the following devices: email, fax, printer and scanner.

Recently, I mentioned this to a colleague, who replied by saying that only very high-end copiers are digital. Alas, they were mistaken. Digital copiers are ubiquitous. That means that nearly every copier now contains a hard disk – similar to your personal computer – capable of storing images of every document copied, scanned, or emailed by the machine. And most of us do not know about it.

Some field investigations

A few years back, CBS News chief investigative correspondent Armen Keteyian went to a warehouse in the state of New Jersey to see how hard it would be to buy a used photocopier loaded with documents. What he found was "a digital time-bomb packed with highly-personal or sensitive data such as social security numbers, birth certificates, bank records, income tax forms". It would be a gold mine for anyone in the identity theft business.

No wonder the US Department of Health and Human Services fined Affinity Health Plan Inc US$1.2m in 2013 for violating the HIPAA Privacy and Security Rules when it failed to wipe data from the hard disks when it returned its leased copiers to the leasing company.

General lessons learned about digital copiers

Now that you know about copier technology, you know that every time you copy, print, scan or fax a document using a digital copier – whether you do it using your office's multi-functional printer or a separate device – a digital copy of your document is stored in that hard disk, including any personal data in that document.

So, therefore, an organisation should securely delete personal data from the hard desk in its copier before parting with possession of the copier. Otherwise you likely do not comply with the requirement of the data protection law to protect personal data in the organisation's possession or under its control.

An additional lesson for mobile workers

If you are a mobile worker – a salesperson, agent or adviser, for example – do you sometimes need to use a copier in a client's office or in a hotel business centre or in some other public or semi-public place? If so, you now know that the copier will more likely than not be a digital copier and that it will retain a copy of your document, including any personal data, on its hard disk.

This involves at least two risks. First, there may be an unauthorised disclosure of personal data to anyone who examines the hard disk in the copier and therefore a failure to comply with the data protection law.

Second, anyone who examines the hard disk will have access to any confidential information that was in the copied document, information that could be incredibly valuable to a competitor of your organisation.

Other operational failures to protect personal data at the copier

In our onsite audits for our clients we have found the following common copier operational failures to protect personal data. These are in addition to copies of documents containing personal data being found on the hard disks of digital copiers.

- Uncollected printouts left in the printer or photocopier
- Original documents left under the scanner or printer cover
- Unwanted prints (with personal data) thrown in the wastepaper basket
- Recycled paper used for printouts with personal data already printed on it
- Unsecured photocopiers with email and recall features

Such careless actions or negligence could put your customers, employees, clients or students at risk due to ineffective or non-existent security practices on your part or your organisation's part relating to your photocopiers and other multi-function peripherals.

Tips for procurement and office administration

In addition to the operational tips above, employees responsible for procurement should include at least the following safeguards to help ensure the safety of data on the hard disk of a digital copier:

- the lease or purchase contract should include a requirement for it to be encrypted and for it to use overwrite protection techniques
- the lease contract should also specify a disposal process for the copier that requires the lessor to remove the hard disk (and return it to the lessee organisation for destruction) when the lease comes to an end
- internal policies should be implemented to ensure that a purchased copier is not sold to a third-party without the hard disk first being removed (and retained by the organisation for destruction) and
- internal policies should set out requirements for secure deletion of data from hard disks removed from digital copiers or for their secure destruction.

Employee training

It goes without saying that another important step you should take is to ensure that your security training and educational materials for employees also cover the potential for data leakage from multi-functional photocopiers and printers.

CHECKLIST OF GOOD PRACTICES

Organisations and individuals who make use of digital copiers should take the following precautionary measures:

- Understand that digital copiers (and printers) contain a hard disk and ensure that it is removed or that all data is securely deleted from it before your organisation parts with possession of the device.
- If you are a mobile worker, you should not use copiers at your client's premises or any copier available for use by the public generally. You should make copies of documents only at your own office.
- Ensure that personnel are not careless about leaving personal data exposed in, on or around the office copier. Discarded copies must be securely shredded.
- Ensure that the necessary due diligence with the copier vendor or lessor is in place from a contractual perspective.
- Put in place security measures within the copier unit that prevent data leakage.

37 Using personal data from unclear or unauthorised sources

Marketers live and die on lists – hundreds and thousands of names and contact information of prospects, referrals, ex-customers and current customers. If they can get additional profile information of these individuals, marketers segment their lists into sub-groups so they can do more specific, targeted marketing.

Today, companies in the business of selling lists to marketers might seem to make marketers' dreams come true. Marketers like the idea that they can use the ready-made lists to find and contact potential customers without doing the tedious and laborious task of "harvesting" and compiling the lists themselves.

But little do these "quick-fix" marketers know – or they know and choose to ignore it – that some of the lists they purchase come from dubious or unauthorised sources that fail to comply with the data protection law.

Some common ways of failing to comply with the data protection law

Here are some common examples of failure to comply with the data protection law we have seen in our consulting work:

- Personal data of individuals who have not given relevant consent for the collection, use and disclosure of their personal data
- Personal data of individuals who have given consent for the collection, use and disclosure of their personal data for a specific purpose (for example, participation in a lucky draw) but not for marketing or other purposes

- Personal data of individuals who have withdrawn consent to their personal data being used for marketing purposes
- Personal data that is inaccurate or outdated
- Personal data that includes phone numbers on the national Do-Not-Call (DNC) registry
- Publicly available information collected from government departments and public agencies and sold despite specific terms of use that might include a ban on selling the personal data and/or restrict the purposes for which the data can be used

Obviously, marketers should purchase ready-made lists with their eyes open to avoid failing to comply with the data protection law.

Tips about how marketers can protect their organisation

Whenever they consider purchasing a ready-made list, marketers should conduct appropriate due diligence to satisfy themselves that none of the names on the list suffers from any problems such as those listed above. They should get written evidence from the seller and keep it on file. This might include, for example, getting the seller to produce evidence of consent and any other necessary permissions relevant to the marketer purchasing the personal data and using or disclosing it for marketing purposes.

Generally, the evidence provided by the seller that is least open to legal challenge about its validity is the written contract between the seller and the marketer. It should include representations and warranties by the seller about compliance with the data protection law.

While notoriously difficult to negotiate, marketers should require the seller to provide an indemnity to their organisation to cover damages, costs and losses resulting from any failure by the seller to comply with the data protection law. These measures will likely not protect the marketer from regulatory action for any failure to comply with the data protection law by purchasing and using the list, but may go some way towards mitigating culpability in the regulator's eyes.

The biggest "red flag"

In practice, most list sellers will not provide the various assurances mentioned above. Either they cannot do so because there are problems

204 88 Privacy Breaches

of the types listed above – they do not have evidence of consent, for example – or there is some other unknown factor in play. Either case is a big "red flag" for marketers and their organisation.

In any case, getting the suggested assurances takes a lot of time. From the perspective of both regulatory risk and time, it pays for marketers to "harvest" and compile their own lists through their own effort and in compliance with the data protection law. Then they can have sweet dreams instead of nightmares.

CHECKLIST OF GOOD PRACTICES

Before marketers make use of ready-made contact lists from third-party sources, they should check that the following have not been contravened:

- Personal data of individuals where consent for collection, use and disclosure has not be obtained.
- Personal data of individuals where consent for collection, use and disclosure has been obtained for a specific purpose, but is now being used for a different purpose.
- Personal data of individuals who have withdrawn their consent.
- Personal phone numbers that have been registered with the national Do-Not-Call (DNC) registry.
- Publicly available data from government departments and public agencies that have specific terms of use on who can have access to such data and for what purposes.

🔒 38 Watch your spreadsheet – spreading personal data in a data breach

Many of us use spreadsheets in our everyday work. A single Excel spreadsheet file, for example, can contain up to one million lines of records so they are a convenient way to store records and perform useful calculations and transactions.

Very often, spreadsheet users store account, membership, health records and transactional information that includes sensitive data such as identity card numbers, payment card numbers, birthdates and addresses.

Under the data protection law, using a spreadsheet negligently can get the user's organisation into trouble. Here are some examples of data breaches involving spreadsheets:

Accidental email attachment #1

Willis North America Inc. is an insurance broker and risk adviser. On 19 March 2014, one of its employees who was sending a reminder to all of the organisation's employees about an upcoming deadline to earn wellness credits "accidentally attached a spreadsheet to the email that was not meant to be included"[1].

The information on the spreadsheet included names, email addresses, dates of birth, social security numbers, employee ID numbers, and office locations by city/state/zip. It also included wellness credits, individuals' credit status codes, insurance coverage codes and other personal data relevant to medical insurance.

---

[1] https://www.privacyrights.org/content/willis-north-america-inc

In short, the spreadsheet included all the personal data necessary for identity theft. While the organisation believed that the personal data in the spreadsheet was not improperly accessed it nevertheless offered all employees two years of identity theft protection at no charge.

Accidental email attachment #2

An employee of the University of Mississippi Medical Center[2] accidentally attached a spreadsheet with sensitive information to an email that went out to students. The email was meant to alert students to changes being made to the school's health insurance scheme.

The spreadsheet contained student names, social security numbers, GPAs, race, gender, dates of birth, mailing addresses, and phone numbers. Upon discovering the breach, the university used a combination of asking students to delete the email and manually removing the email from students' webmail accounts.

Accidental email attachment #3

In Singapore, Henry Park Primary School mistakenly sent a spreadsheet containing students' personal data to around 1,900 parents when it updated them about a school event.[3]

The school was not within the scope of the data protection law, but the incident caused it embarrassment and immediately attracted unwelcome publicity. A day after the mistake, the school principal had to send an email apology to all parents, asking them to delete the spreadsheet and not to use the personal data in it.

Spreadsheet information published online without checking

In the UK, the Information Commissioner's Office (ICO) fined the Islington Council £70,000 for disclosing the personal data of more than 2,000 local residents when it inadvertently published the data on its website, which allows people to search through responses to similar requests from public authorities.[4]

---

[2] https://www.privacyrights.org/node/57529

[3] http://news.asiaone.com/news/singapore/details-more-1900-pupils-henry-park-primary-school-leaked

[4] www.itpro.co.uk, Spreadsheet error leads to £70K data breach fine for London council, Aug 23, 2013. http://www.itpro.co.uk/security/20465/spreadsheet-error-leads-£70k-data-breach-fine-london-council

The source of the information was three spreadsheets that accidentally disclosed details about whether or not the residents had a history of mental health issues or had suffered from domestic abuse. It also contained details of 2,375 council tenants or those who had applied for council housing. These were contained in pivot tablets, which are used in Microsoft Excel to summarise large amounts of data.

According to the investigation, "The person who released this data did not have sufficient knowledge of spreadsheets to recognise the error or to put it right." As a result, the council staff responsible had to receive additional training on how to prepare data for public release.

Bringing spreadsheets home from the office

Be wary if you bring your work home from the office, especially when it comes to spreadsheets.

An employee from the Hospice of the Chesapeake[5] emailed spreadsheets with sensitive patient information to a personal account in order to work from home. The spreadsheet contained names, ages, dates of service, diagnoses, and medical record numbers.

The breach was initially suspected to have been caused by a computer intrusion. Hospice of the Chesapeake investigated the breach for two months before revealing it to the 7,035 patients who were affected.

Protecting personal data in spreadsheets

The data protection law requires an organisation to protect personal data in its possession or under its control. Therefore, an organisation should require its personnel to password-protect each spreadsheet or the folder in which it is filed. It makes no difference if the file or folder is saved locally or on a shared network drive. The file may also be encrypted to give a higher level of protection, particularly if the personal data in it is sensitive.

Many reported data breaches involve unsecured spreadsheets that were saved on laptop computers that were subsequently stolen. For example, when a laptop computer was stolen from the vehicle of an employee from Yusen Logistics Americas it contained an unencrypted

[5] https://www.privacyrights.org/content/hospice-chesapeake

spreadsheet with payroll deduction information of former and current employees including names, social security numbers, addresses, and payroll benefit deduction[6].

Most spreadsheet software provides an option for password protection. That way an unauthorised individual will not be able to gain access to the file. Not securing spreadsheets containing sensitive personal information will put your organisation at risk.

CHECKLIST OF GOOD PRACTICES

Organisations and individuals who make use of spreadsheets to process personal data and other confidential information should take the following precautionary measures:

- Ensure that all personnel at least password-protect all spreadsheets that contain personal data. Encryption is advisable, particularly where the personal data is sensitive.
- Whenever you attach a spreadsheet to an email always double-check to make sure that it is the correct attachment.
- Whenever you attach a spreadsheet to an email always double-check to see if it contains any personal data and, if so, whether or not that personal data may be disclosed to the recipient(s) of the email.
- Whenever you attach an email with a pivot table to an email check that the recipient is permitted to see any personal data that is included in the source information and, if not, make sure that the source information is not still embedded in the pivot table.
- If you want to work at home, make sure that your organisation's information security policies permit you to email documents to your personal email so that you can work on them. Alternatively, make sure that your organisation's information security policies permit you to download documents to a tablet and work on them at home or permit you to take your workplace laptop home.
- If your organisation publishes personal data online in certain circumstances, make sure that you have a fail-safe system in place (such as a second line of verification) to ensure that only the correct/relevant personal data is published.

---

[6] https://www.privacyrights.org/content/yusen-logistics-americas-inc

🔒 39 "With great power comes great responsibility" – access to employee personal data

As an employee or manager, do you have access to personal data about your organisation's clients, customers or even employees so that you can do your job? Are you sometimes tempted to look at that personal data for reasons not connected with your job? If so, watch out.

Your position of authority gives you access to important personal information, but there are responsibilities associated with exercising that responsibility. As in the Spider-Man comics, "With great power comes great responsibility". Looking at personal data other than for the purpose of doing your job:

■ can lead to disciplinary consequences for you because most organisations' internal policies prohibit that type of snooping and

■ can constitute a failure of your organisation to comply with the data protection law (because it fails to protect the personal data) – and that too will have unpleasant, if not disciplinary, consequences for you.

Here are a couple of real-world examples:

Ex-wife illegally accessed husband's social welfare records

An individual complained to the data protection regulator[1] that an organisation had failed to comply with the data protection law by failing to protect his personal data from unauthorised access. His ex-wife happened to work for the organisation and his claim was that

---

[1] Case Study 3 (2013) from the Office of the Data Protection Commissioner, Ireland. https://www.dataprotection.ie/docs/CASE-STUDIES-2013/1441.htm

it had allowed her to have access to his personal data for a purpose other than doing her job.

The organisation's access logs showed 12 instances of unauthorised access between February 2004 and July 2009. The organisation took disciplinary measures against the ex-wife. The regulator required the organisation to put stricter measures in place to ensure personal data was protected from unauthorised access.

Employee obtained data from customer file for their own use

An individual complained to the data protection regulator in March 2010, alleging an inappropriate access to customer personal data by an employee of Aviva (an insurance company)[2]. The complainant had received a phone call from someone the previous evening. The caller accused him of scratching his, the caller's, car the previous evening while parking his own car. The caller said that he had noticed that the car was insured with Aviva and, as he worked for Aviva, he had looked for the complainant's phone number in Aviva records.

The regulator investigated the complaint. The Aviva employee confirmed that he accessed the complainant's policyholder data for the purpose of contacting him to discuss the incident and to see if he wished to settle the matter directly. Aviva acknowledged that the incident should have been pursued in the normal manner through its claims procedure. (In that case, only Aviva's claims employees would have seen the complainant's personal data and they would have used it only in connection with the allegation.)

The caller, the Aviva employee, was warned of the seriousness of the incident. Aviva used this complaint to draw the attention of other Aviva employees to the importance of complying with its data protection policies and practices.

Aviva issued a letter to the complainant explaining what had occurred. Aviva apologised for the distress and inconvenience caused to the complainant and sent him a voucher for €100 towards his next renewal premium. Fortunately for Aviva and the employee, the complainant accepted this amicable resolution.

---

[2] Case Study 16 (2010) from the Office of the Data Protection Commissioner, Ireland. https://www.dataprotection.ie/docs/Case-Studies-2010/1195.htm

Banker accessed colleagues' bank accounts for salary and bonus information

An individual worked in a bank's suspicious activity reporting unit, which meant he was able to view customer accounts. He admitted that he used this access to look at eleven colleagues' accounts to get information about their salaries and bonuses. He was fined by the regulator,[3] which stated in its report that the individual had been given clear training by the bank about the data protection law, but chose to ignore that training.

Hospital employee disclosed health information about a patient to a mutual friend

A local hospital treated a woman for a serious illness[4]. A hospital employee happened to be her close friend. She had access to the case notes about the woman's illness and the proposed treatment.

With good intent, the hospital employee told a mutual friend that the woman was unwell. The mutual friend contacted the woman to express concern. The woman was upset that her health condition had been disclosed as she had not then told anyone about it. She complained to the regulator, which considered it a breach of the data protection law and that the hospital had caused emotional harm to the woman.

As a result, the hospital apologised to the woman for the stress that had been caused to her. It also paid her some financial compensation.

Health services individuals prosecuted for unauthorised access to personal data

An employee of a medical centre[5] accessed the medical records of colleagues and family members without consent. The (now former) employee was fined £300, and ordered to pay costs of £434.73 and a victim surcharge of £20.

---

[3] "Birmingham banker fined for reading colleagues' bank accounts", 22 Aug 2014, ICO. https://ico.org.uk/about-the-ico/news-and-events/news-and-blogs/2014/08/birmingham-banker-fined-for-reading-colleagues-bank-accounts/
[4] "A hospital employee disclosed health information about a woman to a mutual friend", 24 Aug 2012, Privacy Commissioner's Officer New Zealand, https://privacy.org.nz/news-and-publications/case-notes-and-court-decisions/case-note-235915-2012-nz-privcmr-5-a-hospital-employee-disclosed-health-information-about-a-woman-to-a-mutual-friend/
[5] https://ico.org.uk/action-weve-taken/enforcement/zita-driaunevicius-cookson/

In another case, a (now former) employee of a health care trust was found during a routine internal audit to have unlawfully accessed the medical records of family members, work colleagues and local health professionals. The employee was fined £1000 by the regulator and ordered to pay a £100 victim surcharge and £608.30 prosecution costs.

Important tips for employees

- Remember, you signed a confidentiality agreement with your organisation, and probably an undertaking to safeguard personal information according to your local data protection law.
- For whatever reasons, do not access personal information outside your official duties, even if you have good intentions.
- Follow the procedures and practices as outlined in your organisation's internal privacy policy.

Important tips for managers and employers

- Organisations are entrusted with a huge amount of personal data which they have a responsibility to keep safe and secure, whether it involves disclosure to third-parties outside the organisation, or in the above cases, internal misuse as well.
- Ensure that access to personal information is granted on a need-to basis, which must be continually reinforced through training and reminders.
- Implement access rights controls, based on the individual's roles and responsibilities.
- Put an audit trail in place on computer systems to capture both "read-only" and "edit" accesses to official records.
- Continue monitoring audit trails and follow-up actions to ensure effective protection of records stored on your organisation's computer systems.

CHECKLIST OF GOOD PRACTICES

Organisations should adopt the following safeguards when accessing, using or disclosing employees' personal data:

- Ensure that access to personal information is granted on a need-to basis, which must be continually reinforced through training and reminders.
- Implement access rights controls, based on the individual's roles and responsibilities.
- Put an audit trail in place on computer systems to capture both "read-only" and "edit" accesses to official records.
- Monitor audit trails and follow-up actions to ensure effective protection of records which are stored on your organisation's computer systems.

Employees should be aware of the following guidelines when accessing, using or disclosing their colleagues' personal data:

- Do not access personal information outside your official duties, even if you have good intentions.
- Follow the procedures and practices as outlined in your organisation's internal privacy policy.

"

It takes less time to do a thing right
than to explain why you did it wrong.

"

Henry Wadsworth Longfellow

"

I tell my students that they don't need
to be accurate to communicate. They do
need to be accurate to be respected.

"

Zoe Morosini

SECTION D:

Data Accuracy & Integrity

🔒 40 Identity verification – the wrong way

It was one of those days. I was queueing patiently in front of an ATM (automated teller machine) to withdraw some cash. When it came to my turn, the machine would not accept my ATM card, displaying a message on the screen that read, "There is an error reading your card".

Disappointed, I walked over to the bank branch to have the problem rectified. At the customer service counter, I was attended to by a young female rookie (her badge was inscribed with the word "Trainee"). She ran my ATM card through her machine and certified that the magnetic strip on my card had reached the end of its lifespan. She could issue me a new ATM card within 10 minutes, but she would first have to verify my identity. I thought that was a good security practice and dutifully abided by her instruction.

Identity verification – the wrong way

In a jiffy, the young rookie extracted my record from the bank's database. This was how the verification process went:

Rookie: "Sir, is your name <and she said my name>?"

Me: "YES!"

Rookie: "Is your NRIC (National Registration Identity Card) number Sxxxxxxxx?"

Me: "YES!"

Rookie: "Is your date of birth dd/mm/yyyy?"

Me: "YES!"

Rookie: "Thank you, sir! I will now issue you a new ATM card. You may key in your new PIN number on this device."

Alarmed, I gave the young rookie a piece of free advice on how she should have conducted the identity verification. I told her, instead of phrasing the three questions in the way she had, she should have asked them in reverse:

"Sir, what is your name?"

"What is your NRIC number?"

"What is your date of birth?"

I explained to her the reason for doing this was so that she could verify, with a much higher degree of confidence, that I was really the owner of the ATM card. Someone could have picked up my ATM card and then requested for a new ATM card without even knowing who the card actually belonged to. The rookie would have just given a masquerader an open door into my bank account to withdraw all my savings!

I was further alarmed to learn from the young rookie that the bank branch was short of staff and she had been placed on her job without much training. That explained why she had phrased the three questions in that manner.

Is your organisation doing it correctly?

Organisations should be aware that human beings are often the weakest link in an entire security system. They should therefore ensure that all their employees are educated and made aware of the control measures and verification procedures that are in place to prevent unauthorised access to their customers' personal data or unintended disclosure of their customers' data to the wrong person(s). There should be no compromise in giving proper training to staff who have to handle personal and sensitive data of their customers, especially when verifying their identities and allowing them access to their data.

CHECKLIST OF GOOD PRACTICES

When verifying the identities of customers, organisations should:

- Let the customers supply their own personal data and verify these against the organisation's records.
- Train all customer-facing employees to ask the right questions.

41 Identity verification – the right way

I seem to have a "love affair" with banks and other credit card issuers. Every so often I have to call their hotline to address some inaccuracies in my account statement, such as additional charges that I have not actually incurred, charges that are not waived despite agreement to waive them, and changes that they have not made despite agreement to make them.

In the past, every time I called the hotline, the customer service officer (CSO) at the other end would ask me three standard questions to verify my identity: NRIC (National Registration Identity Card) number, date of birth and mobile phone number. Once these three pieces of information were checked against the organisation's records, I was able to discuss whatever I wished regarding my account.

In recent years, banks and other credit card issuers have tightened their identity verification processes. This is because they realise that it is relatively easy to obtain the three pieces of information mentioned above. For example, individuals often provide them for lucky draws or when signing up for loyalty programmes.

An additional question is now often asked by the banks and other credit card issuers to verify a customer's identity. For example, "How many accounts do you have with us?", "How many supplementary cards do you have on this account?", "How many ATM (automated teller machine), credit and debit cards do you have with us?", etc.

How strict is your identity verification process?

On one occasion, I was really stumped when I called a bank's hotline to activate the new chip-based ATM card the bank had sent to my home address. "Which year did you open your account with the bank?" asked the CSO. I tried to reason with the CSO that I opened my account many years ago and my memory failed me.

Patiently, the CSO tried to help me recall, by asking me: "Have you any record of this kept somewhere?" When I said I did not, the CSO said to me: "I'm sorry, Sir, I can't activate your new ATM card over the phone. You will need to come to one of our bank branches with your new card, together with your NRIC for identity verification, to have it activated."

Was I annoyed that I had to set aside some time to go to one of the bank's branches to have this simple procedure done? Absolutely not!

On the contrary, I have confidence that this bank handles my personal data with proper care. This is because it used stringent checks to verify my identity, even to the extent of refusing its service to me over the phone. This bank has earned my trust in personal data protection. It has implemented the necessary security measures and verification controls to protect the personal data (both physical and electronic) under its care against:

- unauthorised access and modification to the personal data
- unauthorised use, disclosure or duplication of the personal data and
- loss of the personal data.

And not only that, the bank has trained its staff well on how to deny access to the bank's services if the requester over the phone cannot pass the stringent identity verification procedures.

CHECKLIST OF GOOD PRACTICES

- In verifying the identity of customers, an organisation should go beyond asking the standard questions and include certain questions that are related to the customer's unique dealings with the organisation.
- If customers answer the supplementary questions incorrectly, the organisation should deny service to them until they can show documentary proof of their identity.

42 The trouble with processing personal data inaccurately

Recently, a colleague sent me a joke. It prompted me to think about inaccurate personal data and the trouble it can cause. In the joke, a man received a note from his neighbour:

> "Sorry sir I have been using your wife day and night when you are not present at home – maybe using more than you are using. Now I feel very much guilt. Hope you will accept my sincere apologies."

The man went and shot his wife.

A few minutes later, he received another message:

> "Sorry sir, spelling mistake … wifi not wife."

In the joke, a small spelling mistake caused a horrible catastrophe that could have been avoided. Under the data protection law, silly mistakes such as the one in the above joke and other simple typos can get organisations into trouble with the law.

Accuracy obligation[1]

All data protection laws include an obligation or principle regarding the accuracy of personal data. It requires organisations to make a reasonable effort to ensure that the personal data collected by or on behalf of the organisation is accurate and complete.

---

[1] In some jurisdictions, this would be called the integrity principle.

While it might not get somebody shot, financial and other penalties can be imposed by the regulator. The penalties vary depending on the seriousness of the breach or the damage caused. And relatively minor mistakes can be aggravated by the organisation's manner of dealing with them.

Here are some examples. Unfortunately, they can happen to anybody in your organisation, but should not happen if your organisation develops and implements policies and practices to avoid them and trains employees to understand the risk of errors and how to apply your organisation's data protection policies and practices.

Sending wrong text messages on your mobile device

Beware when you use your mobile device to send a text message that includes personal data. Two factors can easily increase the risk of errors and your organisation failing to comply with the accuracy obligation in the data protection law:

- You are in a hurry and you make mistakes.
- You use the built-in predictive text function on your device. The predictive function may not be as accurate as you think. It can incorrectly substitute words that you do not intend, creating an entirely new meaning – like "wifi" to "wife".

The same logic also applies to names and numbers. Double-check any text messages before you send them, especially when they contain personal data.

Sending personal data to the wrong person

You should use the predictive text function on your mobile device or your email software very carefully. Otherwise, you could be responsible for your organisation breaching the accuracy obligation or principle in the data protection law.

How many times do we key in the first few letters of somebody's email address and wait for the email software to fill in the rest of the email details for us? This is indeed convenient. And risky. We inevitably have several potential recipients with fairly close names or email addresses and certainly with the same first few letters in their email address.

If you often email personal data, you should check carefully the email address that you select from the list that the predictive function gives to you. Or, even better, disable the predictive function and always key in email addresses manually.

How about those of us who use the history or event log function on a phone, fax or email application to recall a previous contact, only to retrieve the wrong information?

I wonder if the predictive function was responsible when I received the following text message. Or if it was a simple case of the sender making an input error for the telephone number.

Dear <given name and family name>,

We have approved your loan for <$amount> to purchase <address of property>. Please contact us to arrange for loan drawdown and settlement.

I felt that I should notify them of their error and texted: "You have sent this message to the wrong person. Please delete my mobile number from your records."

Unbelievably, they responded with "We cannot communicate with you unless you include your PIN in your message." Clearly, their employee sending the response had not received adequate training in compliance with the data protection law. They did not even appear to understand that they had disclosed another individual's personal data to me and that their organisation had therefore failed to comply with the data protection law.

Wrongly assuming two people with the same name are the same person
Be extra careful when processing personal data about individuals with the same name, especially when it comes to common names such as John Tan or Peter Lim. Some people take additional care when it comes to very common names such as John Tan or Peter Lim but then are caught off-guard by less common names. Very few names are unique. Names recur surprisingly often even in relatively small databases.

It is common to match or merge a name in a database for email marketing. Or to search for a particular person to provide a service to them. But there is always a danger that you will introduce inaccuracies. Always verify the information first. Look for other identifiers to give you reasonable assurance that you have chosen the right person.

Some final words

As you know, technology might save us a few productive seconds. But as you can see, technology also exposes us to risks of failing to comply with the data protection law.

The consequences of doing so might linger for a long time in terms of fines, reputational damage or even lawsuits.

Technology cannot replace our need to be careful and accurate when processing personal data. Always check and double-check that it is correct. Avoid hurrying and cutting corners.

When the purpose for processing personal data is important or even critical for some reason, such as for decision-making that will likely affect the individual, an organisation should develop and implement policies and practices to verify accuracy. For example, one employee of the organisation might be assigned responsibility for assembling files for some purpose, but another employee is assigned responsibility for checking it for accuracy and then using it for that purpose.

CHECKLIST OF GOOD PRACTICES

Individuals should exercise care in using or processing personal data to ensure the data is accurate:

- When using the predictive text function on your mobile device or your email software, input your text very carefully.
- Check carefully the email address that you select from the list that the predictive function gives to you.
- Be careful when you use your mobile device to send a text message that includes personal data.
- Be extra careful when processing personal data about individuals with the same name.

43 Process personal data accurately or face unintended consequences

Without fail, every month for the past few years I have received a reminder notice from my bank about my housing loan payment due that month. It is a standard form of notice that informs me that the bank will deduct $xxxx from my account on dd/mm/yyyy. It reminds me to make sure I have sufficient funds in my bank account. I normally do not pay much attention to the details in the notice since they are almost the same every month, save for slight variations in the repayment amount due to fluctuations in the interest rate.

On one occasion, I went through the same monthly ritual of opening the envelope from the bank, retrieving the reminder notice and scanning the contents quickly to make sure everything was in order. I almost fell off my chair when the repayment amount on the notice was much bigger than usual – six digits instead of four! The bank had substituted my monthly repayment amount with the balance of the whole loan! I certainly did not have sufficient funds in my bank account to pay that amount.

I phoned the bank immediately to inform them of the grave error. Their customer service officer (CSO) very calmly assured me that the bank was aware of the problem and would send out new reminder notices to all affected customers. I asked about the cause of the mistake. The CSO said it was due to a printing error. Not satisfied with the reply, I probed further and asked if it was due to a computer or software error. The CSO stuck to the same "party line" and repeated adamantly that it was due to a printing error.

Lessons we can learn from this incident

Reflecting on this incident, I drew a few important lessons about automated processes and the consequences of errors that develop in them and are not detected by timely checking for accuracy.

First, the bank's computer system has been churning out the same reminder notices to its customers month after month without any mistake. So the cause of the error in one month could not be simply a printing error.

Printing reminder notices happens right at the end of a chain of processes. So the cause of the mistake could only have been an error in an earlier upstream process. If mistakes in upstream processes are not identified early and fixed, their impact on downstream processes can be dire.

Second, and worse in this incident, is that the processes are automated. Automated processes should always be sampled periodically for accuracy – in this case, to ensure that the automated process was retrieving customers' loan repayment data accurately, that the data was being incorporated accurately into the printed reminder notices and that the deductions from customers' bank accounts were accurate.

A timely check that had discovered, for some reason, the automated process was not retrieving customers' loan repayment data accurately would have prevented the bank from sending out incorrect reminder notices. And saved both customers and CSOs a great deal of time dealing with the resultant complaints.

Third, imagine the negative impact on the bank's reputation among their customers who, like me, had checked their reminder notice and called the bank about the error. Apart from anything else, most customers find it simply annoying to have to waste their time making calls about things that they expect the bank to have got right.

The negative impact on the bank's reputation would be even worse among customers if they had an incorrect deduction made from their bank account – without their knowledge if they had not been vigilant in checking their reminder notices.

The incorrect deduction would have reduced their account balance to below what they expected. Likely consequences of a lower account balance include cheques being bounced by the bank and the bank not making GIRO payments due to insufficient funds remaining in the account. Consequences for the customer of bounced cheques and failed GIRO payments may include personal embarrassment and loss of reputation, plus penalties imposed by third-parties for late payment to them. Consequences for the bank might even extend to lawsuits by customers to recoup their losses caused by the bank's incorrect deduction from their bank account.

Some speculation on the root cause of the error

Barring any malicious attack on the bank's computer systems by insiders or outsiders, I would hazard a guess on some plausible causes that led to the so-called "printing error":

- The database system was upgraded or modified. That upgrade or modification upset the indexing system. Instead of the index pointing to the monthly repayment amount, it pointed to the total loan balance instead.
- Some modules of the application system were upgraded or modified, which affected the logic of other existing modules.
- Fixing software bugs in one part of the application system affected the logic of other parts of the system.

Unintended Consequences

"Unintended consequences" in the context of automated processes are the outcomes and effects of unanticipated causes that the application or software designer could not have foreseen.

What can be done to prevent them? If one of the causes listed above is correct, the bank obviously did not conduct sufficient "user acceptance testing" of the upgrade, modification or bug fix – which would have detected the error – before "going live".

Testing should not be confined to software modules that have been changed or replaced. It should extend to the whole application system (system testing) and the integration of the new software modules with existing modules (integration testing). Testing should also include the impact of the new software modules on the logic of existing or inter-related modules (regression testing).

Had the bank tested the new printouts it should have discovered the mistakes and not sent incorrect reminder notices to customers. Too often, organisations are in a hurry to launch new application systems as quickly as possible and do not put enough emphasis on rigorous testing and validation. Sometimes organisations cut costs by doing only minimal testing and validation without taking into account the cost of complaints and loss of reputation caused by system errors.

Compliance with accuracy requirements of the data protection laws

The data protection laws include an obligation or principle requiring organisations to make reasonable efforts to ensure the accuracy of personal data, particularly where it may be used to make a decision.

Organisations therefore need to be able to assure individuals that the personal data in their possession or under their control is accurate. This includes personal data in IT systems with automated processing.

There is no shortcut to rigorous IT system testing before the organisation "goes live" with them. Rigorous testing is absolutely necessary to reduce the risk of unanticipated consequences resulting from errors, which can be prevented or avoided before it is too late. It is a mistake to seek to cut costs by reducing system testing without taking into account the risk of reputational loss arising from system errors.

CHECKLIST OF GOOD PRACTICES

Organisations that regularly process customers' data should take the following precautionary measures:

- Ensure that customers' personal data and transactions are processed accurately.
- Beware of unintended consequences that could be caused by changes in internal processes or upgrading of the IT systems.
- Any new software module introduced or any existing software module modified should be thoroughly tested to ensure that there are no unintended consequences.

44 The trouble with a poor customer verification process

Some people like phone banking, and some people dislike phone banking.

I dislike phone banking because it forces me to listen to a long list of options in multi-level menus: "Press 1 for…, Press 2 for…". By the time I get to the end of the options I've forgotten the earlier ones. I have to repeat the cycle all over again.

How I wish I could skip the long list of pre-recorded options and simply "Press 0 to speak to a customer service officer". But that doesn't work for all phone banking systems – I still have to go through the entire rigmarole of listening to all the options until I hear "Press 0…".

On the other hand, I like phone banking because I can speak directly to a person eventually instead of to a machine. This is something that is superior to Internet or online banking, which, though more convenient to use, does not permit any human interaction.

When I finally get to speak to a customer service officer (CSO), there is usually a standard script that sounds like this:

CSO: "Good morning, sir. How may I help you?"

Me: "I would like to…"

CSO: "Before I can do that I need to verify a few details with you. Your name, identity card number, date of birth and bank account number."

I rattle off all these details to the CSO. If what I say matches the bank's database, the CSO then willingly attends to my request.

What if someone masquerades as a customer?

This bank's procedure for verifying the identity of its customers seems like a good practice. But only until I put myself in the shoes of someone – a fraudster – masquerading as a bona fide customer.

If a fraudster sees a cheque issued by the customer, the fraudster can easily write down the customer's name and bank account number.

A fraudster can often get an individual's date of birth from the individual's social media profile, such as on Facebook or LinkedIn. (This alone is a good reason why individuals should not disclose their date of birth on social media. But in some countries it can be obtained from public records anyway.)

In countries that have a national identity card system, the identity card may be used widely for all sorts of transactions so a fraudster might see it in a range of contexts. It may even be obtained from some public records, such as records of property ownership or records of company officers.

Voila! The fraudster has all the necessary information required to pass off as a bona fide customer.

What are banks doing about the shortcomings in identity verification?

The banks are well aware of the shortcomings I've described above. Most banks have tightened the procedure they use to verify the identity of their customers.

One common practice is to ask customers additional questions such as which school they attended, their mother's maiden name or their pet's name. If the customer has been an active user of social media, a fraudster might easily obtain the answers to these questions.

Some banks ask additional bank-related questions that a fraudster is unlikely to be able to answer, such as "What loans have you taken from the bank?" "How many credit/debit cards issued by us do you have?"

Two-factor/multi-factor authentication in phone banking

Some banks have implemented a two-factor or multi-factor authentication scheme. This is more secure than the one-factor authentication mentioned above. But the way my bank does it is rather cumbersome. I have to put my conversation with the CSO on hold, while I call another number provided by the CSO. This second number sends a text message to the mobile phone number in the bank's records. It is a one-time code that I need to send to the CSO to verify my identity.

How I wish I could have dual SIM cards on my mobile phone so I wouldn't have to toggle between two phone connections using a single number.

This phone banking user experience of two-factor authentication is a far cry from that experienced in Internet or online banking. Nevertheless, it is a secure step forward.

Two-factor/multi-factor authentication in Internet or online banking

In Internet or online banking, besides the user ID and password, the customer must key in a one-time code generated from a physical token issued by the bank to the customer. Alternatively, the one-time code can also be sent to the customer's mobile phone number or email address.

Onus on organisations to verify the identity of their customers

Banks must be vigilant in verifying their customers' identity. CSOs must seek to detect any instance where another individual calls in on behalf of the customer or does not personally have all the information on hand to verify the customer's identity. Some banks will terminate a call if the CSO hears the person on the phone asking someone in the background for any information that may relate to the bank verifying the caller.

Sometimes some assistance from another person may be perfectly legitimate — the bank might ask callers about the year they opened their account and the callers might have forgotten but know that their spouses would have kept a record of it. But the bank can't take any chances because a family member or some other person close to the customer can easily get hold of all the customer's verification information. They might even have easy access to the customer's cheque book or identity card. There have been cases of ex-spouses of customers pretending to call on their behalf to enquire about the customers' banking activities or other assets kept with the bank which the ex-spouses are not supposed to know about.

Data protection law requirements apply too

Banks are typically required by banking legislation to keep customers' details confidential. In addition, banks and other organisations are required by the data protection law to protect personal data in their possession or under their control. This of course includes not disclosing it improperly.

In summary, banks and other organisations should verify the identity of their customers carefully before disclosing any personal data or any other confidential information to them. Not to do so thoroughly is to invite trouble or negative consequences, including penalties for failing to comply with the data protection law.

CHECKLIST OF GOOD PRACTICES

Organisations (for example, banks) should implement the following practices to verify the identities of their customers:

- In phone banking, go beyond asking the standard questions; preferably ask bank-related questions which only the customer will know the answers to.
- Use two-factor/multi-factor authentication if feasible.
- Do not allow someone to call on behalf of the customer to enquire about the customer's banking activities or assets kept with the bank.

45 Trusting organisations for the accuracy of our transaction data

I invite you to answer three questions before you read this chapter:

■ Do you keep all the credit card slips you have signed so that you can verify your monthly credit card statement from your bank or other credit card issuer against them? Do you also keep track of any credit card transactions where you do not sign a credit card slip?

■ Do you keep your own records of all the transactions in your bank account so that you can verify your monthly bank statement against them? (Transactions you need to keep track of include ATM cash withdrawals, cash deposited, cheques drawn, cheques deposited, debit card payments at point-of-sale and GIRO deductions.)

■ Do you keep your own records of all transactions on your mobile phone account so that you can verify the monthly bill against them? (Transactions you need to keep track of if you have a post-paid plan include the number of text messages you sent and whether they are local or international, the number of call minutes you used, the volume of data you transmitted or received, the number of call minutes you used on voice roaming and the countries where these were used, the volume of data you transmitted or received on data roaming and the countries where these were used.)

If you answer "yes" to all three questions, you are among an endangered species. In all likelihood, the majority of us would answer "no" to at least one, if not all, of these questions. Not that we are lazy, but it is too tedious and time-consuming to keep such records. Sometimes it is near impossible for us to do the record-keeping without special equipment or computer systems, as in the mobile phone example. So the man-in-the-street wisdom is that "I have to trust the monthly statements from the banks, credit card issuers and mobile phone operators since they have the responsibility to keep track of my transactions".

But can you be 100% sure that your transactional data captured and processed by these organisations is 100% accurate all the time?

Worst-case scenarios for customers

Scary thoughts of "worst-case scenarios" have crossed my mind a few times, and some of these have even turned to reality for me:

- What if the bank or other credit card issuer has overcharged me and I have no documentary evidence to prove it? I have been charged twice for one transaction at point-of-sale. The bank reversed the duplicate charge when I brought it to their attention.
- When hit with a massive mobile phone bill, how do I know whether figures such as the call minutes and the volume of data transmitted and received have been accurately captured and computed, especially when the usage was in an overseas country and recorded by a foreign mobile phone operator?

Here are two personal anecdotes:

- In the first episode, I noticed about 50 voice roaming entries in my monthly bill. These occurred over two days. They all had the same phone number. They all had a call duration of 1–2 seconds.

    When I brought this inaccurate charging to the mobile phone operator's attention they waived the charges immediately, because they believed that the calls could not have originated from a human being. The 50 voice roaming entries obviously arose from an error in their metering system.

■ In the second episode, I was charged for data roaming while overseas when I had switched off the data roaming service on my mobile phone before leaving home. This episode turned out to be a battle of sorts between the mobile phone operator and me. They insisted that the settings on my mobile phone were wrong. I denied that accusation vehemently. I had been to the same country monthly over two years and did exactly the same things before I left home. And this was the first time such an incident happened. The matter was eventually resolved after many weeks when senior management of the mobile phone operator intervened and waived all the data roaming charges.

It sounds ironic but the only way we know how much money we have in our bank accounts today is to *ask* the bank. (The same goes for our accounts with insurance companies and some other organisations, including public agencies.) What if there are inaccuracies in the transactions the bank captures and processes? What if there is fraud by a bank employee – for example, they siphon off small amounts from each bank account and no one is the wiser?

I've had a double deduction of the same amount under a GIRO to the same payee within the same month. This was rectified when the bank admitted it had caused the error.

What can customers do?

Granted that all banks and other financial institutions in Singapore are governed by strict laws to ensure the accuracy of the transactional data of their customers and to prevent unauthorised modification to such data, but nothing is fool-proof.

Even the best processes and technological tools deployed have their limitations. Customers have to be their own watchdogs. Short of the impracticality of 100% verification of statements issued by the banks, other credit card issuers and mobile phone operators, customers should scrutinise their statements to spot anomalies.

Like in the few anecdotes I shared above, I would not have noticed the inaccuracies in the transactional data processed by these companies if not for the "lightning rods" that stuck out.

CHECKLIST OF GOOD PRACTICES

- Organisations that maintain accounts of their customers' transactions, such as banks, credit card issuers and mobile phone operators, have a great responsibility to ensure the accuracy of such data.
- Customers, on the other hand, have to be their own watchdogs to spot anomalies in their monthly statements of account issued by banks, credit card companies and mobile phone operators.

46 Hitting the "send" button and regretting it

Your Honour, I plead guilty to the following offences that I committed by hitting the "send" button too quickly on my PC, laptop and mobile devices:

■ I attached files containing personal data and other confidential data and sent it to the wrong addressee. It happened because I did not check the email address that was "auto-filled" by the email software after I had keyed in the first two letters of the intended recipient's name.

■ When I forwarded an email to a colleague for information, I forgot to delete the earlier discussion thread. It contained highly sensitive personal data that my colleague was not supposed to know.

■ When I sent out an email announcement to a group of recipients I used the "cc" feature instead of the "bcc" feature on the email system. This resulted in numerous personal email addresses being exposed to everyone on the mailing list. An unscrupulous recipient could easily "harvest" the email addresses for marketing purposes, or worse, for ill intentions.

■ I drafted an email message in anger. It had a harsh tone and unpleasant words. I sent it out inadvertently instead of placing it in the "drafts" folder for me to edit later when my anger simmered down.

■ I sent a text message from my smartphone to congratulate a friend on the new addition to his family. It was disastrous. Because I didn't check one of the "auto-corrected" or "auto-completed" words my message was unpleasant and inappropriate for the occasion.

- I bought duplicate items in an online shopping spree because I didn't check the contents of the "shopping cart" thoroughly before I hit the "send" button.

Like me, how many of you have hit the "send" button on your PC, laptop or mobile devices too quickly and regretted it later? I believe the number of you who answer "yes" would be high.

(By the way, it seems many individuals do not understand that the "recall" function in Outlook works only to recall emails within a network, such as within a corporate email network. Where you send an email to an outsider and then try to recall it, all you do is to draw the recipient's attention to it.)

Why we hit "send" and regret it later

We hit "send" and regret it later because we live in a fast-paced, information-obsessed society today. We want to share information (or, dare I say, gossip) and communicate our views to others quickly.

With technologies that allow us to send messages on the move, anytime and anywhere, we tend to multi-task – for example, composing and sending text messages while watching TV or waiting for the meat to be roasted. Because of the many other tasks we are doing concurrently, we tend to be less thorough in checking the correctness of our communication messages before we hit the "send" button.

How to prevent hitting the "send" button too quickly

How can we stop being trigger-happy with the "send" button? Here are some tips:

- Turn off the "auto-suggest", "auto-correct" and "auto-complete" features in your email and text messaging systems.

There is a trade-off between convenience and the danger of errors. If you want the convenience, you must be willing to spend the time necessary to thoroughly check your emails and text messages before hitting "send".

- Adjust your email settings so that the default position is that whenever you forward an email the preceding discussion thread will not be included.

  Then, on a case-by-case basis, when you need to include the preceding discussion thread with a forwarded email, change your email settings for that email. Also take the time to double-check whether the preceding discussion thread is relevant to, or intended for, the recipient(s) to whom you are forwarding the email. After you have sent the email change your settings back to the default position.

  (Some individuals who habitually handle personal data or other confidential information adjust their email settings so that "reply" and "reply all" to an email do not include the email to which they are replying either. They avoid disclosing personal data or other confidential information accidentally, such as in those cases where they add an additional individual to the recipient list. They also check who is included in the "cc" list in the email to which they are replying and delete any individuals who do not need to be included in their reply.)

- Always use "bcc" instead of "cc" when you email a group of recipients. Make an exception only where you have concluded that it is important that all recipients know who else is receiving the same email.

- Remember to save draft emails or messages in the "drafts" folder until you have time to edit and send them out later.

- Compose and send out important and sensitive emails or text messages when you are more focused and less distracted by other simultaneous tasks.

CHECKLIST OF GOOD PRACTICES

Individuals should exercise care before hitting the "send" button on their computing devices:

■ Turn off the "auto suggest", "auto-correct" and "auto-complete" features in your email and text messaging systems. If you still want these conveniences, you have to do thorough checks before you hit the "send" button.

■ Make sure that any preceding discussion thread that is not relevant to or not meant for the eyes of the recipients is deleted before you forward an email.

■ Always use "bcc" instead of "cc" when sending out emails to a group of recipients, unless all recipients on the list have to know who else is receiving the same email.

■ Remember to save draft emails or messages in the "drafts" folder until you have time to edit them for sending out later.

■ Compose and send out important and sensitive emails or text messages when you are more focused and less distracted by other simultaneous tasks.

47 Where data accuracy goes beyond correctness

At my home address, I once received a letter in a sealed envelope from one of the main local mobile phone operators. On the front of the envelope were the words "$100 Voucher Inside", emblazoned in an attractive, colourful font. Excitedly, I tore open the envelope to find a friendly message from the organisation's Marketing Director. The Marketing Director thanked me for being a loyal customer, and as a reward, gifted me with a voucher that I could use to partially pay for a new mobile phone.

Then I discovered that the voucher was intended for someone else, not for me. In my excitement, I hadn't noticed earlier that the addressee's name wasn't mine, although the address was my correct home address. No doubt the name on the letter was also the correct name of one of the organisation's customers.

So here we have a case of a name and an address, each of which was correct on its own, wrongly associated with each other – a clear illustration of two pieces of information that were correct when viewed separately but inaccurate when put together.

Data mismatch – a likely cause of data inaccuracy

My story did not end here. It got more intriguing. I took the letter and voucher to the organisation's customer service centre. I asked to have the data inaccuracy rectified. I also asked whether I could be issued with a new voucher. To my utmost surprise, the customer service officer did not even bat an eyelid and said: "This is a small matter. It's not important as long as your mobile phone number is correct."

Sure enough, when he retrieved my record from the organisation's database based on my mobile phone number, everything was correct and accurate – my identity card number, name, address and billing account number.

But what if this had not been such a happy ending and fees and charges were billed to the wrong individual or sent to a wrong address? The organisation would likely have failed to comply with the data protection law by wrongly disclosing personal data. It would likely also have a negative impact on the organisation's reputation.

How might the mismatch have happened?

In this interesting episode, there seems to have been a data inconsistency between the organisation's Marketing Department and its Customer Service Department. There is a range of possible causes. Here are two of them:

- The Marketing Department did not use the same database as the Customer Service Department – the Marketing Department might have created its own database.This could be rectified easily by the organisation requiring the two departments to share a common database.

- The Marketing Department used the same database as the Customer Service Department but somehow the data was corrupted before or during its use by the Marketing Department (such as during data entry). This is a more insidious problem. The organisation's IT Department should implement safeguards in the IT system to minimise data corruption. These safeguards should be supplemented by administrative measures such as random checks on customer data to ensure they are complete and accurate.

CHECKLIST OF GOOD PRACTICES

- Organisations should beware that even though individual pieces of personal data can be correct on their own, they can become inaccurate when combined, due to wrong associations or data corruption.
- Organisations should therefore make regular, random checks on the combined data to detect any inaccuracies.

48 Your identity card number – a prime vulnerability for personal data breach

In some countries every individual citizen or permanent resident has a unique identifier assigned to them by the government for the purpose of work, taxation, government benefits and other government-related functions. Due to "function creep" it becomes used for other purposes, including commercial purposes. Sometimes it even becomes a substitute for other identifiers, such as membership identification numbers in organisations.

In Singapore and some other countries the national identifier stays with the individual "from cradle to grave", or at least from citizenship to grave. Or while an individual is a permanent resident, or even a temporary resident, of the country. Such identifiers are now considered so important for economic and financial inclusion in the digital age that India, for example, has embarked on a huge project to assign national identifiers to all residents.

Not surprisingly, privacy advocates have raised concerns about unique identifiers. Increasingly, unique identifiers now play an insidious role in identity theft. For these reasons they are typically considered to be sensitive personal data, even in those countries where the data protection law does not draw a legal distinction between sensitive personal data and other personal data.

Nevertheless, in countries that do have national identifiers it is common for individuals to just rattle off their identity card number or whip out their identity card upon request without questioning or batting an eyelid. They freely allow service providers to photocopy their identity card for record purposes or surrender their identity card to the security guard at a condominium or commercial building in exchange for a security pass.

The downside of these practices is that they have inadvertently provided to an outsider, who may or may not be trusted, the "master key" to personal data about them that is sensitive.

Changing practices

Data protection laws have the effect, over time, of individuals becoming more aware of the importance of safeguarding their identity card number – not to disclose it unnecessarily to outside parties without knowing the reason or purpose. Organisations are also changing their practices to not insist on using the identity card number as the default means of identification of individuals. Data protection regulators generally suggest that organisations should use other forms of personal identification as far as practicable in circumstances where an individual's identity does need to be confirmed.

On one occasion, I went to a redemption centre to claim a free gift. The customer service officer (CSO) asked me to produce my identity card. I queried the need for it. The CSO told me that the organisation wanted a photocopy of it for their records. When I said that I felt uncomfortable about handing it over, the CSO said without hesitation that it was optional.

On another occasion, I stepped into a medical specialist's clinic for the first time. The receptionist asked me to fill in a form that asked for my name, identity card number, date of birth, address and phone number. I said that I would prefer not to give my identity card number and the receptionist said that was okay.

Complying with the data protection law

From the perspective of the data protection law, the organisations I mention above need to change their requests and forms. Arguably, simply not pressing their requirements when challenged is better than the alternative, but it is not enough for compliance with the data protection law. In addition, there are other obligations under the data protection law such as the requirement to protect personal data like identity card numbers.

Organisations need to review their business practices:

■ They should not seek confirmation of identity from individuals when it is not necessary.

■ They should not make and keep a copy of an individual's identity card when merely sighting it to confirm the individual's identity would be sufficient.

■ They should use less sensitive forms of identification wherever possible – a mobile phone number, for example, would usually be sufficient to distinguish between individuals with the same name.

CHECKLIST OF GOOD PRACTICES

Organisations should handle individuals' identity card numbers with care:

■ An individual's identity card number is like a "master key" to the individual's identity and other personal data.

■ If possible, they should use other forms of identification, such as a mobile phone number.

"

Security in IT is like locking your house
or car – it doesn't stop the bad guys,
but if it's good enough they may move
on to an easier target.

"

Paul Herbka

"

You can't hold firewalls and
intrusion detection systems accountable.
You can only hold people accountable.

"

Daryl White

SECTION E:

Physical & Environmental Security

🔒 49 Clean desk way to data privacy

One can learn something about people by looking at their work desks. If the desk is neat and tidy, the person tends to be organised. If the items on the desk are well-aligned, the person tends to be organised, systematic and meticulous. On the other hand, if the desk is messy, the person tends to be disorganised and unstructured. But some of these "messy" people would argue that they are creative and non-linear in their thinking.

I once had a colleague whose desk was the messiest I have ever seen. One could never see the surface of his desk. It was buried many layers deep with papers, opened files, opened books and manuals, stationery items, empty coffee cups and other unidentified paraphernalia. One wondered how he could ever find anything in this huge mess. Then one fine day, when he was away on a one-week vacation, a few of us fellow colleagues decided to tidy up his desk for him. We thought we were doing him a great favour. But, lo and behold, when he returned from leave, instead of thanking us, he went on a rampage. The reason was he could not find anything. Somehow, in his state of messiness, he had a system to know exactly where he had placed what things. But I think he is more an exception than the norm. More often than not, we hear people with messy desks complaining, "I can't find this! I can't find that!"

Why am I sharing all these anecdotes? From the information security point of view, if you don't have total visibility of what you own (such as personal data and other confidential documents), you may not know what is missing. And if you can't find what you have (such as your employee access card), it is as good as missing.

And if you don't clear all personal data and other confidential information from your desk when you are absent for more than a few minutes, other individuals may be privy to it – your fellow employees during the business day, and cleaners and perhaps other service providers overnight and on weekends.

That is why expert practitioners of information security often cite a "Clean Desk Policy" as the recommended best practice.

What is a "clean desk policy"?

SANS Institute is a private U.S. for-profit company that specialises in information security and cyber security training. It says that a "clean desk policy" is:

> *an important tool to ensure that all sensitive/confidential materials are removed from an end-user workspace and locked away when the items are not in use or when an employee leaves his/her workstation.*

Elements of SANS Institute's "clean desk policy"

The main elements of the policy, as adapted from SANS Institute, are the following:

- Employees are required to ensure that all sensitive/confidential information in hardcopy or electronic form is secure in their work area at the end of the day and when they are expected to be gone for an extended period.
- Computer workstations must be locked when the workspace is unoccupied.
- Computer workstations must be shut down completely at the end of the work day.
- Any confidential or sensitive information must be removed from the desk and locked in a drawer when the desk is unoccupied and at the end of the work day.
- File cabinets containing confidential or sensitive information must be kept closed and locked when not in use or when not attended.

- Keys used for access to confidential or sensitive information must not be left at an unattended desk.
- Laptops must be either locked with a locking cable or locked away in a drawer.
- Passwords must not be left on sticky notes posted on or under a computer, nor should they be left written down in an accessible location.
- Printouts containing confidential or sensitive information should be immediately removed from the printer.
- Upon disposal, confidential and/or sensitive documents should be shredded in official shredder bins or placed in locked confidential disposal bins.
- Whiteboards containing confidential and/or sensitive information should be erased.
- Portable computing devices such as laptops and tablets should be locked away at the end of the work day.
- Mass storage devices such as CD-ROMs, DVDs and USB drives must be treated as sensitive and must be secured in a locked drawer.
- All printers and fax machines should be cleared of papers as soon as they are printed; this helps ensure that sensitive documents are not left in printer trays for the wrong person to pick up.

Some additional elements of a "clean desk policy"

Here are some elements to add to the SANS Institute's list:

- Lock your computer screen when you leave your desk unattended, even if for just a short while, with a password required to unlock it.
- Do not throw any documents with personal data or other confidential information into the wastepaper basket.
- Do not leave any security devices (such as an employee access pass or bank security token) on your desk when you leave it unattended, even for a relatively short while.

Clean desk, clear conscience

It makes a lot of sense to have a "clean desk policy". It minimises the risk of personal data or other confidential information being misplaced, lost, or accessed by unauthorised individuals.

If all employees of an organisation conscientiously play by the rules of the "clean desk policy", they can leave their workplace at the end of the workday with a clear conscience. And the integrity of information security practices at the organisation is safeguarded.

CHECKLIST OF GOOD PRACTICES

- Organisations should have a "clean desk policy" and ensure that their employees are trained to understand it and abide by it.
- A "clean desk policy" minimises the risk of personal data or other confidential information being misplaced, lost, or accessed by unauthorised persons.
- Every employee of the organisation should conscientiously play by the rules of the "clean desk policy" to safeguard the integrity of the organisation's information security practices.

🔒 **50** The dangers lurking in public computer terminals

Many individuals work "on the road" – for example, real estate sales people, financial advisers and independent sales agents. For them, it's often quick and easy to rely on public computer terminals or work stations belonging to their agency to carry out transactions and administration work.

Five important questions to answer when working on public terminals
If you are a mobile worker, here are five questions for you:

1. Do you ensure that your user name and password are not saved in any web applications?

2. Do you delete your browsing history before you log out of the computer?

3. Do you refrain from processing financial or sensitive personal information (such as banking transactions)?

4. Have you cleared everything you loaded or downloaded into the computer (including any USB drive and any documents you have sent for printing, and, if you deleted any files, have you emptied the terminal's electronic recycling bin)?

5. Do you always remember to log out when you leave the computer?

If your answer to any of the above is "no", you may fail to comply with the data protection law. For example, you might unintentionally expose your own and your clients' personal data to individuals who are not authorised to see it.

And if that's not bad enough, given that competition is very high among property agents and financial advisers, you might unintentionally expose valuable commercial information to your competitors. They might "steal" your clients' personal data when you inadvertently leave it for them to find.

Never save passwords in a browser, web form or application
"Why would I be stupid enough to save passwords when I'm using a public terminal?", you may ask. The answer is that you could be doing it unintentionally. Especially when you are in a hurry or are distracted by multi-tasking, like speaking to someone on the phone while you are using the public terminal.

Saving passwords can happen when you sign into an account or submit a web form. The browser prompts you about whether you want to remember your sign-in ID and password. Particularly if you routinely say "yes" at home, you instinctively say "yes" without thinking when you are using a public terminal and are in a hurry or are distracted.

If you do, you make your sign-in ID and password available to other individuals using the same terminal after you. You give them the keys to gaining access to your password-protected account or website, for example.

If you happen to make this mistake, here is how you can rectify it (if your agency has not already turned off the auto-save feature – you can find more detailed instructions for the various browsers if you search online):

- **Firefox**: Tools > Click on Options, Security tab, "Saved Passwords", delete specific ones or all of them.
- **Internet Explorer**: Tools > Click on Internet Options, Content tab, Autocomplete [> settings], delete autocomplete history.
- **Google Chrome**: Click on Chrome Control Panel Button > Settings (chrome://settings/) > Show advanced settings... > Passwords and forms > Offer to save your web passwords (uncheck)
- **Safari**: Click on Safari > Preferences > Autofill > Uncheck box for User names and passwords

Make it a habit never to auto-save your user information and password. In this way you may secure your online privacy and presence. Don't forget to inform your agency or organisation if you notice that the auto-save browser feature is turned on while browsing the Web. The IT administrator and person in charge can take action and implement this for all the public terminals.

Delete your browsing or search history and cookies before you log out of the computer

Why should you care about deleting your browsing or search history and cookies before you log out of a public computer terminal?

Let's say you visit a website offering cancer advice or one offering loans. If you do not delete your history, the next individual who uses the terminal can pretty much infer your intent from looking at your search history. This is because the browser's predictive search feature immediately reveals previous sites visited.

Maybe you care whether the next individual knows what sites you have visited; maybe you ordinarily do not. But it could create a big problem for you, especially if you had been on, say, an Internet banking site and you had also inadvertently saved your ID and password.

(You can easily find instructions online about how to clear your browsing history.)

Better safe than sorry – use the private browsing feature

All popular web browsers have a private browsing feature. Sometimes it is called "privacy mode" and sometimes it is called "incognito mode". It enables an individual to disable their browsing history and the web cache resulting from their browsing. The individual can browse the web without storing local data that could be retrieved later, including by a stranger.

To be safe, always use the private browsing feature when using a public terminal to visit websites.

In addition, it is a good idea to delete cookies in the terminal. A cookie is a small piece of software or mechanism that allows the server (website) to store its own information about a user such as preferences and what web pages were visited on the user's own computer. You can view the cookies that have been stored on your hard disk (though they may not make sense to you).

In short, you should leave no traces of your identity or actions.

Refrain from processing financial or sensitive personal data

For at least the following three reasons, you should refrain from processing financial or sensitive personal data when you are using a public computer terminal.

The first reason is a simple practical one: shared public terminals are rarely located in areas that provide a reasonable level of privacy. If you are doing a banking transaction, for example, the information you input into your bank's online banking portal can be exposed to prying eyes easily. In addition, you could easily misplace sensitive documents or lose security tokens issued to you by your bank.

Second, an unauthorised individual might have installed malware such as a key-logger on the public terminal so that they can track what you type into the computer. If that is your bank account details, bank ID and password, the consequences for you might be very serious.

Finally, if you really have no choice but to do an online transaction on a shared public terminal and are confident that you can do so privately, you should proceed only if the URL of your destination site has got "https" displayed in your browser's address bar. HTTPS is a protocol for secure communication over a computer network which is widely used on the Internet so you can be assured that the data you submit over the Internet is encrypted.

Clear everything you have loaded or downloaded into the computer

It seems obvious, of course, that an individual using a public computer terminal would clear it of everything they have uploaded or downloaded into the computer. But we are surprised how often we find documents and files copied into a computer, in that an individual who sends an email or prints the document and then forgets to delete it.

In our audits we find terminals that are littered with documents that contain personal data. They include transaction documents, application forms and even images of identity cards. Typically, these documents easily identify the agent or salesperson concerned and implicate them in the failure to comply with the data protection law that arises from failing to protect the personal data.

Then there are the confidential documents, including loose sheets of paper, or items such as USB drives left behind at the terminals. The contents of the loose sheets of paper are obviously easily accessible. The USB drives are rarely password-protected or encrypted, so personal data or other confidential information on them is usually easily accessible too. It is very evident that the negligent culprit – again, often identifiable by what has been left behind – has not taken any reasonable security measures to protect the relevant personal data or other confidential information.

Log out when you leave the computer

Finally, please log out of your account when you leave the terminal. It is such a basic requirement but we do find many individuals forgetting to do so – or simply being too lazy to do so. If you are fortunate, your agency or organisation may have a reboot or auto-log out function, which immediately resets the account and initiates the log-out process. You should also log out even when you need to leave the shared terminal for a short while, such as to go into another room to fetch a document or file, to get a cup of tea or even to go to the restroom. It's better to be safe than sorry.

CHECKLIST OF GOOD PRACTICES

Individuals should exercise great caution when using public computer terminals:

- Never save passwords in a browser, web form or application.
- Delete your browsing and search history and cookies before you log out of the computer.
- Use the private browsing feature within the browser to maintain privacy of your browsing history.
- Clear everything you have uploaded or downloaded into the computer. Don't forget to empty the recycle bin.
- Log out when you leave the computer.

🔒 51 Open office, open invitation to snoop

Walk into any modern office and what is a common sight you behold? A labyrinth of tightly compacted, adjoining cubicles. Each employee who is "resident" there can proudly call a small space their own private space. This open-office concept is said to improve employee interaction and teamwork (although it has the benefit of maximising usage of expensive office real estate too).

We have done many "onsite" audits for our consulting clients, walking through our clients' offices, to identity potential information security risks. Here are some tips from what we have learned during these audits:

Office cubicle layouts

The first thing we often notice is that employees from different departments of an organisation or employees working on different projects are seated in cubicles next to each other. They can easily interact to collaborate and to socialise. But they can also peer over cubicle walls to snoop at whether their colleagues are working hard enough and to see what they are working on. In either case, employees of an organisation may inadvertently or deliberately view personal data and other confidential information on paper documents or on computer screens that they are not authorised to see.

Organisations should configure their cubicle layouts so that:

- employees with the same "need to know" access to certain classes of personal data and other confidential information are seated next to each other and

- preferably there is some physical separation from other employees without that "need to know" access.

Sometimes this is not possible, for example due to space constraints. In that case, the organisation must make a risk assessment and balance the costs of such a layout against the risks of failing to comply with the data protection law – personal data being disclosed to unauthorised individuals – that is, to employees who do not have the "need to know".

In large part, an organisation might decide that the risk can be well managed by training each employee to exercise "self-safeguarding" of personal data and other confidential information. And then conducting regular audits to ensure that they actually exercise such self-safeguarding. Some examples of self-safeguarding include requiring employees to:

- use special privacy filters on their computer screens
- keep confidential documents covered in paper files and
- lock personal data and other confidential documents in drawers or cabinets when they are away from their desks.

Highly confidential and sensitive information – good office configuration

Employees in Human Resource (HR) and Finance Departments typically handle highly confidential and sensitive information. In some organisations their cubicles are in separate rooms, one room for the HR Department and another for the Finance Department, for example. Entry to these dedicated rooms is by means of special door access passes issued only to those employees who work in the relevant department.

This is a good practice for reducing the risk of non-HR Department employees or non-Finance Department employees gaining unauthorised access to highly confidential and sensitive information. However, the comments above under the heading "Office cubicle layouts" continue to apply within the HR Department and the Finance Department – that is, not all HR Department employees and not all Finance Department employees have the same "need to know" access to personal data and other confidential information.

We see in some organisations the HR Department and the Finance Department housed in the same room, though separated from other employees. Again, the comments above under the heading "Office cubicle layouts" apply to separating HR Department employees and the personal data and other confidential information that they "need to know" from the Finance Department employees. And vice versa.

Highly confidential and sensitive information – when implementation doesn't quite work

In some organisations with separate rooms for the HR Department and the Finance Department, we see that the doors to these dedicated rooms are left open during office hours. This is typically because employees from other departments may have to submit their medical certificates (MCs) to the HR Department or their expense claim forms to the Finance Department. We hear that constant door opening and closing is inconvenient and disruptive to HR Department employees and Finance Department employees.

In addition, the employee who is responsible for processing MCs or expense claim forms is sometimes seated a long way from the door of the HR Department or Finance Department. Employees from other departments who come to deliver MCs or expense claim forms have to walk through long rows of cubicles to reach that particular person. They may chance upon personal data or other confidential information on HR Department or Finance Department employees' desks – particularly if they stop for a chat with an HR Department employee or Finance Department employee along the way.

Organisations should avoid this situation by making the HR Department and the Finance Department strictly out of bounds to employees from other departments. This policy must be enforced. There should be a sign on the door to say "Access for Staff of XX Department only" so that other employees cannot plead ignorance.

As far as practicable, other employees who wish to submit their MCs or expense claim forms should do so by a one-way drop-in slot into a locked container, similar to that of a post-box. The slot should be narrow enough so that no human hand can go in to retrieve any of the paper forms or documents. By locating the slot on the wall of the main entrance to the HR Department or the Finance Department, other employees can simply drop in their MCs or expense claim forms and need not enter the departmental office at all.

Office security

We have seen some organisations that have taken the open-office concept to the extreme. It is so open that anyone who walks into the office premises need not sign in to the visitors' book because there is no need to do so. All the person needs to do is to appear before the receptionist and ask to see so-and-so, and to wait at the waiting area for the so-and-so to appear.

On paper, this looks like a reasonable practice. But, in reality, there is only one receptionist on duty at any one time, and it is very easy for any stranger to bypass the receptionist and walk straight to any work desk (because all the doors are left open for the convenient movement of the internal staff). And it is a piece of cake for the stranger to just take out any confidential document that is left lying around on desks of employees who have stepped away for a moment.

As its first line of defence, the organisation should have a locked door between the reception/waiting area and the working area in its office. A "Restricted Access" or "Out of Bounds" sign displayed on the locked door means that there is no "I didn't know" excuse if, somehow (such as tailgating an employee), a visitor is able to enter the main office area. And of course the sign gives employees all the justification they need for telling any visitor that they must not tailgate them.

Handling information within the organisation

In an open office, it can be fairly easy for employees to have access to personal data and other confidential information they are not authorised to know. For example, salespersons could approach their colleagues from the Finance Department to get details of their latest commissions earned. In one client's office we were told that top salespersons would sit next to their Finance Department colleague, who would present them with the requested information, either on the computer screen or in a hardcopy file. These salespersons could peek at the information of other salespersons who were their competitors for top honours. The Finance Department employee should at least shield the information of the other salespersons.

A better approach is for the Finance Department employee to ask the salespersons to wait in the waiting area while they extract the requested information for the particular salesperson and then bring it to them. Salespersons should not step into the Finance Department at all. This manages the risk of their seeing confidential information about their competitors or seeing any other personal data or other confidential information held by the Finance Department.

Handling information at public-facing areas

In an open office, if an organisation's employees are not properly trained on the do's and don'ts of information security it can also be fairly easy for outsiders to have access to personal data and other confidential information that they are obviously not authorised to see.

For example, reception counter or service counter employees should ensure that:

- no paper documents are left exposed on the counter
- no paper documents are left exposed in in/out trays and
- computers are placed in such a way that information on screen is not within the line-of-sight of outsiders.

Security guards monitoring CCTV cameras should ensure that their viewing screens are positioned out of the line-of-sight of visitors who come to the security counter to sign the organisation's visitors' book.

Handling information in common areas

In an open office, the organisation should be careful not to display any personal data or other confidential information in common areas – that is, areas open to all of the organisation's employees – if employees are not authorised to know it.

Here are some current practices we observed at our clients' offices as we conducted onsite audits:

- In one client's office, there was a huge electronic screen in a common area displaying the performance data of every salesperson.

  The organisation's intention was to challenge the salespersons to perform better. But the information was displayed to not only the salespersons themselves but also viewable by other employees not from the Sales Department. How would the poorer performers feel?

  Such sensitive information should be kept within the four walls of the Sales Department.

■ In another client's office, we found files containing confidential information arranged neatly on open shelves in the meeting room. There was nothing to prevent individuals – whether outsiders or employees not authorised to see it – from viewing the confidential information in a file if they were alone in the room waiting for other individuals to arrive for a meeting.

Such shelves should be covered with opaque panels that are locked so that no unauthorised individual can see what is on them or take files out and look at them.

■ In yet another client's office, we found open pigeonholes with confidential documents in files. These files could be flipped open easily. We also found sales commission slips of agents in unsealed envelopes.

Organisations should replace open shelf-style pigeonholes with locked letter boxes. They should have one-way slots and only the "owner" of the letter box should have a key to it.

Information security consciousness

From an information security point of view, in an open office there are many ways that personal data and other confidential information may be seen by individuals who are not authorised to see it.

Organisations should:

■ ensure that they are aware of the vulnerabilities and security gaps in their open office

■ develop and implement policies and practices to minimise the vulnerabilities and gaps and train all employees to adhere to them

■ "audit" their offices regularly by walking around and checking compliance with their existing policies and practices and

■ identify any new vulnerabilities and security gaps that have arisen since the last audit, develop and implement additional policies and practices to manage them and train staff in these additional requirements.

An organisation should ensure that all employees are aware of the organisation's information security do's and don'ts and make every effort to carry out self-safeguarding of personal data and other confidential information that they are handling.

CHECKLIST OF GOOD PRACTICES

Organisations and employees should practise the following to safeguard personal data and other confidential information in their offices:

Office layout

- Require employees to practise self-safeguarding of personal data and other confidential information under their care in an open-office concept.
- House employees handling highly confidential or sensitive information in separate rooms with locked doors and restricted access to other employees.

Office security

- Require all visitors to report at the reception counter.
- Restrict visitor movement to the waiting area unless escorted by an employee.

Handling information within the organisation

- Show only the personal data and other confidential information that is relevant to the requesting employee.
- Better still, make the requesting employee wait outside the confidential work area while the information is being extracted.

Handling information at public-facing areas

- Do not leave confidential documents exposed at the reception counter, service counter or in/out trays.
- Shield computer screens from the line-of-sight of outsiders, including the terminals used by security guards to monitor CCTV cameras.

Handling information in common areas

- Do not display confidential or sensitive information openly that is only pertinent to a particular group of employees.
- Do not store confidential files on open shelves that are directly accessible to visitors.
- Do not place in open pigeonholes confidential files that can be easily flipped open or confidential documents in unsealed envelopes.

🔒 52 Remember to clear out

I recall that at the end of my university course many years ago I had to clear out all my personal belongings (including all the accumulated rubbish) from my hostel room. The university expected me to return the room to its original spartan state so that it would be ready for a new student to move in. I had to comb through every nook and cranny of the room meticulously to ensure that I did not leave behind a single item that belonged to me.

Minimising information security incidents

This recollection of my past set me thinking. Can this same "clear out" principle be applied to the way we treat information security?

If everyone consciously remembers to clear out everything belonging to them at the end of every life moment or work session, we might minimise information security incidents.

Some failures to "clear out"

Here are some examples of failure to exercise the "clear out" principle in places where personal data or other confidential information has been used or shared:

- Leaving a laptop computer or mobile phone behind at a public place such as a shopping centre, restaurant or café, or leaving it behind in a taxi or on other public transport
- Leaving a USB drive or other portable hard disk behind at a shared terminal in a common work area

- Leaving behind paper files and documents at a public place or on public transport
- Dropping a security access pass on the way to some destination or leaving it behind at a public place
- Forgetting to delete uploaded/downloaded confidential files or to empty the recycle bin from a shared public terminal after using it
- Forgetting to collect a confidential document from the photocopier/scanner after photocopying/scanning the document
- Sending a confidential document to the printer and then forgetting to collect the printout
- Forgetting to remove extra copies of confidential documents from the meeting room at the end of a meeting
- Forgetting to erase the whiteboard or remove the flipcharts in a meeting room at the end of a meeting

What the organisation can do to help employees "clear out"

Organisations should have clear policies and written practices assigning responsibility for protecting personal data and other confidential information to employees according to their job roles. These policies and practices should form part of their standard employment contract and there should be disciplinary consequences for failure to comply with them.

Organisations should then remind their employees to "clear out". One way of doing this is by putting up signs near shared terminals in common work areas, at printers/photocopiers/scanners and in meeting rooms.

If an employee fails to "clear out", either by deliberately ignoring these reminders or by carelessness, they will have to bear the resulting disciplinary consequences. These could be particularly serious if there is any misplacement or loss of personal data or confidential information under their care.

What employees should do to "clear out"

Including policies and practices about information security in employment contracts and applying disciplinary consequences for failing to adhere to them tend to focus employee minds. Training is an important ingredient too.

This should instil in individuals the habit of conscientiously having a mental or written checklist of what they have brought with them to the various places they work at or visit.

The organisation cannot help individuals who leave their valuables and personal belongings behind in public places or on public transport. The individual must take responsibility. A mental or written checklist helps, but individuals are solely responsible for their own negligence or carelessness.

Individuals should always be aware of their surroundings and the risks, such as the risk of theft. They should take the necessary precautions against placing their belongings or anything containing personal data or other confidential information in unguarded positions that are tempting to thieves.

Discipline to "clear out"

The personal discipline of practising the "clear out" principle does not come naturally to some people.

The "clear out" principle has to be constantly nurtured and drilled into individual consciousness.

Employees of an organisation quickly learn to "clear out" if there are disciplinary consequences when they misplace or lose personal data or other confidential information in their possession or under their control. An approach that incorporates "clear out" and other information security policies and practices into employment contracts may also mitigate any regulatory penalties on the organisation for failing to comply with the data protection law.

CHECKLIST OF GOOD PRACTICES

Organisations should do the following to minimise loss or theft of personal data and other confidential information:

■ Remind their employees to adopt a "clear out" mentality so as to minimise the risk of information security incidents occurring.

■ Display signs prominently at shared terminals in common work areas, at printers/photocopiers/scanners and in meeting rooms to remind employees to "clear out".

■ Include policies and practices on information security in employment contracts, with disciplinary consequences for non-compliance.

Individuals should have a mental or written checklist of what they have brought with them to the various places they have visited or worked at, so that they know what to "clear out".

53 Smart devices – new challenges for data privacy

The comedy science-fiction radio series, "The Hitch-Hiker's Guide to the Galaxy", was first broadcast in 1978. It was later adapted to other formats, becoming an international multi-media phenomenon that was translated into more than 30 languages. The centrepiece, the "Hitch-Hiker's Guide" was a small portable device used to look up pretty much any information about anything in the galaxy, the Milky Way.

By 2017, over a third of the world's population – an estimated total of almost 2.6 billion individuals – is projected[1] to have a portable computer in their pocket or handbag. This is a dream come true and science fiction turned into reality, albeit earthbound. Of course, we call this class of computing devices "smartphones".

Since Apple Inc. introduced its first generation of the iPhone in 2007, today's smartphones have been able to do almost anything a much larger personal computer (PC) can do. In addition, smartphone users can make phone calls around the world through cellular networks, which a PC can't do.

Smartphones have revolutionised our lives so much that they have become indispensable to us. We can't leave home without them. A smartphone is at once:

- our mobile office where we can access our organisation's emails and databases
- our learning centre where we can tap on the wealth of information around the globe and

[1] See http://www.statista.com/topics/840/smartphones/.

■ our social media platform where we can share our private lives and experiences with friends, and something with tempting features that can get us into trouble.

Tendency for individuals to "capture and post"

"C & P" refers to "cut and paste" or "copy and paste" when we work on electronic documents. With smartphones, "C & P" refers to "capture and post". Trigger-happy users of smartphones use them to snap photos, record voice conversations and capture video footage. They then post them online or to social media platforms in a matter of seconds. Nothing can escape their attention, all for the sake of being the first to post the most "juicy" news or gossip. Or even news of an emergency, as shown in the sign in a public building warning the occupants to exit the building quickly in a fire instead of staying behind to tweet about it on social media.

New privacy challenges brought about by smartphones

Smartphones raise a host of new challenges for organisations and their employees responsible for privacy and information security.

The camera and voice recorder built into smartphones provide users, including every employee of the organisation, with instant "tools" for capturing personal data and other confidential information that they are not permitted to take out of their offices. Worse, a visitor walking within the office unescorted can easily take photos of confidential files or documents lying around on unattended work desks, or of confidential information displayed on computer terminals.

At meetings, individuals can surreptitiously turn on the voice recorder on their smartphones to record conversations concerning sensitive matters. Attendees can quickly whip out their smartphones to capture images of personal data and other confidential information presented on the large screen when the presenter's back is turned or is looking down.

At one board meeting, I was quite intrigued to observe that the minute-taker was hardly taking down any notes while conversations were going on at rapid pace. The answer? The voice recorder on the individual's smartphone recorded every relevant bit – as well as every juicy bit – of the conversations, including the grunts, groans, sighs and coughs. I did not notice that the voice recorder was turned on because the smartphone was placed inconspicuously on the conference table, encased in a wraparound cover.

What should organisations do?

Organisations should adopt at least the following basic measures to prevent employees and visitors alike from taking photos of confidential documents or recording conversations using smartphones, while in the office premises:

- Display notices at prominent places, especially in meeting rooms where outsiders are present, to remind people not to take any photos or record any conversation without the permission of the person-in-charge, such as the chairman of the meeting or the most senior person present.

- Remind employees to shield their confidential documents and computer terminals from being viewed by those without a "need to know" whenever they are away from their work desks, even for a short period of time.

  They can do so by covering or closing their files or locking them in drawers or cabinets. They can lock their computer terminals using a software utility.

- Have visitors deposit their smartphones at the receptionist's counter when they need to enter highly secure and restricted areas of the organisation.

Dawn of wearable computers

Having addressed the privacy concerns brought about by smartphones, organisations and their employees responsible for privacy and information security cannot afford to rest on their laurels. More and more innovative "smart" devices are being introduced to consumers at a steady stream.

Are you old enough to remember the crime-solving detective, Dick Tracy, from the American comic strip and later film versions? His two-way wrist radio was a centrepiece of his stories and a "brand icon" – not least because the idea was so unbelievable when the comic strip was introduced in 1931.

Now wearable computers in the form of smart watches, for example, have entered the mainstream. While the current functions of these smart watches are rather limited, they may already include two-way voice communication. If not, it is surely only a matter of time before two-way communication, as well as camera and voice recorder features, are incorporated into them. (Indeed, it may happen between my writing this and your reading it.)

Highlighting pens that can scan paper documents and digitise them line-by-line are already available in the market.

Google Glass[2] was introduced to consumers as a prototype in May 2014. It resembles a pair of eyeglasses. It displays information to the user in a smartphone-like hands-free format. Wearers communicate with the Internet using natural language voice commands. Because of its ability to take photos or record videos, Google Glass caused quite a stir among those people concerned with its invasion of privacy. In January 2015, Google Glass was pulled off the shelves. In December 2015, Google commenced work on the next version of Google Glass.

Looking ahead to the not-too-distant future, we can anticipate yet more sophisticated types of wearable computers, long the dream of science-fiction writers, coming onto the market. Buttons, cuff-links or brooches on jackets that function as cameras and voice recorders, and special hand gloves that can digitise paper documents with a wave of the hand, are already within scientific capabilities.

The final word

Organisations and their employees responsible for privacy and information security must keep up with technologies to stay relevant and remain on top of new data protection/privacy challenges.

---

[2] Source: Wikipedia, under the entry "Google Glass"

CHECKLIST OF GOOD PRACTICES

Organisations should do the following to prevent people from taking photos of confidential documents or recording conversations using smartphones:

- Display notices at prominent places to remind people not to take photos or record conversations without permission.

- Remind employees to shield their private and confidential documents and their computer terminals from being viewed by those without a "need to know".

- Have visitors deposit their smartphones at the receptionist's counter when they need to enter highly secure and restricted areas.

" We've seen a ton of archiving companies developing data-protection technologies during the last six months ... We've seen a lot of search engine companies looking at ways to access this information too. **"**

Brian Babineau

" Phishing is a major problem because there really is no patch for human stupidity. **"**

Mike Danseglio

SECTION F:

Security, Storage, Retention & Disposal of Personal Data

🔒 54 Do you value privacy on your mobile devices?

I was on Facebook when a sponsored advertisement "New App Knows Where All Your Friends Are?" caught my attention. According to the advert, the application, which is available on iPhone and Android, notifies you "when your friends happen to be around so you can hang out together!".

I clicked on the "comments" and was surprised to read negative postings:

> *"dis link is nonsense"*
> *"Hahaha, the concept of privacy has disappeared"*
> *"no privacy… at all"*
> *"This is dangerous & risky… who knows I invited a stalker or killer"*
> *"This is way too dangerous"*
> *"Scary"*

While the developer of this mobile app paid to advertise on Facebook, the promotional efforts backfired because of the perception that the app invaded an individual's privacy.

Privacy and security issues on mobile applications

Many of us will have voiced the same concerns about invasions of privacy in this type of app and will be turned off by the advertisement. But still we don't think twice when we download apps into our mobile phones or tablets. Ironically, we could already be facing the same privacy and security issues without even knowing it.

In fact, a HP Mobile Application Security Vulnerability Report[1] which examined more than 2,000 mobile applications from more than 600 companies revealed the following:

- 9 in 10 of the mobile applications tested revealed some form of serious security vulnerability
- 97% of the apps contained some sort of privacy issue
- 86% of the apps lack basic security defences
- 75% fail to properly encrypt data

While the report focused on custom business apps, we can apply the same issues to commercial apps that we download from the Apple's App Store or Google's Play Store. We ignorantly grant permission for many apps to access our data and to perform functions that are unnecessary for the purpose of the app's functionality.

Do you read the terms of use or privacy policy when you download an application?

Why does a game app need to have access to your contacts? Or a weather app need permission to send email on your behalf? If you read the terms of use or privacy policy of an app before you download it, you will find these types of permissions being required.

Many apps require us to give permission for our personal information to be revealed to third-parties. A few of these apps may even sell our personal data with our permission already given!

How else do you think we get to use the app for free?

To aggravate matters, apps such as the one I saw on Facebook require that their users agree to "indemnify, defend and hold harmless" the organisation "from and against any and all claims, liabilities, damages, losses, costs, expenses, and fees of any kind (including reasonable attorneys' fees and legal costs)".

What are the implications for organisations?

Many organisations allow their employees to use their own mobile devices to access their corporate email and applications. In such BYOD (Bring-Your-Own-Device) scenarios, these security and privacy risks

---

[1] HP Mobile Application Security Study – 2013, HP (http://ww8.hp.com)

have serious implications for both the employer and the employee.

In most cases, we mix our business and personal needs. So the installed apps can easily blur that line and put both organisation and personal data at risk.

The problem is exacerbated by the fact that many of the downloaded apps are free and have been programmed by developers who may not value privacy or security. Their apps are written in such a way that they access everything in your mobile device because it's easier than writing more specific code. Their lazy coding also paves the way for any future enhancements that might actually need it.

According to a Statista report[2] published in 2013, the average smartphone user has 26 apps installed. However, this is a global figure. The average is much higher in some countries, with Korea topping the list at 40 – of which 37 apps are free downloads, which means that the privacy risks are much higher.

So how many applications do you have installed on your mobile device? What about privacy and security?

CHECKLIST OF GOOD PRACTICES

Individuals should exercise caution in downloading and installing mobile apps:

- Be aware of intrusive mobile apps that invade your privacy.
- Avoid downloading free mobile apps into your mobile device.
- Ensure you read the terms of use or privacy policy before downloading an app.
- Comply with your organisation's Bring-Your-Own-Device (BYOD) Policy.

---

[2] http://www.statista.com/chart/1435/top-10-countries-by-app-usage/

🔒 55 Guess what I found when I sent my notes for photocopying?

Recently while conducting an in-house data protection training course, I witnessed a data breach real-time. It happened while I was distributing the notes for the day's lessons!

The dividers that separated the course notes had personal data on them. One recycled paper divider had someone's loan balance sheet, complete with name, identity card number and the name of the institute.

I showed it to a participant who was from the local regulator. He shook his head in disbelief.

Beware if you are photocopying confidential information

The personal data was on the paper divider because the photocopy service provider blindly used recycled paper when they printed the notes. They did not even check if there was confidential or personal data on the paper. Or perhaps – and even worse – they did know it was there and had no idea that it mattered.

This incident shows the extent that personal data is being processed by all kinds of organisations including those providing photocopying services. Organisations and their service providers can get into trouble under the data protection law.

Organisations using personal data, including where they do so on behalf on other organisations, should ensure that they put in place security safeguards. They should also ensure that they securely delete or destroy any personal data when they have fulfilled their business purposes.

And they should ensure that all of their employees are trained in, and understand, the organisation's security safeguards and other processes connected with collecting, using or disclosing personal data – that is, all employees are aware of their responsibilities under the data protection law.

Before an organisation sends documents containing personal data to an organisation that offers photocopying services they should find out whether or not that service provider is able to comply with the data protection law – whether, for example, it has fully educated its employees about protecting personal data under their care. If not, an organisation should not send personal data to them. Or, if there is no option but to do so, the organisation might decide to seek to manage its risk by having one of its own employees personally witness the service provider doing its work to guard against leakage of the organisation's personal data.

The perils of doing your own photocopying

You are not entirely safe even if you happen to have a photocopying machine or MFD (Multi-Functional Device) in your office. Here are some things that an organisation's employees should do to reduce the risk of an inadvertent disclosure of personal data:

- Handle highly sensitive information with care.
- Do not leave sensitive data unattended or uncollected on a copier.
- Do not email sensitive data to unauthorised recipients.
- Shred sensitive documents when no longer needed.

Employees are always busy and must often multi-task. In addition, it is easy for them to be distracted by a phone call or by another employee interrupting them with a request or question. In our PDPA readiness audits, we often find employees leaving their original documents containing personal data on the copier. Or forgetting to collect their prints. These failures to protect personal data can be overcome by employee awareness and diligence.

A final word: Not many employees are aware that today's sophisticated copiers use a hard disk that stores a document every time they make a copy of it or fax it, just like a computer stores a copy of a document. An organisation should ensure that these hard disk are physically reformatted before the copier is turned-in (such as at the end of its lease) or disposed of (such as by sale).

In short, everyone in the office has a part to play in ensuring information security within the organisation.

CHECKLIST OF GOOD PRACTICES

Organisations and individuals should exercise care when using photocopiers in-house or when using a photocopy service provider:

- Practise care when using a photocopying machine or MFD (Multi-Functional Device) in your office.
  - Handle highly sensitive information with care.
  - Do not leave sensitive data unattended or uncollected on a copier.
  - Do not email sensitive data to unauthorised recipients.
  - Shred sensitive documents when no longer needed.
- Beware if you are using a service provider to photocopy personal and confidential documents. Make sure the service provider does not recycle papers containing personal data.

🔒 **56** Lock it or lose it

Why do we consciously take pains to ensure our valuables at home are kept securely locked in strongboxes, drawers and cabinets, even though our front and back doors are locked?

Why is it that paper documents and files containing personal data and other confidential information are often NOT kept securely locked in file cabinets and drawers in offices? This is one of the most common findings when we audit our clients' offices in the course of our consulting work. When we ask them why, these are some of the reasons we hear:

- "We have space constraints. There is not enough room to put in additional file cabinets. Some of our files have to be placed into cardboard boxes beneath our work desks."
- "It is too tedious to unlock the file cabinets, take out the files we need to use, put them back into the cabinets after use and lock the cabinets. We would rather put the current files on our work desks or place them on the open shelves."
- "The main door to the office is locked after office hours or when no one is around. So it should be secure enough."

These reasons seem legitimate enough, at least on the surface. But, because of the data protection law and because confidential information may be valuable commercially, organisations should not be complacent.

A laissez-faire approach risks the organisation losing or misplacing important files containing personal data or other confidential information. At a minimum, organisations should do a risk assessment of the types of confidential information, including personal data, which should be protected strongly. A strong protection means that paper documents and files should be kept under lock and key around the clock.

Examples of personal data and other confidential information requiring a higher level of protection include:

- employees' personnel files and performance appraisal reports
- personal information of high net worth individuals
- market-sensitive information and
- customer lists, contracts and other valuable business information.

Lock and key

An organisation should ensure employees make a conscious effort to lock those file cabinets that ought to be locked. And to protect the keys used to lock them. Here is what we often observe in our onsite audits of clients:

- File cabinets are locked but the keys are left in the keyholes for convenience – so that there is no need to hunt for them next time.

- File cabinets are locked but the keys are taped to the top or the side of the cabinets, again for convenience.
- Keys are left in the keyhole. The locking mechanism is broken.
- File cabinets do not have a lock.

Keypress

An organisation should maintain a secure keypress where all the keys can be kept safely. Keypress records should properly account for each key. The master key to the keypress must be assigned to a responsible person who is accountable for its safekeeping.

Here are some practices that we have observed in our client audits. They are not acceptable in a good information security programme:

- No one is accountable for the master key. It is left in the keypress. Therefore, anyone has access to the keys in the keypress.
- The master key to the keypress has been misplaced, so the keypress is not locked (or cannot be locked).
- There is no record of the movement of keys. No one knows whether some keys are lost. No one knows if someone has taken a key out of the keypress – or when they took it out – and not returned it. So employees who are not authorised to see personal data or other confidential information may actually have unfettered access to it and no one knows!

In some organisations, guess who has access to the master key – the cleaner! The reason is simple: the cleaner arrives at the office first to unlock the doors and do the cleaning, and is the last to leave the office after clearing the rubbish for the day.

Little do these organisations realise the risks to which they are exposing personal data and other information in their possession or under their control (albeit in some organisations the security guards follow the cleaner around). What better way to steal an organisation's secrets than to pose as a cleaner and be handed the master key to the keypress.

Classification and inventory

Other areas of concern we usually observe and highlight to our clients are:

■ Files are not classified into categories such as "Confidential", "Restricted Access" and "Public".

Employment contracts should require employees to protect the organisation's confidential data. But if files are not classified, anyone caught with, or misusing, information that the organisation considers to be confidential can easily plead ignorance. They can thus use this as an excuse to avoid the consequences of breaching their employment contract.

Data protection policies and practices should restrict access to personal data, as well as confidential information. If files are not classified, anyone who accesses files containing personal data either accidentally or deliberately can similarly plead ignorance. Again, they can use this as an excuse to avoid the consequences of failing to comply with the organisation's data protection policies and practices.

■ There is no inventory list of files kept in the cabinets – no one will be the wiser if a file is misplaced, lost or stolen.

Concluding remarks

Locking file cabinets, classifying files and maintaining file inventories to protect an organisation's valuable paper documents may be administratively inconvenient or burdensome for its employees. Locking strongboxes, drawers and cabinets and locking our doors at home may also be inconvenient too, but we do it to protect our own valuables.

If an organisation is serious about protecting its valuable paper documents it should require its employees to bear with administrative inconveniences or burdens to help it achieve that aim. As the title of this chapter says, "Lock it or lose it". It is better for the organisation to be safe, even at the expense of employees being inconvenienced, than to be sorry.

CHECKLIST OF GOOD PRACTICES

Organisations should implement the following practices to protect their documents containing personal data and other confidential information:

- Ensure that their employees make a conscious effort to lock the file cabinets when they are not around.
- Have a secure keypress where all the keys can be kept safety and for which a proper accounting is maintained. The master key to the keypress must be assigned to a responsible person who is accountable for its safekeeping.
- Classify paper documents and files according to the level of confidentiality and maintain an inventory of documents and files that are kept in their filing cabinets.

🔓 57 Lost and found – selfies in your mobile phone

I was driving and tuned in to a radio programme when a DJ mentioned an incident that caught my attention. He was complimenting flight stewards for returning a mobile phone belonging to one of their passengers – but with the addition of some selfies. When the owner of the lost phone turned on his device, there were several photos that the flight crew had taken of themselves with the phone as a fun gesture.

The DJ went on to say that he also did the same thing for fun when he returned a mobile phone or tablet he had found.

Selfies and the data protection law

"What have selfies got to do with the data protection law?", you may ask. The issue is not about the selfies being taken by the flight stewards. Rather, it is about how it was possible that the flight stewards and the DJ were able to take selfies when they found the mobile phones.

Obviously, the devices were not screen-locked! They were not password-protected. And this is the data protection issue, at least where individuals use their mobile devices to access personal data in the possession or under the control of, say, the organisation for which they work.

Mixing personal and business use of mobile devices

Today, many employees mix personal and business usages of their mobile devices. They use their personal mobile devices to get access to emails sent to them as employees of an organisation and they share their organisation's files with their business associates.

Mobile workers, such as property agents, and to a certain extent, financial advisers, might use their mobile devices for business purposes but also receive personal data through email or WhatsApp. They may even use the built-in camera to take photos of identity cards or other client documents.

Now imagine you find a mobile phone belonging to the employee of an organisation (particularly if it is a senior employee) or a business owner or some prominent person or well-known celebrity. What kind of personal data or other confidential information would you expect to find on their mobile devices?

Is your mobile device screen-locked?

It is important to remember that your hand-held devices are actually personal computers and should be protected adequately.

Having a password-protected screen-lock is probably the most important security measure that can be taken to prevent unauthorised access, let alone allowing someone to include his or her selfie. If you haven't locked your mobile device with a password, do it now. Detailed instructions for locking it are readily available online.

A final word

The lucky individuals whose mobile phones were returned to them received an extra selfie from the finder. What if the finder had malicious intent and decided to make use of the hundreds of personal contacts stored on the phone, complete with personal details – and whatever information they found in email and photos?

CHECKLIST OF GOOD PRACTICES

Individuals should take the following precautionary measures when using their mobile devices containing personal and confidential information:

- Ensure that mobile devices such as mobile phones and tablets are screen-locked at all times.
- When implementing screen locks, choose the password option which has a higher security or the biometrics option (thumbprint recognition) if it is available.
- Refrain from using "Swipe" or "PIN" codes that are easy to guess.

🔒 58 Operational compliance: the importance of the human factor in preventing data breaches

We decided to analyse all the recent mega data breach cases to see if human error was either directly or indirectly the main cause.

2014 was the year of mega breaches

Take a look at the following data breaches which involved millions of accounts, all of which happened in 2014. (At the time of writing, results were not all in for 2015.)

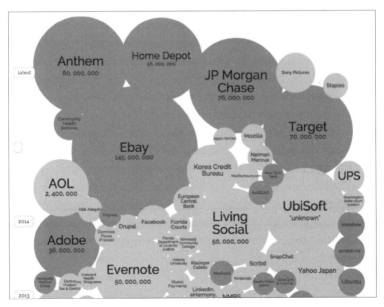

Source: http://www.informationisbeautiful.net

- JP Morgan Chase & Co (76 million households and 7 million small businesses affected)
- eBay (145 million people affected)
- Home Depot (56 million unique payment cards affected)
- CHS Community Health Systems (4.5 million people affected)
- Michaels Stores (2.6 million people affected)
- Nieman Marcus (1.1 million people affected)
- Staples (point-of-sale systems at 115 retail stores affected)

No wonder a commissioned report by the Ponemon Institute was called "2014: Year of the Mega Breaches".[1]

Human error, the trigger of data breaches

Let's take a look at a few of the breaches in a little more detail.

- **JP Morgan Chase**

  An employee of JP Morgan Chase, working from home, was a victim of phishing.

  Phishing is a common hacking technique where the victim is lured into clicking on a malicious link masquerading as a trustworthy entity. Behind these links are various electronic methods of stealing user credentials or malicious codes designed to clandestinely give the attacker control of the user's computing devices.

  The hapless employee, making a human error, clicked on such a link. Hackers then penetrated the bank's network through the employee's infected computer.

- **eBay**

  According to eBay, their data breach occurred when cyber attackers compromised a small number of employee log-in credentials. This allowed unauthorised access to eBay's corporate network.

  Again, we can attribute this to human error. We don't know if the credentials were compromised by keylogging malware or by a phishing attack. But it was obvious that there were no added security measures such as two-factor authentication.

- **Home Depot**

  Home Depot suffered the largest retail card breach on record. It involved malware that infected its point-of-sale system. The

---

[1] http://www.ponemon.org/local/upload/file/2014%20The%20Year%20of%20the%20Mega%20Breach%20FINAL3.pdf

malware was designed to siphon data from payment cards when swiped at infected points-of-sale.

The question is, how did the malware get into the point-of-sale system? Was it because there was a download from an infected website or because somebody clicked on a malicious link? Either way, it seems clear that there was human error.

■ **Target**

Target's data breach happened in late 2013. It affected the personal data, including payment card numbers, of more than 70 million individuals.

An air-conditioning contractor working in Target stores had access to its IT system. A successful phishing attack compromised the contractor's log-in credentials. They were used to access Target's internal contractor billing system. From there, the hackers accessed Target's server that managed the billing system application, changed the access permissions, and gained access to Target's internal networks. The hackers then uploaded their malware to Target's point-of-sale system and used the malware to collect millions of credit card numbers, which were then sold on the black market.

This attack may have involved at least two human errors: the contractor's error that allowed a successful phishing attack and, possibly, insufficient internal system controls that allowed the malware installed by the hackers to move through Target's IT system from the contractor billing system to the point-of-sale system.

Your employees can get your organisation into trouble with the law

The above data breaches happened in organisations that individuals would trust to take the greatest care of their personal data. Yet the breaches happened.

Did they necessarily mean that there were no security policies, practices and technology systems in place? No. The common denominator was the human factor.

Employee negligence or error, the cause of data breaches

We then looked at available research to see the extent to which employees or other insiders were the direct or indirect cause of data breaches. Here are our research results:

- According to the IBM Security Services 2014 Cyber Security Intelligence Index[2], over 95% of all incidents investigated recognise human error as a contributing factor to data breaches.
- A very high percentage was also reported by Experian's Data Breach Industry Forecast Report[3], where "employees and negligence are the leading cause of security incidents but remain the least reported issue." According to one of its executives, of 3,100 incidents that Experian Data Breach Resolution surveyed in 2014, "81% had a root cause in employee negligence".

The most common issue was the loss of administrative credentials – user name and password. But there were also lost media, firewalls left open and lost laptops.

The report also highlighted that "employees and negligence are the leading cause of security incidents but remain the least reported issue".

- From a regulator's perspective, figures from the Information Communications Office (ICO) in the UK, in a Freedom of Information (FoI) report, reveal that humans, not machines, are responsible for 93% of data breaches.

A quarter of all data breaches between April and June 2014 involved the accidental loss or destruction of personal data.

- In a study by Ponemon Institute of 584 IT professionals whose organisations had been breached in 2012, the following causes were revealed:
  - 34% were caused by a negligent insider
  - 16% were caused by malicious insiders
  - 19% were a result of outsourcing data to a third-party
  - 11% were a result of systems glitches
  - 7% were the product of a cyber attack
  - 6% were triggered by a failure to shred confidential documents

So, in this study, 50% of breaches were caused by insiders. Taking insiders of third-parties into account, the number is likely close to 70%.

Whichever report you choose, the human factor is a major cause or trigger of data breaches.

---

[2] See http://www-03.ibm.com/security/services/2014-cyber-security-intelligence-index-infographic/index.html
[3] Experian's 2015 Second Annual Data Breach Industry Forecast

Implications on data protection law – and the importance of operational compliance

We expect that mega breaches and emerging technologies such as big data, cloud computing, social media, mobility and the "Internet of things" will create regulatory pressures that bring about stricter data protection laws.

Organisations in Asia and the European Union will need to deal with new legal requirements. But legal compliance is not enough, as the above cases demonstrate. The key for organisations is to achieve operational compliance – to overcome the human factor.

If organisations adopt operational compliance practices and an employee fails to comply with them, resulting in a data breach, the regulator might take their existence into account. For example, a regulator might count them as a mitigating factor in assessing any penalty for the organisation failing to comply with the data protection law. Or it might not, depending on the circumstances of the lapse.

Generally, regulators require organisations to demonstrate some sort of accountability – defined as responsibility, ownership and evidence – for their operational compliance policies.

The final word

The conclusion is a simple one: humans are the weakest link in any organisation. An organisation may have implemented the best data loss prevention software, end-point security or encryption technology. But all it takes is just one ignorant, careless or disgruntled employee to ruin all the good work done from an operational perspective.

Effective internal training can help manage the risk of ignorant employees. Regular auditing of compliance with policies and practices can help to manage the risk of ignorant employees too, as well as the risk of careless employees. Restricting access to personal data on a "need to know" basis might assist in managing the risk of disgruntled employees.

Good automated methods to track access to, and use of, personal data and diligent review of their records to monitor compliance with policies and practices may identify problems at an early stage and even stop disgruntled employees in their tracks.

> ### CHECKLIST OF GOOD PRACTICES
>
> Organisations should be aware of the main causes of data breaches and should implement precautionary or mitigating measures to minimise the occurrence of data breaches:
>
> - Understand that more than 50% of data breaches are the result of the human factor.
> - Ensure the your organisation implements operational compliance practices – legal compliance is not enough.
> - Train employees and raise their awareness in operational compliance and information security.

🔒 **59** Out of sight, out of mind

What do organisations do when they have more paper documents and files than they have space enough to store them?

I have observed how some organisations, especially small and medium enterprises, come up with ingenious ways to create extra storage space. Here are some examples:

■ Put the less-current paper documents and files into cardboard boxes and stash them away on top of file cabinets, in the printing room, under work desks or even in the tools storeroom.

■ Have files from different departments share the same storage space. Larger organisations with bigger budgets invest in compactus-style cabinets and filing systems to maximise the limited storage space. Some send out their archived documents and files to commercial warehouses offsite.

Onsite storage

Where organisations store their paper documents and files onsite, do they:

■ think about whether the manner or place in which they are stored could give rise to personal data and other confidential information being accessed by employees without a "need to know" or even by individuals from outside the organisation? Or

■ worse, after some time, forget what is in the cardboard boxes and where they are kept?

Here are some ways organisations might address these two concerns:

■ Segregate those files with higher levels of confidentiality and sensitivity from the rest of the organisation's files. For example, an organisation might assess that the personnel files of ex-employees and (if the organisation has a business or legal reason for needing to retain them) the résumés of unsuccessful job applicants attract higher levels of confidentiality and sensitivity than other files.

Even if these files and documents have to be kept in cardboard boxes and placed on top of file cabinets, the organisation should require that they are at least placed within the Human Resource (HR) Department. The organisation should require the HR Department to mark the boxes as "Confidential" and to ensure that only HR employees with a "need to know" (as opposed to *all* HR employees) can have access to these files and documents. The job titles of such individuals (for example, Director of HR and Assistant Director of HR) should be clearly marked on the boxes so that other employees without a "need to know" will not open the boxes accidentally.

■ Other departments responsible for storing their cardboard boxes of files and documents in various nooks and corners should have the boxes clearly marked with the names of the departments that own them and with a "Confidential" notification. This is so that employees from other department will not open the boxes accidentally.

Again, marking the boxes with the job titles of individuals with a "need to know" might help to avoid other employees without a "need to know" opening the boxes accidentally.

■ As far as possible, files from different departments should not be put in the same storeroom, especially where files contain personal data and other confidential information that is highly sensitive.

For example, HR Department files and Finance Department files should not be co-located in the same space.

If there is no choice, due to space constraints, then a deliberate demarcation should be made so that employees from either department do not cross the line (for example, Shelving Unit A is for the HR Department and Shelving Unit B is for the Finance Department).

In any case, the boxes should be marked as indicated above.

- An organisation should maintain a written inventory of what is contained in each box and where it is stored. (This should include documents stored offsite, such as by attaching the separate records of them to the inventory.)

  This is because an organisation cannot expect anyone in the organisation to remember these details after some time. Where there is seldom a need to refer to non-current files in the boxes it is even harder to rely on anyone's memory.

- An organisation is required by the data protection law to dispose of personal data when it is no longer necessary for a legal or business purpose.

  If possible, organise the files in each box according to the retention period so that when it comes to dispose of them it is easier to locate the right boxes.

Storage at warehouse

Some organisations send their archived paper files and documents for storage at offsite warehouses. From the perspective of the data protection law the organisation remains responsible for them, although the warehouse operator may have some statutory responsibilities too.

The organisation should ensure that the responsibilities and obligations of the warehouse operator are clearly spelt out in the storage contract with the warehouse operator, which may include defined service levels. Such responsibilities and obligations should include those things that the warehouse operator must do or must not do to enable the organisation to remain in compliance with the data protection law.

Ideally, the agreement between the organisation and the warehouse operator should include a contractual indemnity covering any costs, losses or damage suffered by the organisation as a result of a breach of the agreement by the warehouse operator. This should extend to any misplacement, loss of, or damage to, the cartons of documents placed by the organisation at the warehouse. It should also cover any other action or inaction by the warehouse operator that may result in the organisation failing to comply with the data protection law.

Again, an organisation should maintain written records of the paper files and documents that are stored at warehouses so that:

- the organisation can ensure that it disposes of, or destroys, these paper files and documents appropriately at the expiry of the retention periods applicable to them and
- these paper files and documents may be accounted for in inventory records lest they become forgotten – "out of sight, out of mind".

Concluding remarks

The volume of paper documents and files maintained by organisations is expected to grow as their businesses expand. Storage space will never be enough.

Organisations should do housekeeping regularly to dispose of those documents that are no longer needed for any business or legal purpose, in accordance with the organisation's document retention policy.

The more documents an organisation keeps, the more personal data the organisation must protect, and the more the more the organisation's employees have to remember where the documents are stored.

CHECKLIST OF GOOD PRACTICES

For storage of confidential documents onsite, organisations should adopt the following practices:

- Segregate files with higher levels of confidentiality/sensitivity from the rest.
- Mark storage boxes clearly with the owners' names to prevent accidental opening by persons without a "need to know".
- Do not keep files from different departments in the same storeroom.
- Maintain an inventory record of the contents of each box and where it is stored.

For storage of confidential documents at warehouse, organisations should adopt the following practices:

- Spell out clearly the responsibilities and obligations of the warehouse operator in the service level agreement, including indemnity clauses.
- Maintain an inventory record of the contents of each box and the document retention schedule.

🔒 60 Sending sensitive documents – learning from data breaches by law firms

You would think that law firms would be the last organisations to get into trouble with the data protection law since they know the legal requirements inside out. Right? Wrong.

And this illustrates that compliance is not just about legal compliance – for example, ensuring that the various legal contracts, data protection policies and consent clauses are in place. There needs to be operational compliance too. And it's operational compliance that has tripped them up.

Here are a few data breaches that happened to law firms due to operational compliance failures. We can learn from them because they might also happen to any other type of organisation delivering or sending confidential documents.

Unsecured trial documents delivered

An employee of a law firm delivered documents relating to a matrimonial trial to its client. The documents contained sensitive personal data about the client. The employee left the documents in a gap between the front door and the metal gate at the client's residence. To aggravate matters, the documents were not sealed in an envelope and were easily accessible to passersby and unrelated parties. It happened that a security guard on patrol picked them up.

The client complained to the regulator.[1] It found the law firm, being the employer of the negligent staff, liable for the privacy breach. The

[1] Office of the Privacy Commission of Personal Data, HK, Case No.:2002C07, https://www.pcpd.org.hk/english/enforcement/case_notes/casenotes_2.php?id=2002C07&content_type=&content_nature=&msg_id2=164

investigations by the regulator revealed that the firm had no written guidelines advising its employees about compliance with the relevant requirements of the data protection law, especially with regard to delivering sensitive documents.

Careless disclosure of sensitive information through acknowledgement receipt

A law firm arranged for documents relating to a matrimonial case to be delivered to a party to the case at that individual's office. The original documents were placed in a sealed envelope. However, there was a duplicate of the documents for the recipient to sign to acknowledge receipt. The duplicate was not covered in any way. It contained the suit number of the proceedings and the names of the parties to it.

When the messenger arrived at the office he placed both the sealed envelope and the duplicate copy of the documents on the reception desk and took a seat to wait for the recipient. The receptionist inevitably read the front page of the duplicate documents. They could also be read by any person passing by the reception desk.

When the recipient discovered this, she was upset that her involvement in divorce proceedings had been disclosed to others in her office and complained to the regulator[2].

The law firm argued to the regulator that the front page of the duplicate documents showed merely the suit number of the proceedings and the names of the parties. It said that these details were accessible to the public at the court registry. It argued that therefore this was not confidential personal data.

The regulator said that:

- the law firm failed to take practical steps to safeguard the personal data in this context
- the data was still of a sensitive nature to the individual concerned, particularly in her workplace and
- such "information was unnecessarily brought to the notice of persons who in all likelihood would not otherwise have had knowledge of it and this had caused distress to the complainant".

[2] Office of the Privacy Commission of Personal Data, HK, Case No.: 1997C18 https://www.pcpd.org.hk/english/enforcement/case_notes/casenotes_2.php?id=1997C18&content_type=4&content_nature=&msg_id2=112

Therefore, the regulator considered that the law firm had failed to comply with the data protection law. The case was settled by mediation after the law firm accepted the regulator's findings.

Letter without cover acknowledged and read by receptionist

A messenger for a law firm hand-delivered a letter to a client of the law firm without any cover to the client's office. The messenger asked the receptionist to sign a copy of the letter as acknowledgement of receipt.

The receptionist called the client and read out part of the letter to the client. This upset the client. The letter contained reference to court actions involving the client and, as a result of the messenger delivering the letter from the law firm, the receptionist now knew about them.

The client complained to the regulator[3] that the law firm had disclosed her personal data to the receptionist and the messenger. The law firm admitted to the breach and undertook to put remedial measures in place. These included not disclosing a client's personal data whenever delivering any document or when getting any acknowledgement of delivery. The law firm also undertook to give clear instructions to its employees about the purposes of complying with these requirements.

Confidential legal documents faxed by lawyer without checking with recipient

A solicitor in a law firm sent confidential legal documents to a private fax number of the Chief Executive Officer of an insurance company meant for an employee[4]. But here is the problem: this employee had set up their own private business, presumably without their company's knowledge. The solicitor apparently obtained the fax number by searching through the Internet. The number was the general fax number of the insurance company. As a result, the documents were delivered to the CEO, prompting the employee to complain to the regulator against the law firm for disclosing their personal data without consent.

[3] Office of the Privacy Commission of Personal Data, HK, Case No.: 2009A03 https://www.pcpd.org.hk/english/enforcement/case_notes/casenotes_2.php?id=2009A03&content_type=4&content_nature=&msg_id2=321
[4] Office of the Privacy Commission of Personal Data, HK,Case No.:2013C06, https://www.pcpd.org.hk/english/enforcement/case_notes/casenotes_2.php?id=2013C06&content_type=&content_nature=&msg_id2=416

The law firm confirmed that sending legal documents containing personal data to a fax number, which would enable persons other than the intended recipient to have sight or easy access to the documents, contravened its policy. It told the regulator that it had reminded its solicitors of such policy during internal meetings. However, there was no written policy.

The regulator served an enforcement notice on the law firm requesting it to prepare a written policy to prohibit sending legal documents that contain personal data to an insecure fax number (that is, without encryption or to a fax machine accessible to other users).

Lessons learned

While the above case studies relate to law firms, they are common data breaches that can happen whenever confidential documents containing personal data or other confidential information are delivered, sent or transmitted by organisations.

The data protection law requires that organisations take adequate measures to safeguard and protect personal data from unauthorised access. Organisations should ensure that their employees are trained on what security measures the organisation requires them to take when handling documents that contain personal data and other confidential information. Any third-parties entrusted with delivery should be similarly briefed.

Verbal instructions or reminders are not enough. An organisation should have a formal written policy in place.

Always deliver or send confidential documents in a sealed envelope marked "Confidential" and marked to be opened by the named addressee only. Do not include in any acknowledgement receipt any information from which an unauthorised recipient can infer personal information of the intended recipient.

It is risky to fax confidential documents. If they need to be faxed, a cover sheet should be used. This will let anyone know who the information is for and whether it is confidential or sensitive, without them having to look at the contents. Before faxing the document, the sender should confirm that the recipient is ready to receive it.

CHECKLIST OF GOOD PRACTICES

When handling documents containing private, confidential and even sensitive information, organisations should take the following precautionary measures:

■ Ensure there are security measures and procedures in place when confidential or sensitive documents are delivered, sent or transmitted. For example, using sealed envelopes and acknowledgement of receipt.

■ Ensure there are written policies and guidelines in place to ensure no sensitive documents are disclosed during delivery or when acknowledging receipt.

■ Ensure all personnel including messengers and delivery service providers are trained.

■ When faxing confidential documents, use a secure procedure, such as:

　● Double-check the fax number

　● Use a cover sheet to shield the sensitive information

　● Confirm that the recipient is ready to receive the document

　● Call or email the recipient to confirm that the document has been sent and received intact

61 The pack rat syndrome – and how it can bite you

A pack rat is a rodent that is noted for its habit of collecting bright, shiny objects and leaving other objects, such as nuts or pebbles, in their place. Individuals who store everything they acquire and won't discard any of it and individuals who collect things they do not need are a close human equivalent. In data protection, pack rats are particularly common in three areas:

- job applications
- proposals for services (e.g. insurance) that are rejected by the potential customer and for financial advice that are rejected by the individual seeking advice
- photos

My all-time favourite pack rats

The clear winner of my own "who's the worst pack rat" competition is an HR manager. This HR manager's organisation recruits for about 500 open positions each year. They told me they keep unsuccessful job applications for five years "because we might want to call them about another job in the future".

A runner-up in my competition is a public relations manager whose organisation provides community services, including sporting and other events, to teenagers. At every event they take dozens of photos. They publish a couple of them in their next newsletter and might even use a photo in their Annual Report. They told me they never discard any photos because "we might want to use them in the future".

In both cases, it seems highly unlikely that even a single job application or photo would be used after the role had been filled or the newsletter and Annual Report had been published. There is no point from a business perspective in retaining the personal data in job applications and in photos for a very long time on a "just in case" basis.

The downside of retaining personal data

We've seen that there's no upside – no point – in retaining personal data in job applications and photos for a very long time on a "just in case" basis. Now let's look at the downside – how it can bite you – in doing so. And this is all about failing to comply with the data protection law.

First, the data protection law requires an organisation to dispose of personal data when it is no longer necessary for a business or legal purpose. Organisations should develop and implement a data retention policy so that documents containing personal data are securely shredded or deleted periodically to comply with this data protection requirement.

Second, where an organisation retains personal data it must comply with other obligations under the data protection law. It makes no sense from a business perspective for an organisation to burden itself with them in connection with personal data that it does not really need to retain:

■ It may be unlikely that an individual will seek access to personal data in an old job application, proposal or photo. Nevertheless they have the right to do so and an organisation must have processes in place to respond to any such request. And the process will need to extend even to personal data that the organisation retains on a "just in case" basis.

■ The same point applies to the right of an individual to obtain information about how an organisation has used their personal data in the previous 12 months. Again, an organisation may receive requests (and incur the administrative burden of dealing with them) in connection with personal data that serves no useful purpose for the organisation, except for any "just in case" benefit.

■ The same points apply to the right of an individual to correct any error or omission in the personal data that an organisation holds about them.

A disgruntled, unsuccessful job or insurance applicant might make these requests simply to cause administrative hassles. They may delight in the idea that the organisation has to go back through its records to find their personal data so that it can respond to the request. They could then report to the regulator that the organisation retained their personal data when it was no longer necessary for a business or legal purpose.

In addition, the data protection legislation requires an organisation to protect the personal data in its possession or under its control. It makes no sense to retain personal data "just in case" it is required and thereby assume the obligation to protect it. Much better to cease to retain personal data when it's no longer necessary for a legal or business purpose than to worry about how to protect it.

CHECKLIST OF GOOD PRACTICES

Organisations should put in place safeguards to protect the personal and confidential documents in their possession or under their control:

■ Implement reasonable security measures and controls.

■ Develop and implement a data protection policy and comply with it.

■ Implement processes to enable individuals to exercise their access and correction rights to their personal data.

62 Beware – don't ever lose or misplace your USB drive or other portable storage device

The data protection law requires organisations, which includes individuals, to protect personal data in their possession or under their control. Any failure might result in a data breach with consequences under the data protection law. But any failure might also result in loss of confidential information, including competitively sensitive information.

If you have a USB drive or other portable storage device and you use it for office or business purposes, you run the risk of a data breach under the data protection law. If you use it only for personal purposes, you run the risk of personal embarrassment or worse. If you use the same device for business and personal purposes – perhaps you should stop doing so.

For a mobile salesperson such as a real estate agent or a financial adviser or other individual who is generally "on the road", you are particularly exposed as you may easily lose your USB or other portable storage device.

High probability that your storage device could be misplaced or lost

Have you ever forgotten to take your portable storage device out of your pocket before putting your clothes in the washing machine or sending them to the dry cleaners? Or have you forgotten to remove it after using a public or other shared computer terminal? Or have you ever lost a portable storage device and concluded that it must have fallen out of your pocket in a taxi?

Surveys by Credant Technologies, a London-based data security company, have revealed that:

- At more than 500 laundromats and dry cleaners in the UK, 17,000 USB drives were left behind between December 2010 and January 2011. This was a 400% increase in lost devices compared to the year before.[1]

- In 2011, travellers left behind 8,016 mobile devices at seven of the largest airports in the United States. This figure comprised smartphones and tablets (43%), laptops (45%) and USB drives (12%).[2]

Data from Transport for London (TfL) has revealed that Londoners left almost 25,000 devices such as phones, laptops and USB sticks on buses, taxis and tube trains in 2013.[3]

You might fail to comply with the data protection law

If you lose a portable storage device, the loss may, depending on the circumstances, result in a data breach that is a failure to comply with the data protection law.

Protecting personal data on a portable storage device by a strong password and/or by encryption should prevent an individual who

---

[1] See http://blog.allusb.com/2011/03/rising-trend-in-lost-usb-flash-drives/
[2] See http://www.businesswire.com/news/home/20120703005106/en/Credant-Survey-Finds-Travelers-Left-8000-Mobile
[3] See http://www.v3.co.uk/v3-uk/news/2384295/londoners-left-21-000-phones-in-buses-tubes-and-taxis-in-2013

finds the device and happens to have malicious intent from getting access to the personal data on it and using it.

An organisation that fails to comply with the data protection law may be fined or face other penalties if they suffer a data breach as a result of someone accessing and using personal data on a portable storage device used by an employee of the organisation.

For example, a local government authority was fined £80,000 after a special education needs[4] teacher lost a USB stick which held personal and sensitive data of children with special educational needs. The USB stick was unencrypted and the regulator decided that "Personal data and sensitive personal data were lost due to the inappropriate technical and administrative measures taken by the data controller".

In another case,[5] the regulator fined a US Government Department $150,000 for privacy and security breaches when an employee lost an unencrypted USB drive. (It was stolen from the employee's vehicle.) It contained the health information of 2,200 people. The regulator also required the organisation to develop and implement a corrective action plan. It was required to include a risk analysis and a risk management plan to address and mitigate any security risks and vulnerabilities.

Questions about your USB drive and other portable storage devices

- Do you protect your USB drive and other portable storage devices by a strong password and by encryption?
- Do you minimise the risk of a data breach by deleting from your USB drive and other portable storage devices any documents containing personal data or other confidential information when they are no longer needed?
- Do you ensure that you keep your USB drive and other portable storage devices safely?
- Do you make sure that you account for your USB drive and other portable storage devices at all times?
- Do you regularly scan your USB drive and other portable storage devices for viruses and malware?

[4] See http://www.out-law.com/en/articles/2013/October/lost-unencrypted-usb-stick-costs-council-80000-data-breach-fine/
[5] See http://www.healthcareitnews.com/news/lost-thumb-drive-leads-150k-fine

If the answer to any of these questions is "no" you should take remedial action.

Protect your devices and their contents with strong passwords and encryption

Encryption can be done at either the device level – that is, every file on the device is, in effect, encrypted – or it can be done on a file-by-file basis.

It is easy to encrypt devices. Bundled utility programs for doing so are included in popular computer operating systems or can be purchased separately. Information about how to find and use them is readily available on the Internet. These applications can also encrypt the entire hard disk of your computer. They work in the same way as for your portable storage devices.

If you decide not to encrypt at the device level, then you should at least password-protect the device or the specific documents that contain personal data or other confidential information.

Delete any sensitive documents containing personal data when no longer needed

The data protection law requires organisations to dispose of personal data when it is no longer necessary for a business or legal purpose. An alternative is to anonymise it (which is not as straightforward as it seems).

The requirement applies to personal data on USB drives and other portable storage devices in the same way as it applies to personal data in an organisation's IT system or stored locally on computer hard disks.

An organisation's Bring-Your-Own-Device (BYOD) policy should require employees to delete documents containing personal data or other confidential information from their USB drives and other portable storage devices, as well as from their phones, tablets and any other mobile devices.

Because USB drives and other portable storage devices are at risk of loss, an organisation should require its employees to delete personal data and other confidential information from them when it no longer needs to reside on them – for example, after it has been transferred to the organisation's IT system and the employee no longer needs it "on the road".

Secure your USB drive and other portable storage devices

Keep your USB drive and other portable storage devices safe and secure. Do not leave them unattended or unsecured when they are stored – whether it is at home, in your room or at your work desk.

Know where your devices are and keep an inventory

So how many storage devices do you have altogether? Where are they? Have you misplaced any of them or loaned any of them to family, friends or colleagues? What's in those devices?

Scan your USB drive and other portable storage devices for viruses and malware

USB storage devices have become so popular that cyber criminals have written viruses and worms that specifically target them. If, for example, someone plugs an infected USB drive into your home computer, these criminals could inadvertently upload the bug and potentially cripple the machine.

If you use the same device in your organisation, the malware can connect to the office network and upload the worm to replicate itself on the network, putting it and everyone at risk.

Therefore, you should regularly scan any USB drive or other portable storage device for viruses and malware. And don't forget to ensure that your scanning program has the latest updates.

Final words of caution

Even if you have the precautionary measures in place, it is best if you avoid storing sensitive personal data, such as identity card numbers and credit card numbers, and other confidential personal data on a USB drive or other portable storage device.

I once met a property agent who panicked because they'd lost a USB drive which was not protected at all. For whatever reason, the property agent had stored all their tenancy agreements on it. And didn't have a back-up copy.

Do not use the same USB drives for home and work to avoid accidentally introducing a virus you picked up from an infected device into your company's office network. (Or vice versa!)

And be sure to find out about policies adopted by your organisation about what external devices can be plugged into its network. Failing to comply with them generally has disciplinary consequences up to and including termination of employment.

Using a USB drive or other portable storage device is just one of many ways a data breach can happen to you or your organisation. You should be aware of the risks and how to manage them, especially if you are a mobile warrior. The "enemy" is lurking quietly everywhere, waiting to pounce on you when you least expect it. The data protection law also changes the rules of the game.

CHECKLIST OF GOOD PRACTICES

Organisations and individuals should take due care to protect and secure USB drives and other portable storage devices:

- Protect your devices and their contents with strong passwords and encryption.
- Delete any sensitive documents containing personal data when no longer needed.
- Do not leave storage devices unattended or unsecured when they are stored – whether it is at home, in your room or at your work desk.
- Know where your devices are and keep an inventory.
- Scan your USB drive and other portable storage devices for viruses and malware.
- Regularly conduct a risk assessment exercise to address and mitigate any security risks.

63 Call centres – a treasure trove of personal data

Why do customers and members of the public contact call centres operated by private organisations, government agencies or outsourced entities acting on behalf of private organisations or government agencies? There are numerous purposes for such calls, but the most common ones might be to:

- enquire about products, services or promotional items (for private corporations)
- enquire about policies and schemes (for government agencies)
- compliment employees who have rendered good service to them
- complain about employees who have rendered poor service to them
- clarify items on bills, invoices or statements of account
- give feedback on inefficient processes or procedures and
- offer suggestions on how to improve existing processes or procedures.

My experiences interacting with call centres
I, for one, often contact call centres for any of the reasons listed above. Sometimes it could be an enquiry on issues or matters of concern when I don't get satisfactory answers from the FAQs on websites. Other times, it could be to clarify certain incorrect or inaccurate entries in the bills from telcos and utility companies, or statements of accounts from banks and other payment card issuers. At other times, it could be to give feedback on the quality of service, or to offer suggestions for improving existing processes and procedures.

Most times when I get through to the call centre number (sometimes after numerous attempts or long waits), I am usually greeted by a pre-recorded message:

This conversation may be recorded for coaching and quality purposes.

That sets me thinking: Where are all the recorded conversations stored? Who has the right to access them? For how long does the organisation keep them? Mind you, some of these conversations may contain highly sensitive personal data or other confidential information, especially when customers complain about the quality of service of certain employees and say unpleasant things about them. And what if some of the "juicy" conversations are leaked and become fodder for common gossip? How can organisations ensure that this does not happen, especially among their outsourcing vendors?

Call centres should protect against leakage of recorded conversations

Organisations operating call centres, either for themselves or as a vendor for another organisation, should take at least the following preventive measures to minimise the leakage of recorded conversations:

- Keep the servers containing the recorded conversations in a secure place with restricted access.
- If practicable, encrypt the more sensitive recorded conversations.
- Limit employees' access rights to the recorded conversations to those with a "need to know" in order to do their jobs. Document the purposes for which these employees may use the recorded conversations, including details of any third-parties to which the employees may disclose them.
- Develop and implement a policy about the time period after which the recorded conversations are to be destroyed and monitor compliance with the policy.
- Educate call centre employees of the requirement under their employment contract to comply with data protection policies and practices, and about their confidentiality obligations under that contract.

Where an organisation's call centre services are provided for it by an outsourced service provider, the organisation should ensure that it has a service contract with the vendor that includes at least the above points in connection with personal data and confidentiality.

Before entering into the contract, the organisation should satisfy itself that the prospective vendor is capable of complying with the obligations and any other applicable requirements of the data protection law. The service contract should give the organisation the right to audit the vendor's compliance with the above practices, and the right to audit the vendor's physical premises, if necessary.

CHECKLIST OF GOOD PRACTICES

Organisations operating call centres should adopt the following practices when handling sensitive personal information in recorded conversations:

- House the servers containing the recorded conversations in a secure place with restricted access.
- Encrypt the more sensitive recorded conversations if practicable.
- Limit the right of access to the recorded conversations on a "need to know" basis.
- Determine a time period after which the recorded conversations are to be destroyed.
- Educate the call centre employees on their obligations to maintain confidentiality of information, as per their employment contract.
- Have a service contract with the outsourced vendor to abide by the above practices, auditing their compliance and physical premises if necessary.

64 Do you trust the PC repairman with your personal data and other confidential information?

It was one of those things I wished would not happen to me – but it did! One fine morning, the hard disk in my home PC crashed. With my limited knowledge of the innards of the PC and the lack of the right software utilities, it was well-nigh impossible for me to get the hard disk to work again. Fearing the worst, my main concern was how to salvage the personal data and other confidential data I had stored in the hard disk. The last full data back-up I did was many moons ago!

In desperation, I had no choice but to send my PC to a self-proclaimed "PC Doctor" to seek help to recover the precious data buried in the hard disk. The PC Doctor opened up the chassis of my PC and took out the hard disk in a jiffy. He then inserted my hard disk into a gigantic chassis that looked like it was meant for a large server. He performed a few diagnostic tests with his special utility software and pronounced the demise of my hard disk.

But he had good news for me, though. He declared with a lot of self-confidence that he could recover at least 80% of the data stored in my hard disk. He would first have to copy the data from the good sectors of my newly-dead hard disk to another hard disk in his gigantic chassis. Once that operation was completed, he would transfer the salvaged data from his hard disk to a new hard disk he was going to sell me. Of course I bargained for a discount on the price of the new hard disk and the labour costs of recovering the data from my old hard disk.

Alas, the entire operation of recovering the data from my old hard disk and copying the recovered data to a new hard disk would take at least two hours. The PC Doctor encouraged me to do some shopping and come back two hours later to collect his finished masterpiece.

Dare I trust him with my personal data and other confidential information? What if he were to duplicate my precious data he had copied to his hard disk? I then chose the most risk-averse approach by staying by his side and watching his every movement for the next two hours!

After all, I did not know anything about the PC Doctor as a person before that day – the only thing that attracted me to his shop was his huge array of equipment that gave me the confidence that he would have the right tools.

After a very draggy two hours, the job was done. The PC Doctor managed to recover more than 90% of the data from my old hard disk, beating his own boast. I heaved a great sigh of relief! I thanked the PC Doctor for a job well done. But before I left his shop, I made sure that he deleted all my copied data on his hard disk.

Whatever happened to my dead hard disk? I kept it as a memento at home.

Useful lessons to be learned

There are a few useful lessons we can learn from my experience:

- Always back up your hard disk regularly, especially when it contains valuable data you can't afford to lose. Were your hard disk to crash unexpectedly, you now have a back-up set of data which you can quickly restore to your new hard disk. There is no need to send your hard disk to any PC repairman for data recovery if you are confident that almost all your precious data can be restored from your back-up copy.

- If you have to send your PC to a repairman to recover the data in the hard disk, choose one who is reliable, preferably based on referrals by friends. If you really can't trust the PC repairman then you have to do what I did – sit beside him and watch him closely.

- There will be occasions when parts of your PC become faulty and you have to send the PC to a repairman for repairs or replacement of components. Again, you have to take precautionary measures to ensure that the repairman does not make unauthorised copies of your private and confidential data.

CHECKLIST OF GOOD PRACTICES

Organisations and individuals should take the following precautionary measures when sending computers for repair or for data recovery:

- Always back up your hard disk regularly so that you have a back-up set of data that can be used quickly to restore your valuable data.
- Choose a repairman who is reliable, preferably based on referrals by friends.
- Take precautionary measures to ensure that the repairman does not make unauthorised copies of your private and confidential data.

🔒 65 Mishandling physical documents containing personal data can get you into trouble

Have you lost, misplaced or accidentally exposed any physical documents containing personal data – especially those with sensitive information? If UK's data protection law is anything to go by, you too could be prosecuted under the local data protection law.

Case #1: Sensitive documents left behind in a plastic shopping bag on a train

A monetary penalty was served to the London Borough of Lewisham after a social worker left sensitive documents in a plastic shopping bag on a train, after taking them home to work on. The files, which were later recovered from the rail company's lost property office, included medical and police reports and allegations of sexual abuse and neglect.

Case #2: Documents with personal data stored in transparent bags

An undertaking to comply with UK's data protection law was sent to Thamesview Estate Agents Ltd after the company continued to leave papers containing personal information on the street despite a previous warning. The papers, meant for disposal, were stored in transparent bags and the information was clearly visible to anyone who walked past.

Case #3: Folder containing personal data left in a café

An undertaking to comply with UK's data protection law was signed by Foyle Women's Aid. This followed the temporary loss of a folder belonging to a Criminal Justice Support worker employed by Foyle Women's Aid that was left in a café. The folder contained confidential client information.

Case #4: Recycled paper with personal data
A monetary penalty of £250,000 was issued to Scottish Borders Council after former employees' pension records were found in an over-filled paper recycle bank in a supermarket car park.

Important checklist when handling personal data
- Is your physical file or folder containing personal data marked as "Confidential"?
- When in transit or in meetings, do you secure any file or bag containing sensitive data (e.g. loan application forms) so that it is not exposed?
- When recycling paper, do you ensure no personal data is exposed?
- Do you ensure that all unwanted documents containing personal data are securely disposed of or shredded?
- When submitting or archiving documents with personal data, do you take reasonable security measures to protect the document?

Mark all files or folders containing personal data or other confidential information as "Confidential"
If you are constantly on the move and handling personal data of clients is part of your job, ensure that your confidential documents are placed in a non-transparent folder or envelope with "Private and Confidential" stamped on it.

"Why warn people that you are carrying a sensitive document?", you may ask. If you are in the office environment, anyone who views a confidential document without any authorisation will be considered to be violating the human resource policy which requires employees to respect confidentiality. If you lose a confidential folder in a public place, the confidential warning – hopefully – will be noticed by a good Samaritan who might return the document to your office. Pray that he or she doesn't complain to the regulator. Now imagine if there is no "Confidential" notice.

Secure any file or bag containing sensitive personal data

Instead of carrying loose sheets of paper around, or worse, putting them in transparent folders or plastic bags, ensure any documents concerning personal data are secured in a bag or preferably a sealed envelope. Take extra precautionary measures to avoid losing or misplacing the bag.

No personal data should ever be exposed on recycled paper

One of the most common findings in our onsite audits is finding recycled paper with personal data on it. While saving the environment is an important initiative, protecting other people's personal data is even more important.

Unwanted documents containing personal data should be securely disposed of or shredded

Always dispose of documents with personal data by shredding. Never throw them into the wastepaper basket or recycle bin. When making copies of sensitive documents, ensure that discarded or imperfect prints are not left behind at the copier.

If you are a mobile salesperson or an independent agent, beware when you move house. People tend to get careless when getting rid of old stuff – which could happen to be your old transaction records containing other people's confidential personal data.

Beware when submitting or archiving personal information

Whether you are in a hurry to meet a submission deadline or handing over documents to another party, take steps to ensure there are proper security measures in place. Never leave a document containing personal data on someone's desk or even an exposed tray for incoming documents.

If you have to submit documents to your agency or company and the medium is not secure, inform the management that the data protection law requires organisations to take reasonable measures to protect personal data under their care. The submission box should be secured and documents must not be retrievable by unauthorised personnel.

CHECKLIST OF GOOD PRACTICES

Organisations and individuals should take the following precautionary measures when handling documents containing personal data and other confidential information:

- Mark all files or folders containing personal data or other confidential information as "Confidential".
- Secure any file or bag containing sensitive personal data. Do not lose or misplace it!
- No personal data should ever be exposed on recycled paper.
- Unwanted documents containing personal data should be securely disposed of or shredded.
- Beware when submitting or archiving personal information. Make sure it is done securely and that the information is not exposed to or retrievable by unauthorised persons.

🔒 **66** The data protection law also applies to freelancers

First things first. By "freelancer" I mean individuals who are self-employed and not necessarily committed to a particular employer. In some countries they might be called "independent contractors" rather than freelancers. It's the same thing.

At the end of 2014 I conducted a series of data protection law training sessions for more than 50 freelance travel guides engaged by a travel agency. The agency wanted to ensure that all its travel agents comply with the data protection law. I asked them how many of them were aware that it existed in the first place – the data protection rules in it had been in force in Singapore for about six months.

Only one person was aware of its existence. (And this person happened to be a property agent. This is not uncommon as freelancers take on multiple jobs.)

So, more than 90% of the course participants were totally unaware of the data protection law. And so they were equally unaware that it governs how they collect, use, disclose and care for individuals' personal data in their possession. And that if they fail to comply with it, they may incur penalties, including fines.

Freelancers are considered organisations

We find that when individuals are employees of an organisation they have no difficulty with the concept that the data protection law applies to the organisation. They may not like it, but when they know that there is a data protection law, they understand that the organisation that employs them must comply with it.

Even when they know about the data protection law, we typically find that individuals who are self-employed, including freelancers, do not think that it applies to them, especially if they have not set themselves up as a company or other registered business. They are wrong.

The rules about when the data protection law applies can be complicated, but here's a rule of thumb in connection with individuals:

- If an individual is collecting, using or disclosing personal data in a personal or domestic capacity, the data protection law does not apply. So it does not apply to individuals swapping personal data such as contact details to arrange a party or to start a book club that will meet at their house or to invite guests to their child's wedding.
- If an individual is collecting, using or disclosing personal data for a business purpose or in a business context, then the data protection law does apply. If the individual is an employee of an organisation, it is the organisation that must comply with it. If the individual is not an employee, the individual is considered to be an "organisation" and must comply with the data protection law.

Hence, whether you are freelancing as a tour guide, a financial adviser, a property agent, a consultant, a tutor, a multi-level marketing salesperson or an individual involved in making money part-time, the data protection law applies to you.

Failure to comply with the data protection law can result in penalties, including hefty fines. Individuals can file a complaint with the regulator and, in some jurisdictions, even sue the freelancer to get compensation for any loss to them from the freelancer failing to comply with the data protection law.

Common data protection law exposures for freelancers

Here are some things done by tour guides which can get them into trouble under the data protection law – they apply equally to other freelancers with a tweak of the context:

- In situations where they handle a lot of personal data, making mistakes (such as mixing up personal data of different individuals or writing it down incorrectly) or accidentally disclosing personal data to someone who is not authorised to see it – for example, when helping individuals to check in and check out of hotels or to join a sightseeing tour

■ Carelessly repeating individual's credit card numbers when booking their tours – this includes calling them out in front of other members of the group or talking about them over the phone when they can be overheard

■ Gossiping about individuals, such as members of a tour group that they suspect are having a secret romance (or who are having a less than secret, but illicit, romance!)

■ Writing credit card numbers down in the travel itinerary list or on scraps of paper that can be seen by unauthorised individuals or lost

■ Losing personal data about individuals, such as guest travel lists containing their travel itinerary and their rooming information

■ Failing to dispose of personal data about individuals after their travel guide assignment is done, or disposing of it but failing to do so securely

Data protection law obligations for freelancers

Most freelancers process personal data on behalf of the organisations that hire them to provide their services. They should always make sure that they have a contract in writing with the organisation that hires them because this may reduce their liabilities under the data protection law.

Typically, the organisation will be liable under the data protection law for what the freelancers do (or don't do) too. This is the reason why organisations should require freelancers to sign a contract that includes an undertaking to comply with the data protection law. Some organisations also require the freelancer to indemnify the organisation against the monetary consequences to the organisation of the freelancer failing to comply with the data protection law.

In Singapore's case, the data intermediary need only comply with two obligations – the protection obligation and the retention limitation obligation – if they have a contract in writing (or evidenced in writing).

In any event, a freelancer that processes personal data on behalf of an organisation will have at least two obligations under the data protection law.

Obligation to dispose of personal data

The freelancer must dispose of the personal data (or anonymise it[1]) when it is no longer necessary for the freelancer to retain it for a business or legal purpose. Depending on the terms of their contract with the travel agency, a freelancer who is a tour guide might need to keep it for a few months in case of any disputes. Otherwise, the freelancer may only need to retain the personal data for a very short time after each separate tour engagement.

The point is that the tour guide should take care not to forget to dispose of personal data when they no longer need it. Retaining it exposes them to unnecessary risks, especially if the documents containing the personal data are stored unsecured at home. This is because they have to protect the personal data for as long as they retain it.

Obligation to protect personal data

The freelancer must protect the personal data that they collect for and on behalf of the organisation (if the freelancer is an insurance agent, for example) or the personal data that they receive from the organisation (if the freelancer is a tour guide, for example).

In one of my engagements, I was told about a case where a tour guide absent-mindedly left a clear folder of the entire list of his guests containing personal data and hotel-rooming information at a Starbucks, only for someone to call the agency to return it. Imagine what would have happened if that person called to complain to the regulator?

Use of personal data

When an organisation collects personal data from individuals they do so for specified purposes – in the case of a travel agency, for the purpose of providing travel services to them.

---

[1] Refer to chapter 28, "Anonymising personal data ... but is the individual really not identifiable?"

Freelancers should bear in mind that when the travel agency passes the personal data on to them they may use it only for the purpose that the travel agency specifies (which the travel agency must ensure is within the scope of the consent that the individual gave them). All of this is a long way of saying that freelancers are not permitted by the data protection law to use the personal data passed to them by a travel agency for any other purpose. Of course they are not permitted to use it for personal gain.

The bottom line for freelancers

Putting the above three things together, it is obvious that a freelancer should dispose of personal data as soon as they no longer need it for a business purpose. There is no upside in keeping it for a longer time because:

- they must protect it for as long as they retain it and
- they must not use it.

Did I waste my breath training the tour guides?

Here is what happened when I ended my session with the tour guides. One of them innocently came to me and asked:

> "You know, I enjoyed your session. I have a question. Can I reveal my clients' names to my friends so that my friends can claim free parking at the hotel where my clients are staying?"

What part of "you must protect personal data and not disclose it for any purpose except providing your tour guide services" did they not understand?

CHECKLIST OF GOOD PRACTICES

Organisations that hire freelancers should ensure that the freelancers comply with the data protection law when they process personal data on behalf of the organisation:

■ Make sure that there is a written contract with your organisation. This may reduce your liabilities under the data protection law.

■ Make sure that freelancers understand and carry out their obligations under the data protection law:

- ● Protect the personal data collected for and on behalf of your organisation.
- ● Do not use the personal data for any other secondary purposes, other than those where consent has been given.
- ● Dispose of the personal data (or anonymise it) when it is no longer necessary to retain it for a business or legal purpose.
- ● Securely dispose of or shred unwanted documents containing personal data.

🔒 67 Do you do regular email housekeeping?

I recall in the early 1980s when computer memory was very expensive, having 1 MB (one million bytes) of storage in the hard disk was a luxury. We had to be very stingy when we used computer memory. We had to constantly debate with ourselves which e-files to keep and which to delete.

This applied to email usage too. We had a strict quota of memory space allocated to us by the IT Department. Again, deciding which emails to keep and which to delete was tough as we had the tendency to treat almost every email as important. Data and email housekeeping was a conscientious effort in those days.

Today, the prices of computer memory have plummeted so much that we are no longer awed by gigabytes (10^9 bytes) of storage in tiny memory sticks or USB drives, or terabytes (10^{12} bytes) of storage in portable hard disks. Email systems like Gmail and Yahoo Mail provide allocated memory space in the order of gigabytes. Many users now assume that the storage space will not run out on them and are doing little or no housekeeping of their data files and emails.

Importance of emails to organisations

Today, emails have gone beyond their original use as a convenient and efficient mass communication tool. Organisations and employees use the email system as a platform for brainstorming, sharing ideas, evaluating proposals and even decision-making.

There is now a ton of valuable information embedded in emails and their attached files, comprising both company proprietary information as well as personal data and other confidential information of employees and customers. Such information in emails can be forwarded to individuals both within and outside the organisation easily, thus rendering emails a vulnerable source of information leakage. With little or no disciplined housekeeping of emails, there could be gigabytes of information residing in the personal email accounts of employees that have passed their retention periods. And what happens to such information when employees resign and leave the organisation?

What should organisations do?

Faced with these twin challenges of safeguarding against information leakage and managing data retention in email systems, what should organisations do?

Organisations should implement policies and processes to address at least the following:

- Have a strict data and email housekeeping regime. It should seek to ensure that employees make a conscientious effort to delete those e-files or emails that are no longer needed.

  Some organisations have reverted to the old practice of allocating a fixed quota of memory space to employees so that they have no choice but to do regular housekeeping.

  Other organisations have taken the more draconian approach of automatically deleting emails that are more than xx days old or email accounts to which the relevant employee has not logged in for more than yy days.

- Mandate important e-files and email attachments to be deposited in a central shared drive. This makes it is easier to manage the retention schedules of these e-documents.

  A central shared drive also ensures that the organisation has access to the e-documents of ex-employees.

  Some organisations do not allow file attachments in emails. Instead they allow hyperlinks only to the relevant e-documents in the shared drive. The consequence is that only employees can gain access to e-documents. Even if the emails are leaked, the unauthorised recipient cannot access the e-documents in the shared drive.

Final Word

Regular data and email housekeeping is everyone's responsibility. Organisations must constantly drum into their employees the need to do regular housekeeping and remind them of the risks of not doing so.

CHECKLIST OF GOOD PRACTICES

Organisations should be aware of the importance of emails and should adopt the following practices:

- Be aware that emails present a vulnerable source of information leakage if not properly managed.
- Understand that emails and their attachments, when retained by individual employees, have implications on the retention schedules of e-documents.
- Implement a strict data and email housekeeping regime for employees to delete e-files or emails conscientiously when they are no longer needed.
- Mandate that important e-files and email attachments are to be deposited in a central shared drive so that it is easier to manage their retention schedules.

🔒 68 Beware of your laptop or home computer

These days most people have at least one computer at home, either a laptop or a desktop computer. Sometimes more than one member of the family uses it to surf the Internet, to store their photos, to send emails to friends and relatives and to download and play games. Sometimes a member of the family uses it for work purposes too, to store documents related to their work and to send work emails, for example.

Many employees of organisations use their home computer for work purposes sometimes. Those who are mobile workers, such as real estate sales people, financial advisers, freelancers and individuals who work from home, almost always use a home computer for work purposes. If you use your home computer for work purposes you will have personal data and other confidential information in the work documents you store on it and in the work emails you send and receive from it. The data protection law requires organisations to use reasonable measures to protect personal data. This includes personal data on a home computer. Or to put it another way, do not think that there is no need to protect personal data because it is not on an office computer.

If you use your home computer only for personal or domestic purposes the data protection law likely does not apply to you. But protecting the information on your home computer is still a good idea. You want to minimise the risk of someone hacking into it and destroying information on your hard disk or stealing information and releasing it publicly.

You should consider the following checklist for your home computer. If the answer to any of the following questions is "no", you should take remedial actions immediately.

Five questions about your home computer

■ Are you the only individual who uses the home computer? (Hint: the answer is "yes" only if you never allow someone else to use your home computer, so for most people the answer is "no".)

■ Is your home computer password-protected?

■ Does your home computer have a firewall installed and is the firewall turned on?

■ Have you installed anti-virus software on your home computer and is it up to date?

■ Are the documents on your home computer protected and backed-up?

Using your home computer

In our security audits of real estate agents and financial advisers, for example, we often notice that they share the same computer with their children at least some of the time. Even if they do not allow the children to download or play games on their computer, there are always school projects and homework assignments where they need to use a computer.

The danger is that your children or other family members who use the same home computer as you do might accidentally leak personal data or confidential documents connected with your work. And malware might find its way into your computer when they browse the Internet, install new applications or read emails. Malware can cause a data breach.

Here are some tips to reduce the risk:

■ Create a separate account for each person who shares your home computer.

■ Separate your home-related documents and emails from your office work. It may make sense for you to create two separate accounts for yourself – one for work and the other for everything else.

■ As an added precautionary measure, you might want to separate your Google accounts[1].

Password-protecting your home computer

You should always protect your computer, including your home computer and particularly your laptop (because it is more likely to be lost), from unauthorised access.

This does not mean that you do not trust other family members. It simply means that password-protecting your computer is a good security practice. And it protects your data from other visitors, such as people who come to your home to provide various services, such as cleaning, air-conditioner servicing and general maintenance. Oh, and password protection should include a screensaver password for those times when you leave your computer unattended.

Password protection sounds very basic, right? Not true, based on our findings during security audits we have done for our clients.

Even if there is a password, guess what it is? You're right, it's either "123456" or "password". According to Splashdata, these two were the top passwords in both 2014 and 2015.[2] And that's what we have found during our security audits too. Plus we often find passwords written on yellow sticky notes and pasted to the computer monitor or under the keyboard.

You should protect your home computer, including your laptop, with a strong password – not just a password, but a *strong* password. So if you lose your laptop or if someone otherwise gets unauthorised access to your home computer they cannot get access to the personal data you have stored on it.

If you are a mobile worker, data on your computer might include personal data like transactions with clients and commissions. If you fail to take reasonable measures to protect it, you could be fined for failing to comply with the data protection law.

---

[1] You can find out online how to do so. See, for example, http://www.pcworld.com/article/2597432/three-easy-ways-to-separate-work-and-play-on-the-same-pc.html and, for Macs, http://www.cnet.com/how-to/how-to-set-up-multiple-user-accounts-on-os-x/

[2] For the full list, see https://www.teamsid.com/worst-passwords-2015/ or numerous other similar lists that you will find if you Google for "worst passwords".

In the US in April 2013 a property management firm was fined $15,000 after the theft of a company laptop containing the personal data of over 600 Massachusetts residents.[3] The reason for the fine? The user did not even have the basic password protection!

So if your home computer, including your laptop, is not already password-protected you should make remedying this a priority. You can easily find out online how to do it.[4]

Is a firewall installed and turned on?

A firewall is software or hardware that checks information coming from the Internet or a network. A firewall either blocks information from coming to your computer or allows it to pass through to your computer, depending on your firewall settings. (All computers have this as a standard installation, but check to make sure it has not been removed from your computer by someone who found it inconvenient.)

Firewall settings are intended to help prevent hackers or malicious software (such as worms) from gaining access to your computer through a network or the Internet. A firewall can also help stop your computer from sending malicious software to other computers. Make sure the firewall settings on your home computer are turned on and active. Again, it is easy to find information online about how to do this.[5]

Do note that a firewall isn't the same thing as an anti-virus program. To help protect your home computer, you need both a firewall and an anti-virus/anti-malware program – which is the next point.

Have you installed anti-virus software and is it up to date?

Anti-virus software is not expensive compared with the value of the information stored on most home computers. (Even if your photos have no monetary value, they are valuable to you, right? You would hate to lose them all.) And if you store work documents and emails on your home computer, they almost certainly have a monetary value from your perspective.

[3] http://www.realtor.org/articles/property-management-firm-pays-15000-fine-following-data-breach
[4] See, for example, http://windows.microsoft.com/en-us/windows/protect-computer-with-password#1TC=windows-7 and, for Macs, https://support.apple.com/en-us/HT202860
[5] See, for example, http://windows.microsoft.com/en-us/windows/turn-windows-firewall-on-off#turn-windows-firewall-on-off=windows-7 and, for Macs, https://support.apple.com/en-us/HT201642

Anti-virus software comes bundled with most new computers, but it expires. You should check the expiry date to find out if the anti-virus software on your home computer has expired. We do see individuals who are confident that they are protected by anti-virus software (because they see the icon in their toolbar), but they are wrong because the protection has expired.

If you find anti-virus software too expensive to buy, including to extend or renew anti-virus software that came bundled with your computer, there is anti-virus software you can download from the Internet for free.[6] (If you take this route, check to satisfy yourself that the free product is adequate for your needs.)

Ensure you scan your computer for viruses regularly. When was your computer last scanned? Do yourself a favour, do it now! And check to see if your anti-virus software has an option for a regular auto-scan schedule. If so, set the regular schedule right after you do a scan now.

Protecting your documents and backing them up

Protecting your documents is your last line of defence. Even your spreadsheets, presentations and PDF documents can be protected. You can easily find information online about how to protect them – it depends on the software you use and the type of document, but it is usually quite easy to do.[7]

Note: You will need to remember the passwords or you will not be able to gain access to the respective documents again!

And when you send password-protected files to your business contacts or clients, never send the password in the same email (or other medium for sending the document). The email can be forwarded to another person. They will immediately see that password – which defeats the purpose of having a password! Always take care to stop and think about what you are doing and what the recipient of your document might do – it is scary to know what some people do out of ignorance or inattention.

---

[6] See, for example, http://www.pcmag.com/article2/0,2817,2388652,00.asp and, for Macs, http://www.digitaltrends.com/computing/best-free-antivirus-software-for-mac/

[7] See, for example, http://www.digitaltrends.com/computing/password-protect-pdf/ about password-protecting PDF documents in various formats. If your budget is tight, you might consider password-protecting PDFs by uploading them https://www.pdfprotect.net.

Here is a tip about protecting images. We know that mobile workers, in particular, find it very convenient and efficient to take photos of identity cards, application forms and even contracts using their smartphone camera. You cannot protect images in the same way as you can protect documents, spreadsheets, presentations and PDFs. But what you can do is to:

- paste them into a Word or PowerPoint document and password-protect that document or
- paste them into a document and convert that document into a PDF document – not many people seem to know that as you save the document containing the image using the PDF format you can click on options to give you the ability to encrypt the file with a password.

Password protection is particularly important if you are sending and sharing documents that include personal data or other confidential information, especially in the cloud (for example, in Dropbox). If anyone hacks into your account, your documents should still be safe from harm if you have used strong protection.

Go ahead, try it. Make it a point to always protect documents that contain personal data or other confidential information! (Of course, you should always protect physical documents as well.) Others might ridicule you for being over-protective when sending documents with passwords. (Nothing ever goes wrong, right? Wrong. And you don't want to be the person who gets caught out.)

Clients might wonder why you are doing this. Here's your chance to build up trust with them by showing that you do carefully protect their personal data. And you might also share with them the importance of complying with the data protection law too.

Suffering a data breach may be a failure to comply with the data protection law that results in a fine or other consequences. You may also lose the trust of your clients.

A final word while we are on the subject of protecting documents in your home computer. Do not forget to back them up regularly too. Some individuals rely on storing a copy of their documents "in the cloud" using a commercially available cloud solution; others buy various types of portable storage devices. Some individuals do both.

CHECKLIST OF GOOD PRACTICES

Individuals should take the following precautionary measures when using their computers or laptops for storing and processing personal data and other confidential information:

- When you use your home computer for work purposes, do not allow your children to download or play games on it. This is to prevent accidental leakage of personal data or confidential documents connected with your work or the introduction of malware.
- Protect your home computer or your laptop from unauthorised access with a strong password.
- Ensure that a firewall is installed, turned on and is the latest version.
- Install anti-virus software and ensure it is up to date.
- Protect your documents, spreadsheets, presentations and PDF files with passwords if they contain personal data, and ensure you have back-ups.
- Embed images containing personal data into a Word document or PowerPoint presentation and save them with the built-in password.

69 Beware when connecting to public WiFi – don't trust the postman!

Do you sometimes or often use public WiFi to connect to the Internet?

Many of us do this to save on the limited data plan that we subscribe to through our telecommunications provider. So we will not hesitate to connect to WiFi networks in places where we can get free Internet access. Places where we sit to chat and work such as McDonald's and Starbucks and places that we visit such as shopping centres. And even in convention centre ballrooms and meeting rooms when checking our email is more diverting than paying attention to our purpose in being there.

And some of us simply seize any opportunity to connect to any open network just to get free online access.

Did you know?

Did you know that it is possible to access the personal data of every person (at a certain place) who is connected to a public WiFi at any particular time?

Here's how. Hackers go to a public place and create a fake – or maybe "unofficial" would be a better description – hotspot network. Other individuals at that place connect to the hotspot network so that they get free online access. Then the hacker intercepts their connections. By using certain tools, like a WiFi sniffer or analyser[1], the hacker spies on the data sent to and from the devices of individuals who connected to the hotspot network. In so doing, the hacker can collect user names, passwords, email addresses, hotels where someone is staying, etc.

[1] See https://en.wikipedia.org/wiki/Packet_analyzer

For example, an Android application called DroidSheep looks for and lists any unsecure log-ins to popular websites. While it doesn't capture the passwords to those sites, it can exploit a vulnerability that allows you to open the site using another person's current session, giving you full access to their account in the process.

Now imagine the types of places where a hacker might find particularly valuable data. For example, a café in a financial district where employees of financial institutions connect to the hacker's hotspot network. Or at crowded conferences where participants are keen to log in to any free WiFi offered by the conference organisers (just to catch up on unfinished work), which understandably becomes congested. It would be relatively easy to set up an alternative WiFi name such as "Conference X - 2" to fool individuals into connecting to the wireless network and then siphoning the Internet traffic to eavesdrop and steal personal data.

A "man-in-the-middle attack"

So, having intercepted the connections of an individual who logs in to a public WiFi network, what does the hacker do next?

Well, the problem with most WiFi networks is that when data is sent – for example, an email – it is not encrypted, allowing what is called a "man-in-the-middle attack". This is the vulnerability that the hacker exploits.

Here is the parallel in the physical world. Imagine you're mailing a letter. You put that letter in your mailbox and then the postman picks up the letter and delivers it to the addressee. A man-in-the-middle attack is when an unauthorised person, not employed by the post office, intercepts the letter before the mailman arrives to pick it up. This person could read the letter and even make changes to its contents before putting it back into the mailbox.

Important checklist

- Do you ensure that you do not log in to any open (unsecured) WiFi network?
- When you log in to WiFi, is it always a source you trust and is the connection encrypted?
- Do you refrain from processing personal data or other confidential information (such as banking transactions) on an open WiFi network?
- When you tether or use your own hotspot, is your device always password-protected?
- Do you ensure that you do not broadcast your full identity on your WiFi and Bluetooth connection?

If your answer to any of the above is "no", please read on to learn what you should be doing.

Refrain from logging into public WiFi

You should not connect to any open public WiFi network. Ensure your computer or mobile device is not set up to connect automatically to unknown WiFi networks. Alternatively, set it to ask you before connecting – so you're sure you know what you're connecting to when you connect.

Log on to trusted sources only and if possible use VPN

Your organisation's WiFi is one example of a trusted source or provider of Internet access. When logging into public WiFi services of reputable companies, for example at the airport, you will often be authenticated in terms of a passcode being sent to you via SMS or there could be a WiFi passcode you must first enter. Ensure that the connection is encrypted by looking for a "lock" icon beside the WiFi connection. If the connection is not encrypted, refrain from performing any sensitive transactions such as online banking.

If your organisation provides a VPN (virtual private network) service, ensure you use it. This is because VPN services always encrypt data sent through them. Anyone trying to steal your data will see only encrypted data that they can't decipher. If a VPN service is not available to you, you can use VPN services (such as Witopia.net and StrongVPN.com) which charge a fee for their use on a daily or annual subscription basis.

Refrain from processing personal data or other confidential on an open public WiFi network

If you really cannot avoid using an open public network you should ensure that the particular website you want to log on to is secure. In the address bar of your browser window, look for the "https" at the beginning of the web address (or, on some web browsers, a lock icon).

Another alternative is to use your smartphone as a hotspot or do the transactions on your mobile device, which brings us to the next important point.

When you tether or use your own hotspot, ensure it is password-protected

We have come across individuals who are unaware of the dangers of turning on their hotspots without any password protection. And often they don't know how to enable the security feature on their smartphone either. Anyone within the area of their hotspot can use their device to gain free Internet access.

You can find instructions online about hotspots and enabling the security features of your smartphone[2].

Here are some tips:

■ Do not use common passwords such as "password" or "123456".

---

[2] For example, see http://www.techradar.com/news/networking/wi-fi/how-to-set-up-an-iphone-personal-hotspot-964105 and, for Android phones, http://gizmowise.com/forum/topic/wifi-hotspot-tethering-password-and-security

- Turn off your mobile hotspot when it is not in use.
- Do not broadcast your full identity on your WiFi and Bluetooth connection because it may draw unnecessary attention to your presence and be spotted by hackers. Whether you are creating a WiFi hotspot or a Bluetooth hotspot, there is no need to name your device using your full name.

Bluejacking

If you are using a Bluetooth hotspot, be careful. If you have Bluetooth activated, anyone can hack your phone. It is called Bluejacking.

When you're not actively using Bluetooth, turn it off. Also ensure that it is not "discoverable".

CHECKLIST OF GOOD PRACTICES

Individuals should take the following precautionary measures when connecting their computers or mobile devices to WiFi networks:

- Avoid logging into public WiFi networks if you can help it.
- Log on to trusted sources only and if possible use VPN.
- Refrain from processing personal data or other confidential information on an open public WiFi network.
- When you tether or use your own hotspot, ensure it is password-protected.
- Be careful when using Bluetooth. When you're not actively using Bluetooth, turn it off. Also ensure that it is not "discoverable".

🔒 70 Digitising may be efficient, but don't forget the hardcopy

It almost goes without saying that office space is expensive, especially well-located office space in cities. It equally goes without saying that most organisations reduce their overhead expenses as much as possible by limiting the office space they acquire. It then follows that they find ways and means to maximise its use.

Besides carving out space for people, furniture and equipment, office planners have to create storage areas for paper documents and files. One means of reducing physical storage space is to digitise the paper documents and store them in computer servers or magnetic media that take up a fraction of the space.

Besides the saving in storage space, digitisation brings about a number of efficiencies and benefits. For example:

- the same e-document can be shared with a number of users concurrently at any time and at any place
- it is easier to index and retrieve e-documents
- an organisation can implement secure access controls to e-documents and
- e-documents do not deteriorate over time.

Far from paperless office environment

Organisations may dream of a paperless – or at least a "less-paper" – office environment. However, even with digitisation, many organisations still maintain lots of compactus filing systems and storage cabinets for paper documents. Why is this so?

In some instances and due to legal or statutory requirements, original paper documents bearing original authorised signatures, seals or company stamps must be maintained. It makes no difference that digital versions have been created. Examples of such documents include certificates and licences and, in some cases, even contracts and more informal documents such as memoranda of understanding.

What should organisations do?

Organisations are faced with having two systems to manage their valuable and confidential documents – one for paper documents and one for e-documents.

For e-documents, there are a number of proven document management systems in the market. Some of them even include an authentication function so that e-documents can be produced in court in lieu of producing an original (paper) document.

Managing paper documents is more challenging, particularly where an organisation adopts digitisation, as it involves a number of manual processes. Here are some tips:

■ **Version control**

The paper version of each document and any e-version of it must be consistent. This is obviously easy where the organisation creates the document electronically. Whenever there is a new version of a paper document, either created by the organisation (such as by having an individual complete a paper form) or received from a third-party, a digitised version should be created as soon as possible.

■ **Indexing and cataloguing**

Paper documents have to be indexed and catalogued in a file inventory so that the organisation knows at any time where these documents are kept.

The file inventory also helps the organisation to retrieve any document efficiently when needed. This is important in enabling an organisation to comply with the access and correction requirements of the data protection law. It is usually necessary in enabling it to comply with its document retention policy, as required by the data protection law.

■ **Access control**

The organisation must develop and implement policies to classify documents (such as "Confidential", "Public") and to control access to personal data and other confidential information on a "need to know" basis among its employees.

This too is an important element in enabling an organisation to comply with the data protection law.

■ **Retention and storage**

The paper documents have to be stored in a safe and secure place to enable an organisation to comply with requirements of the data protection law to protect personal data. The storage place should have appropriate environmental controls to prevent the deterioration of the paper.

If the paper documents are stored offsite, such as in a warehouse, the organisation should first satisfy itself that the warehouse operator is capable of storing the documents safely and securely. The organisation should include requirements in its contract with the warehouse operator about safety and security of storage and audit, particularly where documents contain sensitive personal data or highly confidential information. The organisation should ensure that the warehouse operator abides by these stringent requirements, including by exercising any inspection or audit rights under the contract.

The time period of storage should follow the organisation's document retention policy for each type of document.

■ **Disposal and destruction**

The paper documents that contain personal data have to be marked for secure disposal or destruction when the retention periods adopted for compliance with the data protection law are reached.

The retention schedule for each such document has to be recorded in the file inventory to ensure efficient tracking of the life of the document.

CHECKLIST OF GOOD PRACTICES

In managing paper documents, organisations should adopt the following practices:

- Version control – consistency between the versions of paper documents and e-documents.
- Indexing and cataloguing – file inventory to help in organising and storing the paper documents and in retrieving them when needed.
- Access control – policy to spell out who can have access to what document.
- Retention and storage – safe and secure place for storing paper documents, preferably with environmental controls. Same requirements apply to paper documents that are stored offsite at warehouses.
- Disposal and destruction – secure disposal or destruction of the paper documents when the retention periods are reached.

🔒 71 Don't be social engineered!

Today, the term "social engineering", as used in the context of information security, has taken on a very different meaning from its original conceptualisation. One definition is:

Social engineering is a non-technical method of intrusion used by computer hackers or cyber-criminals that relies heavily on human interaction and often involves tricking people into breaking normal security procedures.[1]

How do social engineers work?

Social engineers use a variety of methods to trick unsuspecting individuals into disclosing their personal data and other confidential information (such as their identity card number, password, bank account number or payment card number). They use social engineering to get the information necessary for them to be able to gain illegal access to confidential databases or to carry out unauthorised transactions.

In this chapter I will share from my personal encounters a few methods that are commonly used by social engineers. In all of them, the social engineer does something to impersonate, or to masquerade as, genuine organisations or individuals.

Data verification over the phone

I received a phone call from a sweet voice at the end of the line saying that she (it is usually a female "bait") was from ABC Bank and that the bank was doing a data verification exercise.

---

[1] Source: TechTarget

It sounded legitimate enough since I was a customer of ABC Bank. Her first question was to verify whether she was speaking to "<my name>". I confirmed positively as asking the question portrayed professionalism on her part.

Then she asked me for my bank account number. Immediately my defensive "antenna" stood on end. I threw the question back at her, "If you say you are from ABC Bank, how come you don't know my bank account number?"

There was a long pause at the end of the line as she did not expect this kind of response. Then her voice came back again, less confident now, saying, "Oh, never mind", and she quickly terminated the call.

Had I blurted out my bank account number to her, I could have risked my bank account being accessed illegally by a social engineer or any unscrupulous person.

Password verification online

I tried to log in to one of my web-based subscription accounts with my user ID and password. I was surprised to be greeted with this message:

Your account has been reset. You have to re-enter your password.

This had never happened to me before. And I did not request for my account to be reset.

Immediately I became suspicious and decided to check out the actual URL of the web portal. The URL turned out to be an unknown name with a ".com" behind it. Obviously someone had masqueraded as the real content service provider to acquire subscribers' passwords.

Had I not been alert enough I could have been deceived into giving away my password to a social engineer.

Official commercial company correspondence

I received an email from PayPal with the subject header "Unauthorised Use of Your PayPal". The email said:

We've completed investigation on your account and have discovered an instance of unauthorised account activity. Someone recently tried changing sensitive Credit Card information on your account. Thus we have Limited Your Account, Kindly Verify your information.

This was followed by a clickable button that said "Check Now".

This immediately aroused my suspicion as my PayPal account had been dormant for quite some time. I did a quick investigation and found out that although the sender's name said "PayPal", a simple "mouse over" revealed that the actual name was something else – nothing resembling PayPal at all. So I had the good sense not to click on the button that said "Check Now".

As I scrolled further down the email, I made an amazing discovery. There was a paragraph in small print instructing one on "How do I know that this is not a fake email?" The first line after this header read:

An email really coming from PayPal will address you by your first and last names or your business name.

But the reality of this was that the email did exactly the opposite of what it said it would do – it did not address me by first name and last name at all, just to "undisclosed recipients"! What a neat and clever trick to make the email look so authentic! Had I not been alert, I would have easily fallen prey to this social engineer's trick.

Official government correspondence

I received an email from the local tax authority. The sender's email address looked like it was a legitimate tax authority email address. The email said:

Attached is a report on your 2013 tax refund, we need you to go through the pdf attachment to view the tax refund report. Kindly advise your decision regarding this Tax Return Report for immediate processing. Thank you.

The email was signed off by the local tax authority, followed by the full address of this government organisation and its correct website address.

In summary, the email was from an official government organisation and everything checked out – the full name and address of the local tax authority, its website address and its email address were all correct. The content of the email looked perfectly legitimate.

Just as I was about to click the pdf attachment, a gnawing feeling inside me compelled me to read through the email again. I read through the email a second time, this time slowly and one word at a time. Then I made two startling discoveries: the subject header of the email read "Your 2013 Tax Return Report!!!" and the opening word in the email was "Hello".

I immediately smelled a rat as a genuine government tax authority would not have used three exclamation marks in the subject header and would not have addressed a taxpayer so casually with the salutation "Hello".

Sure enough this email turned out to be a hoax when I called the official hotline of the local tax authority to verify it.

Had I not been vigilant, in my haste to clear the numerous emails in my inbox I would have been "conned" into disclosing my personal and sensitive data to such a sophisticated social engineer.

Hijacking an email account

Early one morning, I received email messages from four of my friends on the same subject, "Cheap PCs Going Fast!". When I opened these emails, three out of four of my friends asked me whether I was satisfied with the purchase of my new PC. Puzzled, I scrolled down the email and, to my great surprise, discovered that I had sent out an email to an undisclosed number of my friends, recommending them to take advantage of the cheap PC offers! The email did not originate from me.

Obviously my email account had been "hijacked" and someone had masqueraded as me to send out emails to my friends from my address book.

I had read before that one's email account could be "hijacked" by someone else, who would then impersonate the genuine person and send out emails in that person's name. Such "hijackings" often occur when one accesses a public WiFi network or makes use of an unprotected public terminal.

The simple solution is to change the password of one's email account. I quickly changed my password and the scam was nipped in the bud. Fortunately, the scam email was on a tame subject like cheap PCs.

What if someone had masqueraded me and sent out scam emails that were unpleasant or provocative, which could put me in a bad light?

How to protect against social engineers?

As can be seen in the five personal encounters I had with social engineers, they primarily work on deception. They trick unsuspecting individuals into believing that the emails or phone calls they receive are from genuine organisations. Some of these emails seem so authentic, such as the PayPal and tax authority anecdotes, that they can easily fool many people.

Therefore, online users especially have to be vigilant at all times and be aware of what are some of the prevention and verification techniques they can use.

Here I offer some advice based on my personal experience:

■ Turn on the spam filter in your email account to filter out unwanted emails.

This is not a fool-proof method as certain unwanted emails may still get through while certain emails you want may be filtered out. But it is better to have a spam filter turned on than turned off. Today's smart filters can be trained to recognise new types of spam messages.

When an email looks dubious or suspicious (for example, there is no subject header or there are words spelt wrongly), don't open it or click on the attachment.

Social engineers often make use of click buttons or file attachments to download malware, spyware, Trojan horses or viruses into your computer system.

Verify the authenticity of the email sender by doing a simple "mouse over" if the sender is unfamiliar to you or seems suspicious.

■ Verify the authenticity of the website URL if you suspect something is amiss. You can do this by retrieving the URL information from Page Info > Security under the Tools tab (Mozilla Firefox), Properties under the Page tab (Internet Explorer), or View Source under the More Tools option (Google Chrome).

- Examine the writing style or tone of language, especially for emails from official government or known commercial company sources.

    You should be suspicious if the words used are too casual (for example, "Hello") or the text contains a number of grammatical errors.

- If you have no dealings with an organisation for a long time, you should be suspicious if, out of the blue, they ask you for verification of certain personal information.

- Do not disclose any personal data or other confidential information over the phone if the caller should already know it. (If you initiate the call, the organisation will of course need to verify your identity.)

- Be careful when you connect your computing device to a public WiFi network or if you use an unprotected public terminal.

    Be especially wary if you are asked to reset some settings on your device or email accounts. Change your passwords often, particularly after you have recently connected to a public WiFi network or used a public terminal.

Social engineers are always on the prowl for unsuspecting victims. The best defence against them is to stay alert and vigilant at all times. You should also arm yourself with knowledge and awareness of what to watch out for, especially when you are using email or online services. Protecting one's personal information is one's responsibility. Better to be safe than sorry.

CHECKLIST OF GOOD PRACTICES

Organisations and individuals should take the following precautionary measures to safeguard against becoming victims of "social engineers":

- Turn on the spam filter in your email account to filter out unwanted emails.
- Do not open an email or click on an attachment when it looks suspicious or dubious.
- Verify the authenticity of the email sender.
- Verify the authenticity of the URL on the web.
- Watch out for writing style or tone of language in emails – too casual, poor grammar.
- Be careful when an organisation asks you to verify certain personal information out of the blue.
- Do not disclose any personal data over the phone if the caller should already know of such information.
- Be careful when you connect your computing device to public WiFi networks or make use of unprotected public terminals; change your passwords often.

72 Think that you will never be a victim of cyber theft? Think again!

In May 2015, a journalist wrote in *The Straits Times* in Singapore that she was a victim of cyber thieves. They stole the ID and password of her Gmail account. They also grabbed her list of contacts and their email details.

How could this have happened to a veteran journalist who is pretty tech-savvy and has written dozens of IT-related articles? Simple: she was a victim of phishing. It can happen to anyone.

What is phishing?

Phishing is a type of cyber theft – a type of cyber attack. Wikipedia defines phishing as the illegal attempt to acquire sensitive information such as user names, passwords and credit card details (and sometimes, indirectly, money), often for malicious reasons, by masquerading as a trustworthy entity in an electronic communication.

A sub-set of phishing is spear phishing. In a phishing attack, individuals receive emails more or less indiscriminately. In a spear phishing attack, specific individuals (usually within the same organisation) are targeted in an effort to find a way into that organisation's IT system.

How phishing happened to the journalist

Here is how the journalist described what happened to her:

> *It happened so swiftly. I was browsing through my Gmail account on my iPad when I came across an e-mail supposedly from a dot.com*

entrepreneur I have known for 20 years. I opened the e-mail and it had a link to a document I was supposed to download from his Google Drive account. It was nothing extraordinary because Google Drive is a digital cabinet into which Gmail users put documents they want to share. Since I thought I knew the sender, I proceeded to download the document by keying in my Gmail ID and password. The same prompt appeared again, asking for my ID and password. Thinking I had made a mistake the first time, I typed my details again. And that was my mistake.

The second time round, the hacker had directed me to a new website from which he could grab my credentials and gain access to everything in my Gmail account.

It is scary to think that we can be fooled easily by the contents in an email. But many of us would react in exactly the same way as the journalist when we receive an email that is apparently from someone we know and their request is something that we expect to get from them.

Why organisations should be concerned about phishing

Organisations should be concerned about their employees falling victim to phishing. Intruders can enter the organisation's IT system through a phishing attack and steal confidential information, for example. They can also steal personal data.

The data protection law requires an organisation to implement reasonable measures to protect personal data.

So any theft of personal data – that is, a data breach – may mean that the organisation has failed to comply with the data protection law. The regulator might find that the organisation has not implemented reasonable measures to protect its back-end IT infrastructure, for example.

What organisations should do

Even if an organisation has the most advanced IT protection measures and systems in place, phishing can still succeed and do harm because of an action by an unwitting or negligent employee.

It is therefore important for an organisation to educate its employees about phishing. This includes ensuring employees are aware of phishing, are familiar with common phishing methods and have been trained to avoid falling prey to it.

Examples of phishing methods

The journalist's email was from someone she thought she knew, through an approach called social engineering. Social engineering is the art of manipulating people so they give up confidential information.

Here are some more everyday examples of emails and websites that can deceive almost anyone, especially in the right context or coming from someone you know.

- **Email from a bank**

  Banks generally say that they will never send an email concerning bank account details and ask you to log in to it or to do something in connection with it.

  So if you receive an email that is apparently from your bank, telling you, for example, that your account will be suspended or deactivated if you do not do something, you should never do it. The "something" is usually asking you to click on a link. If you do so, the phishing attack may succeed and the sender gains access to your IT system. Simply delete the email.

  If you are concerned that it might be genuine and that you should not ignore it, call your bank to check with them about whether they sent the email. Or, if you have online access to your bank account, go to the bank's website and log in to your account and check for any messages the bank may have sent to you securely.

- **Email from your organisation's IT administrator**

  If you get an email that is apparently from, say, your IT administrator (such as "You have exceeded the storage limit on your mailbox"), or even from your boss asking you to click a link to perform some action, you should be suspicious about it immediately. Call the sender and check whether the email is genuine. Never click on the link without checking.

- **Email alerts**

  Another common phishing method is an email that alerts you to something, such as the status of your account with an organisation or, an old favourite, the progress in delivery of a parcel to you. These very often look genuine and may appear to come from organisations with which you have a customer relationship.

You should never click on any link in them without checking that they are genuine. Resist the temptation to check on the progress of a parcel when you were not expecting to receive any parcel. Indeed, even if by chance you are expecting a parcel when you receive one of these emails you likely do not need to know the progress of it. You should not click on the link.

■ **Emails from someone you know**

I need not remind you that receiving an email that is apparently from someone you know is the approach to which the journalist fell victim.

Be immediately suspicious of a message such as "Click here for the information we discussed" or "The information you requested is attached". Yes, links are risks but some phishing attacks occur through opening an attachment to an email. So be suspicious immediately when you receive an email with an attachment.

Think about whether you were expecting to receive something from the apparent sender. If so, think about whether what the email says is what you'd expect them to say. In case of any doubt, call the apparent sender and check whether they sent the email.

Sober statistics

In its 2015 Data Breach Investigation Report[1], Verizon Communications Inc. found that more than two-thirds of the 290 electronic espionage cases it learned about in 2014 involved phishing. The bad news is that Verizon found that sending phishing emails to just 10 employees will get hackers inside corporate gates 90% of the time.

A Symantec Intelligence Report issued in February 2015[2] reported that the most common attachment in phishing is a .doc file. The .txt file type came in second. (So beware of clicking on email attachments.) The report said that hackers prefer to target organisations with between one and 250 employees. It said that finance, insurance and real estate are the top industries targeted in spear phishing attacks.

[1] http://www.verizonenterprise.com/resources/reports/rp_data-breach-investigation-report-2015-insider_en_xg.pdf#sthash.qtlsfxaB.dpuf
[2] http://www.symantec.com/content/en/us/enterprise/other_resources/b-intelligence-report-02-2015-en-us.pdf

Tips on how to prevent phishing

Here are some ways to inspect an email to see if it is likely to be genuine:

- **Tip #1**: Check to see the source of the email.

    Don't just read the header – look at the email address to determine the authenticity. Ensure that the email source is valid. For example, if an email is sent from Apple, check to see if the email address is really from Apple, e.g. yourcontact@apple.com.

- **Tip #2**: Beware if the email looks anything like spam email.

    For example, look at whether the email is poorly written, meaning that it has poor wording and grammar. Look at the greeting message. Be suspicious if it is a generic non-personalised greeting. Or if it is not the kind of email you would expect to receive from the apparent sender – where, for example, someone you know only in a social context appears to be sending you an email related to business with them or where someone you have not been in contact with for a long time suddenly sends you an email with an attachment or asks you to click on a link.

- **Tip #3**: If the email asks you to click on a URL link, check the source of the link.

    You can check the source of the link by hovering your mouse over the link. Its source will appear. It is not genuine if the website or domain name does not reflect the identity of the organisation or person apparently contacting you.

- **Tip #4**: Beware if there is an unexpected attachment to the email or if an attachment is a zipped file.

    As mentioned above, be wary if an attachment to an email seems to be out of context. Be careful about all attachments to emails, but be extremely careful if the attachment is a zipped file. Zipped files have genuine uses of course, but they are often used to install malicious code on your computer or mobile device.

- **Tip #5**: Except where you have no doubt that the email is genuine, you should always verify the identity or the source of the email. For example, you could contact the sender by phone.

    As a golden rule, DO NOT click on any download links or email attachments without first checking these 5 tips.

Prevention is better than cure

If you or any of the employees in your organisation get tricked by a phishing attack, the consequences can be pretty nasty, especially when it comes to personal data that you hold.

The root cause of many large data breaches can be traced to someone who fell victim to spear phishing.[3] This is because the spear phisher knows something about the targeted individual – for example, that they are in the organisation's IT Department and have "privileged access" to its IT system.

Phishers thrive on stealing credit card details, bank account numbers, passwords or financial related information. As the journalist put it: "When I found out, I felt no different than if I'd been told that someone had broken into my home, rifled through my correspondence and taken the names, addresses and telephone numbers of my family members, friends and work contacts. It sent a chill down my spine."

A call to action

Stop cyber thieves from breaking into your virtual home or office. Get your employees trained now. In addition to training them not to open email attachments and not to click on download links that they are not expecting, other precautions include the following:

- Always run the latest version of security software.
- Run regular full scans on computers and mobile devices and regularly back-up files.
- Use strong passwords and change them regularly.

[3] Refer to chapter 71, "Don't be social engineered!"

CHECKLIST OF GOOD PRACTICES

Organisations and individuals should adopt the following practices to prevent phishing:

- When inspecting an email and in doubt, check to see the source of the email.
- Beware if the email looks anything like spam email.
- If the email asks you to click on a URL link, check the source of the link first
- Beware if there is an unexpected attachment to the email or if the attachment is a zipped file.
- Verify the identity or the source of the email when in doubt. For example, you could contact the sender by phone.
- Do not click on any download links or email attachments.
- Ensure employees are trained in basic information security and that they comply with the relevant policies.

🔒 73 A-tearing we will go

Here is an easy exercise that is guaranteed to improve your left-right hand coordination and strengthen your wrist and finger muscles. It does not require any brain power and is therapeutically soothing after a hard day's work of burning up your brain cells and staring at the computer screen.

I'm not talking about massage. Rather, it is tearing papers, especially those that contain personal data and other confidential information you do not want others to see. Merely tearing papers can get you into trouble under the data protection law if the personal data printed on them is still partially readable.

Use paper shredders and secure document disposal services

In our work with our clients, one of the common sights we have observed in our onsite data protection audits is hand-torn papers in wastepaper baskets. When we ask employees why they do this, they invariably give one of the following answers:

- "We don't have a paper shredder."
- "The paper shredder is too far away – it is more convenient this way just for a few pieces of paper."

But do they realise that people can easily piece the document back together by retrieving the torn pieces from the wastepaper basket? If the individual who pieces back a document is not authorised to see the personal data the organisation will likely have failed to comply with the data protection law. If so, the organisation risks fines and other penalties imposed by the regulator.

At a minimum, organisations should:

- invest in paper shredders to destroy unwanted documents containing personal data and other confidential information or
- if they find it too time-consuming and tedious to do the shredding themselves, engage a commercial secure document disposal service to do it for them.

Engaging a secure document disposal service

A good – which is not necessarily the cheapest! – commercial secure document disposal service provider leaves a secure, locked bin with a one-way slot for dropping in unwanted documents at their client's premises. When the bin is full, the service provider carts the whole bin away and leaves a new empty one in its place. The service provider destroys the papers inside the bins at its secure disposal facility. Once that is completed, the service provider issues the client a certificate of destruction.

When selecting a service provider, make sure that the lid of the bin provided cannot be opened easily. It defeats the purpose of the secure disposal service if people can put their hands into the bin and retrieve pieces of paper with personal data or other confidential information on them.

In addition, before engaging the service provider, make sure that it will actually destroy the papers and will certify that it has done so. Make sure that the service provider is reputable and that it is reasonable for the organisation to rely on its certificate of destruction. Why? Because we have heard of instances where a service provider promises that it will securely dispose of documents but, in fact, sells as many sheets of paper as possible to ready buyers. The equation is simple. Money received by selling paper plus costs saved by not disposing of it securely equals more profit for the service provider. Oh, and be sure to keep a record of the steps the organisation takes to satisfy itself on these points. If there is ever a problem later, evidence of the organisation's "due diligence" on the service provider may be invaluable.

In-house shredding

If, due to cost or other issues, an organisation prefers to shred the unwanted papers in-house, here are three precautionary measures:

- Invest in a shredder with fine blades so that the resulting strips of paper cannot be easily pieced back together. Or invest in a "cross-cut" or other type of shredder where it is virtually impossible to piece back the document, particularly where documents contain sensitive personal data or highly confidential information.

- If employees are too busy to use the shredder, do not pile the unwanted papers next to the shredder.

   Where papers are piled next to the shredder, employees or other individuals walking past it can easily pick up a piece of paper from the pile and view the personal data or other confidential information on it.

- Beware of employees who are too busy to use the shredder and, perhaps knowing that they must not pile unwanted papers next to the shredder, dump them into the bin inside the shredder.

   These employees might genuinely think that they will come back and do the shredding later. But what if they forget or they do not have time to do it? Or maybe they have no intention of doing it later.

   In any event, the likely outcome is that the whole shredder bin is cleared by the office cleaner. Thus documents containing personal data or other confidential information will end up being taken away with other general rubbish. Such information is then at risk of being viewed by unauthorised individuals by chance.

A final word – a "shred all" policy is safer than going green

Some organisations have committed to going green. In their enthusiasm to save more trees, they use the reverse side of unwanted papers for photocopiers and printers. Some of these so-called recycled papers contain personal data or other confidential information. Of course, there is a high risk of it being viewed by employees who are not authorised to do so. In the worst instances, it may be viewed by individuals outside the organisation. In either case, the organisation may fail to comply with the data protection law.

When in doubt, it is always good practice to have a "shred all" policy – that is, an organisation should adopt a policy to shred all documents, other than materials that are intended for public consumption. Such a policy obviates the need to sieve out documents into a "to shred" pile and a "no need to shred" pile. It also minimises the risk of making a wrong decision on which pile to put the document in.

And there are at least a couple of things that an organisation can do to still maintain a "Go Green" objective.

Other than the cheapest models, most printers are capable of printing on both sides of a sheet of paper. So set the organisation's printers to print "duplex" or "two-sided" by default or train employees to choose this option as often as possible.

Many office printers are also capable of printing, say, "2-in-1" – that is, the output size is shrunk so that two pages of the document appear side-by-side on a sheet of paper. Combined with duplex printing, four pages are printed on one sheet of paper. Train staff to choose this option when they are printing drafts of documents or even some documents that are for internal use only.

CHECKLIST OF GOOD PRACTICES

Organisations should adopt the following practices in disposing of unwanted papers containing personal data:

- Have a "shred all" policy – invest in a good shredder or use a secure document disposal service.
- Do not place unshredded papers next to the shredder if the employee is too busy to shred.
- Do not recycle papers containing personal data or confidential information.
- Make sure that the bin provided by the shredding service provider has a tightly closed lid and one-way slot to prevent anyone from retrieving papers from the bin.
- Do due diligence on the service provider to make sure that they have actually shredded the unwanted papers.

🔒 74 Is that your name, address, phone number in the dump?

"Is that your name, address, phone number in the dump?" was the title of an article in *The Sunday Times* in Singapore in May 2015. The article discussed a data breach involving paper documents that had been discarded together with general office rubbish.

The data breach happened in the central business district. A reporter saw documents containing personal data in the rubbish from offices in high-rise commercial buildings. The documents were in a dumpster in a public laneway, visible to any individual walking down the lane. They were marked as "Confidential" or "Strictly Confidential" and belonged to various organisations, including a bank, a law firm and a real estate company.

The documents included photocopies of passports, résumés of various professionals and details of commissions paid to property agents as well as printouts of emails with addresses, names and telephone numbers. There were also documents of a law firm's business expansion plan, with personal details of lawyers it hoped to get on board, including their photographs, educational background and work history.

The incident involved organisations we trust with our personal data. Yet it happened. The irony is that these organisations – especially the bank and law firm – would have the strictest form of governance, risk management and compliance. The issue here is one of operational compliance. Their employees may not have been trained adequately to comply with the data protection law, or operational aspects of compliance may have been overlooked.

The possible root causes of the data breach

So how did the personal data end up in the dump? We can only speculate, of course. But we do know that the documents containing personal data and other confidential information were not shredded. Why not?

One likely answer is that the documents were simply thrown into wastepaper baskets in the office. Then the cleaners emptied them and the documents thus found their way to the dumpster. Any paper document containing personal data or other confidential information should always be securely destroyed, such as by shredding.

Another possibility is that there were paper shredders in the respective offices, but not all documents were shredded due to lack of time, laziness or pure inconvenience.

- Perhaps the shredder is not a heavy-duty unit, so only 20 sheets of paper can be shredded at once without jamming the machine. So busy employees don't have time to shred large documents.
- Perhaps employees had cleared out old files, but had to first remove sheets of paper from files or folders because the shredder is not a heavy-duty unit. That takes up time and effort.

Doing shredding during office time may also be disruptive because of the noise generated from the unit. So it is left until after hours and doesn't get done at all.

For all these reasons and more, when we do data protection audits for our clients, we often find lots of paper piled up by employees near the shredders, where someone else – presumably a more junior employee – is expected to do the shredding. And it is not their priority!

A few more factors to take into account

The recycling bin within an organisation's office is another potential source of data breaches. In wanting to "Go Green", many organisations advocate recycling.

Unfortunately, recycling paper is rarely a good idea for an organisation that has documents containing personal data and other confidential information.

Beware of discarded or imperfect photocopied documents that are "recycled" by being placed back into the copier tray where they are then forgotten. A newly copied document, which may not contain personal data or other confidential information, is then distributed along with the previous personal data or other confidential information on the other side.

This can cause double-trouble – two data breaches. First, the personal data or other confidential information on the back of the sheet of paper may be viewed by employees who are not authorised to see it. Second, they may throw the paper into the wastepaper basket because the side that they read does not contain personal data or other confidential information and it ends up in the dump.

Finally, organisations should ensure that when they are moving offices or sending documents to be digitised, appropriate security measures are put in place to ensure documents do not end up in the dump.

At the end of the day

A few, if not all, of the possible root causes and other factors listed above likely contributed to personal data being found in the dump where it could be easily accessible to anyone. According to the report:

> "Access to the rubbish bins was easy. One karung guni man [rag-and-bone man], who was seen sorting out the documents into neat piles, said he would sell them to recycling companies."

So organisations are exposed to failures to comply with the data protection law when this happens. If documents are not disposed of securely, the organisations have no control over where they finally end up or how the personal data and other confidential information in them could be used.

Organisations should consider having a "shred all" policy rather then limiting their shredding to documents that contain personal data or other confidential information. That way, they need not worry about employees having to decide which documents should be shredded. In any event, organisations should audit employees' compliance to their shredding requirements to gain assurance that it is carried out.

Otherwise, organisations should consider the benefits in productivity and compliance with the data protection law in engaging a commercial secure paper shredding service that provides a document destruction certificate as proof of destruction.

Some examples of data breaches involving paper documents

- A local government authority in the UK was fined £250,000[1] after employee records were found in a supermarket car park recycle bin. It had outsourced its digitising and had handed large volumes of confidential information to a service provider without performing sufficient checks on how securely the information would be kept and without even putting a contract in place.
- The regulator required a property management company to sign an undertaking[2] to comply with a data protection principle following the loss of 37 employees' details when a filing cabinet was sent to a recycling centre and crushed.
- A restaurant in Hong Kong photocopied a chef's identity card but made two copies due to a copier malfunction. It recycled the second copy by putting it back into the photocopier tray. Later, it photocopied a menu on the back of that second copy and used the menu to record customers' orders. The chef complained to the regulator[3], which then recommended that the restaurant formulate an internal policy on the handling of employees' personal data (especially identity card copies), and ensure that the relevant staff were trained.

---

[1] ICO press release "Council fined £250,000 after employee records found in supermarket car park recycle bin", 11 Sep 2002.
[2] ICO takes further enforcement action using all available tools, http://www.privacylaws.com/Publications/enews/UK-E-news/Dates/2012/8/ICO-takes-further-enforcement-action-using-all-available-tools/.
[3] https://www.pcpd.org.hk PCPD Case No.:2011C04

CHECKLIST OF GOOD PRACTICES

Organisations should adopt the following practices in disposing of unwanted papers containing personal data or other confidential information:

- Mark confidential documents, especially those containing personal data, as "Confidential".
- Train employees not to dispose of documents containing personal information into the rubbish bins.
- When shredding documents with personal information, ensure that they are shredded immediately, instead of piling them beside the shredder.
- When doing recycling, ensure no documents containing personal information are recycled or thrown into the bin.
- Adopt a "shred all" policy, especially if the organisation is in the business of processing personal data.
- Engage a secure paper shredding service to shred documents containing personal information.
- When moving office or sending personal information for digitising, ensure the proper security measures are taken to avoid data leakage or exposure.

75 Whatever happened to your unwanted computers and portable devices?

When organisations are done using paper documents and files containing personal data or other confidential information, they can tear them, shred them, burn them, archive them or store them in warehouses. But what about computers and portable devices containing personal data or other confidential information that are longer wanted or needed?

Here are some possibilities:

- Stack them in the server room, in the IT Department or in a storeroom. They can be used as spares or as standby equipment for temporary staff.
- Sell them to commercial companies that trade in used hardware.
- Donate them to charities for them to use or to give to the needy.
- Discard them by throwing them into the rubbish bins or e-waste disposal bins.
- Engage recycling companies to cart them away for recycling.

If not done carefully – including with compliance with the data protection law in mind – all of these actions may result in the organisation disclosing personal data and other confidential information to individuals who are not authorised to see it. They may also result in the organisation failing to comply with other requirements under the data protection law, depending on the circumstances.

Here we set out some things that organisations should at least do with unwanted computers and portable devices to guard against a data breach.

Securely delete personal data and other confidential information in computers

Whatever means are used to keep, transfer ownership of or discard unwanted computers and portable devices, organisations should make sure that no data, especially personal data and other confidential information, remains in their hard disks.

Erasing or deleting electronic files using computer software is not good enough. Images of these files still remain in the hard disks until they are overwritten by new data, but there is no guarantee that all copies of the old data are purged from the hard disks. Even reformatting the hard disk is not a fool-proof method.

A more reliable method of wiping out all data on the hard disk permanently is to degauss (demagnetise) it.

Another way is to physically destroy the hard disk by using an industrial shredder, by burning it, or by any other means to render it inoperable.

But before you do any of these things, make sure you have backed up any data you still need!

Securely delete personal data and other confidential information in portable devices

Organisations and individuals today own a number and variety of portable devices that may contain personal data and other confidential information. These include smartphones, USB drives, tablets and portable hard disks. What happens to them when they are no longer wanted or needed?

- Smartphones and tablets are typically kept as spares, traded in, given away or discarded.
- USB drives and portable hard disks are typically used as secondary or back-up storage. When they become faulty they are thrown away.

Again, organisations should make sure that there is no data, especially personal data and other confidential information, in the portable device when any of these things are done. And again, remember to back up the data first.

For smartphones, a factory reset on the device is a must. We have heard stories of individuals who traded in their smartphones without a thorough wipe-out of all the data in them. The new owners found bank account numbers and passwords still intact on the devices' built-in memory.

Because portable devices are small compared with computers, there is a tendency to just throw them into a rubbish bin without wiping out all the data stored in them.

We must not forget this step, otherwise the consequences could be severe if sensitive data were leaked. The methods used to erase data from portable hard disks and from USB drives are slightly different:

- Data stored in portable hard disks can be destroyed in the same way as for computer hard disks.
- Data stored in USB drives, which use flash memory technology, can be erased by reformatting the device. But to be absolutely sure that the data is wiped out permanently, you should physically destroy the USB drive.

Not the hardware, but the valuable data

Just as we take a lot of precautionary measures to safeguard our computers and portable devices when they are in active use, we should do likewise when these are no longer wanted and are to be disposed of or destroyed.

What we should be most concerned with is not the hardware itself, but the valuable data that is stored in the hardware.

CHECKLIST OF GOOD PRACTICES

Organisations and individuals should adopt the following practices:

- Before discarding unwanted computers and portable devices, remember to back up the data you need.
- Ensure that the data stored in unwanted computers and portable devices is permanently wiped out before the hardware is transferred to another owner or discarded.
- Check with vendors or experts on how best to destroy different types of computer hard disks and portable devices.

"

We shouldn't ask our customers to make a tradeoff between privacy and security. We need to offer them the best of both. Ultimately, protecting someone else's data protects all of us.

"

Tim Cook

"

Never say anything on the phone that you wouldn't want your mother to hear at your trial.

"

Sydney Biddle Barrows

SECTION G:

Disclosure of
Personal Data

76 Do agents and service providers get too much personal data?

A lot of our personal and sensitive information passes through the hands of agents, for example real estate agents, travel agents or employees of domestic maid agencies. In the course of providing services to their clients, especially when they act as go-betweens between clients and government departments, these agents are privy to personal and sensitive information contained in our national identification cards, passports, income tax assessments, bank statements, credit card information, and even our family members' and dependents' birth certificates and salary slips.

Why should agents and service providers be privy to so much personal data?

In Singapore, for example, all these personal data and other confidential information are required by certain government departments to assess the eligibility of potential buyers of public housing units, applicants for visas or potential employers of domestic maids. The agents are merely acting as "couriers" of such documentary proofs to the government departments that need them.

The agents claim that the "courier" service is part of the value-add they provide to their clients, so that the clients need not go personally to the government departments to deliver the documents. I have even heard horror stories of agents' value-added services that include obtaining their clients' single sign-on user ID and password (for signing in to e-government services) and retrieving their clients' personal data on their behalf. With this single sign-on user ID and password to all e-government services, what is to prevent an unscrupulous agent from accessing other personal data and confidential information of their clients from other government departments?

I often wonder why the agents need to have full view of all the personal and confidential documents that we submit to government departments through them. They do not process the information except to act as a "courier" between the client and the relevant departments. The agents really have no legitimate business or legal purpose to view such personal and sensitive information.

Changing current practice

Granted that clients would still expect the "courier" service to be provided by their agents, can we not change the current practice to limit the disclosure of our personal and sensitive information to the agents? We could put all our documents into a large envelope ourselves, seal the envelope and sign across the envelope flaps to prevent tampering, before we pass the envelope to the agent. The relevant government departments can provide a checklist of the documents to be submitted through the agents to ensure that we don't miss out anything.

Clients have to be educated and made aware that they should not readily hand over their user ID and password to their agents. They should approach someone who is more IT-savvy and trusted if they do not know how to use the online e-government services. Such trusted persons could be their family members or relatives.

CHECKLIST OF GOOD PRACTICES

As individuals, we should limit the exposure of our personal data and other confidential information to agents acting on our behalf by doing the following:

- Put all confidential documents in a sealed enveloped before passing them to the agent if they are merely acting as a "courier" between us and the relevant government department.
- Do not reveal to the agent our user ID and password for signing in to e-government services. If we cannot sign in ourselves, we should use someone who is more trusted, such as a family member or a relative.

🔒 77 Be warned – when it comes to dismissals, resignations and employee warnings

Here is a friendly warning if you work in the Human Resource Department of your organisation or if you have individuals reporting to you or working for you. The data protection law requires an organisation to protect the personal data of its employees. This applies to both disclosure to other employees of the organisation, which should be restricted to a "need to know" basis, and disclosure to third-party individuals and organisations.

So be careful how you treat personal data about your or your organisation's employees. Not surprisingly, lapses tend to be reported to the data protection regulator most often when it comes to resignations and performance warnings.

Limit circulation of warning emails

The supervisor of an executive member (X) of an academic department in a university sent X a warning letter when the supervisor was dissatisfied with X's work performance. The supervisor also acted as secretary of a committee at the university. The supervisor sent a copy of the warning email to all members of that committee. X complained to the regulator[1] on the basis that personal data about X was disclosed without X's consent.

The university explained to the regulator that it was necessary to send a copy of the warning email to all members of the committee

---

[1] Office of the Privacy Commissioner for Personal Data, HK, Case 2005C21 https://www.pcpd.org.hk/english/enforcement/case_notes/casenotes_2.php?id=2005C21&content_type=3&content_nature=&msg_id2=315

because one of its responsibilities was to advise the university on "deployment of human and other resources". Therefore, said the university, committee members needed a copy of the warning email so they could each "assess the deficiency found by the supervisor on X's work performance".

However, the regulator concluded that there was insufficient evidence to show that the committee members were empowered to review X's work performance. This was because X's supervisor "merely forwarded the warning email to the Committee members without requesting the recipients to render their advice and views on the Complainant's performance".

The regulator said that the university's disclosure of the warning email to the members of the Committee should have been on a "need to know" basis. Therefore, it found that the university had failed to comply with the data protection law.

The regulator required the university to "take steps to notify its staff who are empowered to give written warnings to staff members not to disclose the contents of the warnings to any third-party unless the disclosure was for the same purpose as or a purpose directly related to the purpose of collection, or the prescribed consent has been obtained from the data subject".

Do not include excessive information in employee resignation notices to third-parties

It is normal for organisations to send emails or faxes to customers to inform them of the resignation of an employee with whom they have been interacting. This might be done to let the customer know which employee will be dealing with them in the future. In addition, it is usually intended to prevent the ex-employee from soliciting business from the organisation's clients.

However, one organisation included not only the name of the employee but also the individual's identity card number in the notice. It did this without the individual's knowledge or consent. When they found out, they complained to the data protection regulator.[2]

---

[2] Office of the Privacy Commissioner for Personal Data, HK, Notes on Complaint & Enquiry Cases related to DPP3 – use of personal data.

The regulator found that the organisation failed to comply with the data protection law because it had not taken reasonable practicable steps to protect the individual's identity card number from accidental or unauthorised use. It issued a warning notice to the organisation and directed it to delete the identity card number from such messages.

The regulator said:

When an employee resigns, the use of his personal data for the purpose of notifying customers is regarded as being a use of the data for [a purpose directly related to employment]. However, the personal data used for such a purpose should be limited to those data which are sufficient to fulfil the purpose of notification. The disclosure of the employee's name and position in the company should be sufficient to identify the employee in the notification. Disclosing the employee's identity card number is unnecessary and may lead to possible misuse of that number for fraudulent or other improper purposes.

Remote monitoring of employees may be unlawful

An organisation installed a CCTV system. On two separate occasions, an employee received phone calls from their employer followed by written warnings about their performance although the employer was not on the premises. The employer had installed CCTV cameras in the office so as to monitor employees remotely.

The employee complained to the regulator[3] that the organisation was collecting personal data through the inappropriate use of the CCTV system that had been installed without first notifying employees about the reasons for installing it.

As is common, the organisation installed the CCTV system for security purposes. The organisation:

- acknowledged that it had not informed its employees in writing about the CCTV system being installed and the purposes for installing it
- said that the cameras were overt and that the recorder and screen showing views and recordings were in the office in full view of both staff and clients

---

[3] Data Protection Commissioner, Ireland, Case Study 9, https://www.dataprotection.ie/docs/Case-Studies-2011/1212.htm#9

- said that the system was installed during working hours in full view of the employees and that no query, question or complaint was received from either employees or clients
- noted that there was a sign stating that CCTV cameras were in operation, although the sign did not include the purposes for installing them, and
- argued, therefore, that its employees knew about the CCTV system.

The regulator said that:

> *any monitoring must be a proportionate response by an employer to the risk he or she faces taking into account the legitimate privacy and other interests of workers ... To meet transparency requirements, staff must be informed of the existence of the CCTV surveillance and also of the purposes for which personal data are to be processed by CCTV systems.*

The regulator directed the organisation to cease monitoring employees by remotely accessing the CCTV system or by any other means. The organisation confirmed that it would:

- remove the cameras in the office and
- cease any disciplinary actions on foot against the employee on the basis of the CCTV surveillance and ensure that the employee would not suffer as a result of any information seen on camera.

As a general rule, organisations may use CCTV to monitor employees if they do so transparently. For example, employees should be notified, including by a notification in the organisation's employee handbook.

Fulfil requests for documents by dismissed employees

In another case involving a university, an ex-employee made a data access request asking for documents relating to their dismissal. The university satisfied their request. The individual felt that the university had incorrectly edited out certain information in an extract of minutes of a meeting. The individual complained to the regulator.[4]

---

4 Office of the Privacy Commissioner for Personal Data, HK, Ref: 2004C19 https://www.pcpd.org.hk/english/ enforcement/case_notes/casenotes_2.php?id=2004C19&content_type=7&content_nature=&msg_id2=278

The regulator investigated the complaint. The university claimed that the information missing from the extract of minutes was not personal data. Instead, the university said it was information related to the review of the university's internal mechanism of handling the individual's complaint. The regulator disagreed.

Therefore the regulator found that "the complainant should have been entitled to a copy of the whole extract of minutes subject to the deletion of other individuals' personal data". It also required the university to review and revise its internal guidelines and procedures in relation to handling data access requests.

Guidelines for organisations

When processing personal information relating to employees, those with managerial duties or doing HR-related work should be aware of their obligations and principles relating to the data protection law. When it comes to warnings and resignations, ensure that no excessive personal information is collected or disclosed in relation to the HR purpose of employment.

Is it possible for the above scenarios to happen within your organisation? If so, review and revise your internal guidelines as they relate to employee warnings, dismissals and resignations, ensuring that all relevant staff are trained accordingly.

CHECKLIST OF GOOD PRACTICES

Organisations should adopt the following practices when handling the personal data of their employees:

- Limit circulation of warning emails to employees by ensuring that only the relevant supervisors are copied.
- When sending out notices to third-parties about employees who have resigned, ensure there is no excessive information such as identity card numbers.
- There needs to be transparency when using CCTV surveillance for the secondary purpose of employee monitoring.
- Adequately fulfil access requests from dismissed employees or those who have resigned. There is no exception.

🔒 78 Complaints about complaints – the problem with disclosing personal data

One of our clients manages a condominium and shared an interesting incident with us.

The occupiers of a unit – let's call them X – lodged a complaint against the occupiers of a unit above them – whom we'll call Y. To investigate it, the condo manager forwarded X's complaint to Y. The condo manager's intentions were good but the complaint included X's identity and unit number. So Y knew who made the complaint. This, of course, upset X. Not long afterwards, the condo manager received a letter from X's lawyer claiming that, by disclosing X's personal data to Y, the condo manager had failed to comply with the data protection law.

In your organisation, have you received a *complaint about a complaint* similar to the above incident? It can easily happen when employees are not trained to be conscious of the risks of disclosing personal data and to proceed with care. And where the organisation does not have clear policies and practices about disclosing personal data.

Under the data protection law, organisations must put reasonable security measures in place to protect personal data under their care. That includes not revealing the identity of a complainant without their consent. Employees handling complaints must be well trained about the organisation's policies and practices that are intended to protect personal data.

Disclosures such as that mentioned above are not uncommon and regulators around the world have taken action in response to complaints. Some examples follow.

Disclosure of bullying case against co-workers

In Australia, an employee complained to their employer about bullying by co-workers[1]. The complaint included a chronological list of all of the alleged bullying incidents.

The employee handling the complaint said that, as part of the complaints management process, a full copy of the complaint would have to be provided to each of the alleged bullies. The employee making the complaint consented to this initially, thinking that there was no other choice. But, later they changed their mind and withdrew their consent by email. This was because they were anxious about the information contained in the complaint, which had documented their private reactions to certain incidents.

Unfortunately, the complaint had already been disclosed to the alleged bullies, in accordance with the organisation's internal policy for investigating complaints.

The employee complained to the regulator that the organisation had failed to comply with the data protection law when it provided the full complaint documentation to each of the alleged bullies. The complaint was that the organisation had disclosed to each alleged bully the full list of bullying incidents, and the complainant's reaction to each incident, instead of each alleged bully knowing only what was relevant to themselves.

In responding to the complaint, the organisation argued that, even if it had received the withdrawal of consent prior to distribution, disclosing the complaint in full was a necessary part of the organisation's complaints investigation process. Further, the organisation said that it was "not reasonably possible" to edit the complaint documentation before distributing it.

However, the regulator ruled that:

- there was excessive disclosure of the complainant's personal data to the alleged bullies
- by being told that disclosing the complaint to the alleged bullies was part of the complaint investigation process the complainant was not given a real choice about what would happen with their personal data and

[1] Office of the Victorian Privacy Commissioner https://www.cpdp.vic.gov.au/images/content/pdf/privacy_case_notes/case_note_03_11.pdf

■ the organisation had not taken reasonable steps to protect the personal data.

The complaint was resolved by the organisation apologising to the complainant, agreeing to change its policies relating to bullying investigations, and paying compensation to the complainant.

Disclosure of student's personal data by school

A secondary school issued a letter headed "To Whom It May Concern" in connection with a complaint and that included personal data about a student, X. Without the knowledge or consent of X or of a parent of X, the school gave a copy of the letter to Y, a parent of another student.

The parent of X complained to the regulator about the unauthorised disclosure of X's personal data. In the investigation that followed, the school administrator said that when Y requested the letter, they did not know why Y wanted it. They were unaware that handing it over was a failure to comply with the data protection law.

Ultimately, the school resolved the issue amicably with X's parents. The school decided to redraft its data protection policy to ensure compliance with the data protection law – specifically, not to disclose the personal data in complaints to a third-party without consent from any individual who is a subject of the complaint.

CHECKLIST OF GOOD PRACTICES

When handling complaints about the disclosure of personal data of individuals without their consent, organisations should do the following:

■ Investigate what led to the complaint and what steps are required to address the matter, in line with organisational policy.

■ Inform the complainant that the personal information provided could be forwarded to relevant parties as part of the complaint and investigation process.

■ Provide the complainant with a real choice about what will happen with their personal information and an option to withdraw consent.

■ Take reasonable steps to protect the personal information.

■ Keep disclosure of personal information to a minimum – only what the relevant individuals "need to know" in order to respond to the complaint.

386   88 Privacy Breaches

79 Does your notice board contain personal data?

We often see notice boards at work, school and public places. The data protection law means that we must be careful about whether and how we disclose personal data about individuals.

Oh, and don't forget that notice boards are not necessarily physical. Our comments here apply to electronic notice boards too. Even when the electronic notice board is, say, a website that is accessible only to the students in a class or the students in a graduating year. And they also apply to notices published in newspapers and other media.

Beware when posting examination results

Whenever a school, university or other educational institution posts examination results, it discloses personal data of the students – namely, their results, as well as any personal data that identifies each student. Therefore, the organisation must comply with the data protection law.

Here are some data protection compliance tips for organisations that post examination results:

- **Give students options**

  The organisation might prefer to post examination results on a designated notice board, but should give candidates the option of getting their results mailed to them individually. From a student perspective, not everybody wants their results to be shared with others, especially if they perform badly in their exams.

- **Get student consent**

  When students sign up for your courses or examinations, it's a good opportunity to seek their consent to your organisation later publishing their results on a notice board. But make sure your organisation has a good system in place for tracking which students have consented, which have not consented and which, having consented, later withdraw their consent.

■ **Build in security measures**

As a good practice, when your organisation posts examination results on a notice board (with the consent of students) it should build in reasonable security measures. For example, it should not reveal students' full identity card or student numbers. To distinguish between students with the same or similar names, use the last four digits only or use a graduation class reference.

■ **Consider anonymising published examination results**

Students usually like to be able to compare their results with the results of their friends. And of their enemies. Of course, they can only compare if names are published on the notice board.

Some organisations may prefer to avoid the need for getting consent to publish names and the need to keep track of consents given, not given, or given and withdrawn. Therefore they issue each student with a confidential examination number or reference, instructing students to keep their individual number confidential.

Students find out their own examination results by looking for their confidential number in the list of results. They can compare their results with the results of their friends only if they have disclosed their confidential numbers with each other.

Posting a complaint letter on the office's notice board

An employee complained in writing about their supervisor who had set duty rosters. The person responsible for resolving the complaint gave the supervisor a copy of the complaint so they could respond to it in person. The supervisor posted the complaint and a memo setting out the findings from resolving the complaint on the notice board inside the staff rest room. The employee complained to the regulator[1] about disclosure of their personal data.

---

[1] Office of the Privacy Commissioner for Personal Data, HK, Case No.: 2002C05 `https://www.pcpd.org.hk/english/enforcement/case_notes/casenotes_2.php?id=2002C05&content_type=3&content_nature=&msg_id2=162

This was an obvious breach of the data protection law. The regulator found that the supervisor ought to have known that the information was to be used for investigation purposes only. It concluded that even if the employee had given consent for disclosure of personal data to a relevant individual (namely, the supervisor), it was unlikely they would have given consent to the public display of the complaint.

Management company posting a resident's personal data

A resident of a building was involved in two pending litigations, namely, a Small Claim filed by the building's management company and a Lands Tribunal claim filed against the incorporated owner of the building.

The management company for the building called for an owners' meeting to discuss the pending litigations. It mailed the resident a letter inviting her to attend the meeting. In addition, it posted the letter to the resident on the tenants' notice board, which was in a public area of the building. This upset the resident, who then complained to the regulator[2] about her name and address being disclosed publicly by the management company.

The regulator concluded that the purpose for collecting the resident's personal data was for management of the building. However, the public display of the letter inviting attendance at the owners' meeting was unnecessary, as the letter had already been mailed to the resident. Therefore, there was an unauthorised disclosure of the resident's personal data.

[2] Office of the Privacy Commissioner for Personal Data, HK, Case No.:2006A03 https://www.pcpd.org.hk/english/enforcement/case_notes/casenotes_2.php?id=2006A03&content_type=3&content_nature=&msg_id2=254

CHECKLIST OF GOOD PRACTICES

Organisations posting notices on public notice boards with disclosure of personal data of individuals should adhere to the following:

- If you intend to post personal data about individuals on a public notice board (or even as a notice on a website), you must get consent from the relevant individuals.
- Your purpose for posting personal data on a public notice board must be consistent with the purpose for which you collected the personal data.
- Consider the sensitivity of the contents of any notice posted on a public notice board. If the notice relates to a complaint or is potentially embarrassing to the relevant individual, send a private letter or an email instead.
- Do not assume that individuals will not mind their personal data being posted publicly – in your position you may not mind, but from their perspective it may be harmful.

🔒 **80** CCTV footage – to show or not to show... and to warn?

Just take a stroll along the street and wander into any office or shop, and what is one of the most common things you see? If your answer is "closed circuit television (CCTV) cameras", you are absolutely right.

Coming in all shapes and sizes and designs, CCTV cameras have become indispensable technological tools for security and surveillance purposes. But CCTV cameras are non-discriminatory: they capture every inanimate object and every living thing within their video capture zones.

When images of human faces are captured at the right angles, unique individuals can be identified visually and, more alarmingly, by face recognition software. That is why a number of jurisdictions with data protection laws treat CCTV footage with human beings in it as personal data or personally identifiable information. This means that CCTV footage should be protected the same way as any other personal data and individuals have a right to request access to footage of themselves.

Organisations cannot deny individuals' right of access to CCTV footage

Under data protection laws in most of the world, once organisations have personal data in their possession or under their control, individuals have a right to access it. Therefore, organisations cannot deny the right of individuals to access the CCTV footage containing their image.

While satisfying the legal obligation to provide access to such CCTV footage is one thing, the practical difficulties in making such footage available is another thing. This is because when the organisation extracts the relevant segment of the footage for an individual to view, the data protection law requires it to make sure that no images of other individuals are disclosed. It must, for example, mask out at least the faces of other individuals in the same footage. But this is easier said than done. Not all CCTV equipment has the capability to do so, especially legacy systems using older technology. Even with newer CCTV equipment, not all organisations have the in-house expertise to do the masking. Hiring a vendor to do it can be prohibitively expensive. And, sometimes, masking the personal data of another person may defeat the purpose for which individuals want access to their personal data. For example, a parent whose child was pushed to the ground at the school playground and sustained injuries as a result would want to find out the identity of the person who did it.

Figuring out a practical solution

Some organisations have come up with a compromise with individual requesters by working around the practical problems associated with disclosing personal data of other individuals in CCTV footages.

First, the organisation needs to find out from the individuals why they want access to the CCTV footage. This is also one way to weed out frivolous requests. Then the organisation can work with the individual to figure out a practical solution that meets the individual's needs and enables the organisation to comply with the data protection law.

For example, we have clients in the property and facility management business who shared with us the practical solutions they have developed. Some of them have told us that most requests for access to CCTV footage come from owners of cars which have been scratched or dented when parked at the premises' car park. These types of incidents involve an investigation by the property or facility manager. For the purposes of the investigation, the property or facility manager views the CCTV footage and reports back to the car owner the status of the investigation and any action taken against the culprit. A similar approach may be used to investigate stolen property or house break-ins.

Consent required for CCTV surveillance

Ordinarily, an organisation is not permitted by the data protection law to collect personal data about individuals without their consent. An organisation should display a sign warning of the presence of CCTV cameras and their purpose before an individual steps into their range. For example, such a sign might be displayed at the entrance to a building or outside a room where CCTV cameras are installed. If so, and the individuals step into the range of the CCTV camera, they implicitly consent to the organisation collecting their personal data, their image, in the CCTV footage.

However, if the organisation fails to display such a warning sign, the individuals whose images are captured by the CCTV camera can challenge the organisation for failing to comply with the consent requirement of the data protection law. Worse, if the individuals demand access to CCTV footage of their images and obtain them, they can show evidence that the organisation collected their personal data without consent (whether implicit or not).

CHECKLIST OF GOOD PRACTICES

Organisations should adopt the following measures and procedures when handling CCTV footage:

- Display signs at prominent locations to inform visitors that CCTV surveillance is being used.
- When a request to access CCTV footage is received,
  - first determine the purpose of the request to weed out frivolous requesters
  - then mask out the faces of other identifiable individuals
  - view the CCTV footage on the requester's behalf if masking is not possible, especially in an investigation.

🔒 81 Don't disclose employees' personal data without consent, even with good intent

Imagine you are an employee of a large organisation, and out of the blue you receive a personally addressed email from a charity inviting you to participate in a charity run. How would you feel?

If you are in a good mood and think that this is a good cause to support, you may sign up for the event. But if you are conscious of data privacy and vigilant about protecting your personal data, you would want to know how the charity got hold of your name and email address. So you call the charity and learn that someone from your organisation's Human Resource (HR) Department forwarded all employees' names and email addresses to the charity.

Fuming mad, you confront the HR Department. You complain to them about disclosing the personal data of employees without their consent. They explain in a calm voice that the charity approached them for the list of names and email addresses, and they just forwarded the list to them with good intention, without realising the consequences of what they were doing. After all, the organisation has been donating money to the charity for years and has sponsored events which many employees have participated in. So this is merely doing what the organisation has always been doing.

Inadvertently disclosing employees' personal information without their consent

This illustrates the need to seek employees' consent before disclosing their personal data to any third-party. An organisation fails to comply with the data protection law if it discloses employees' personal data to any third-party individual or organisation without their consent, even if the intentions are good. An organisation generally has implicit consent, if not expressed consent, to use and disclose the personal data of its employees for the purpose of managing their employment relationship. But the disclosure of personal data in the example above would not ordinarily be something that falls within the scope of managing an employment relationship.

There could be other instances where, with good intent, an individual discloses an employee's personal data to third-parties without the employee's consent. For example, where another organisation shortlists one of your ex-colleagues for a job interview, the hiring manager might want to find out more about this ex-colleague's job performance and character. The hiring manager approaches you through a mutual friend and wants to find out more from you about the ex-colleague. You disclose to the hiring manager that your ex-colleague is very aggressive in his sales tactics and recently won the bid for a multi-million-dollar Middle East project, thinking that such information would boost the chances of your ex-colleague's selection by the hiring manager. But, unknown to you, the hiring manager is still nursing his wounds from losing out in the bid for the Middle East project to your ex-colleague. Now the hiring manager knows who the person is behind the winning bid. Naturally your ex-colleague misses out on the job opportunity. He is not even called up for the job interview.

These scenarios show that it is so easy to cross the line on how and when to disclose the personal data of employees to third-parties, even with good intent. When in doubt, it is always good to check with the employees concerned whether they agree to have their personal data disclosed to third-parties.

CHECKLIST OF GOOD PRACTICES

In handling employees' personal information, organisations should:

- be careful not to disclose employees' information to third-parties without their consent, even with good intent, and
- check with the employees first what personal information they are willing to share with third-parties that are outside the scope of managing employment.

🔒 82 Landlords beware! You too can get into trouble

If you own any properties – commercial or residential – and earn income from them, the data protection law usually applies to you. It doesn't matter if you do not feel that you are a "business organisation". It doesn't matter either whether this is your only source of income or simply one of two or more sources of income.

As a landlord you need personal data about your tenants to make a decision whether or not to rent the property to them and to enter into a lease with them. There may be regulatory requirements for you to hold copies of their documents confirming their identity and their residency status. You may have a justifiable purpose for collecting and using confidential and even sensitive information about their background and profile.

The data protection law governs the way you collect, use or disclose all such personal data. If you fail to comply with it, the regulator may take enforcement action against you.

Case study of a tenancy dispute

A landlord and tenant got into a dispute over rent payments. The landlord's solicitor issued a demand letter to the tenant. But the demand letter was also copied to the tenant's employer, thereby disclosing the fact of the dispute and the amount of the rent in arrears.

The tenant complained to the regulator[1] on the basis that personal data relating to the tenancy dispute is considered to be collected solely

---

[1] Office of the Privacy Commissioner for Personal Data, HK, Ref: 2004C19https://www.pcpd.org.hk/english/enforcement/case_notes/casenotes_2.php?id=2003C04&content_type=3&content_nature=&msg_id2=199

for the purpose of dealing with or resolving the dispute between the tenant and the landlord. Therefore, argued the tenant, it should be limited to the two parties. There was no reason why the tenant's employer should be involved or even informed about the matter.

The landlord failed to justify to the regulator why it was necessary to write to the employer about the dispute. The regulator accepted that a landlord might wish to put pressure on a tenant to satisfy a demand for unpaid rent but found that such a use of the tenant's personal data was not within the original collection purpose. In fact, the regulator found that the landlord disclosed the tenant's personal information for a purpose that was different from the purpose for which it was collected. The regulator required the landlord to cease its practice of informing tenants' employers about rental disputes.

Lesson learned

As a landlord you have personal data about your tenants that you collect and may use as part of performing your tenancy agreement. That does not mean you have the right to use or disclose it for other purposes, such as complaining to the tenants' employer if there is a dispute.

(Of course, sometimes an employer rents a property and an employee occupies it. In that case, and depending on the circumstances, a landlord may be permitted by the data protection law to provide the employer with details of any dispute with the employee who is occupying the property.)

Remember, tenants – like any individuals covered by the data protection law – have the right to ask you how you have used or will be using or disclosing their personal data collected by you as a landlord.

Tips for landlords

If you are considering using or disclosing personal data about your tenant, you must first consider whether the purpose of doing so is reasonably necessary in order for you or the tenant to perform your respective obligations under the tenancy agreement.

Err on the conservative side and seek the tenant's consent to use or disclose their personal data if a purpose is not clearly reasonably necessary for the performance of the tenancy agreement – even if the use or disclosure is with good intent.

Here is a laundry list:

■ Specific circumstances may vary, but it is usually fine to disclose your tenant's contact details so that maintenance and repair works can be carried out – but check with the tenant about how they prefer to be contacted (such as by mobile phone, email, office phone).

■ Do not pass your tenant's contact details (or any other personal data about them) to anyone such as your insurance agent or a multi-level marketer.

■ If you are unlucky enough to get a demanding or unreasonable tenant, do not disclose personal data about them, including on social media such as Facebook – remember that video clips, photos and digital gossip can all disclose personal data.

Protecting and retaining personal data

Landlords should be extremely careful when storing personal data about tenants. It makes no difference whether the personal data is electronic or is in physical documents.

The data protection law requires you to take reasonable and practical measures to protect any personal data in your possession or under your control. And that includes ensuring any folder containing your tenant's personal data is not lying around at home so that it is easily exposed to your children or to friends or relatives visiting your home.

Once it is no longer necessary for you to retain personal data about your tenants for business or legal reasons, you should securely shred physical documents or securely delete electronic records containing their personal data.

CHECKLIST OF GOOD PRACTICES

Individuals who are landlords renting out properties to tenants should handle the personal data of the tenants with care by adopting the following practices:

- Ensure that personal data collected for the purpose of renting a property is used or disclosed only for that purpose.
- Get consent from tenants before disclosing their personal data outside the context of the tenancy agreement.
- Ensure that the personal data and other confidential information about the tenants are securely kept or stored.
- Securely destroy or delete the tenants' personal data when there is no business or legal reason to keep it.

🔒 **83** People know more about you than you realise

Have you ever Googled your own name? If you have, like what I have done, you would have made some interesting and surprising discoveries. For myself, Google returned about 117,000 results. Fewer than 100 of the results I reviewed refer directly to me. The obvious ones include the links to my personal profiles in LinkedIn and Facebook, which I created when I set up the accounts. Also obvious are the links to universities where I studied, organisations where I worked, and professional societies that I joined.

To my pleasant surprise, I also discovered that some of my past contributions in the course of my professional career have taken on a life of their own. For example:

■ Articles I published in professional journals have been referred to by a number of other professional organisations and translated into a few languages.

■ Speeches I delivered and presentations I made at international conferences and seminars have been quoted by other professionals.

■ Photos of me taken at public events have been posted on organisations' websites and printed in foreign newspapers.

What tickled me is a link to a list of "missing" graduates that an alumni association wants to contact. I am one of the "lost sheep".

To my greater surprise, I found out that there is more than one person with exactly the same name as me among the search results, even though my surname is relatively uncommon. I know with 100% certainty that these do not relate to me at all. But would other people who do a Google search of my name know this or might they form the wrong impression or opinion of me?

Examples of such results include:

- Tweets (both pleasant and unpleasant) on Twitter – I don't even have a Twitter account
- Postings on social media platforms such as Instagram, Foursquare, Pinterest, Naymz – I don't have accounts with any of them
- Comments on other people's blogs, such as protests at the G20 Summit in Australia in 2014, and whether or not it is safe to use non-stick pans

And a range of personas which I am not, such as:

- A business development director at an engineering and construction company
- An academic researcher
- A current undergraduate at the National University of Singapore
- A furniture designer

You are more "exposed" than you realise

Why am I highlighting all these examples of what I found? To bring greater awareness to readers that a lot of personal data is publicly available or is made publicly available unbeknown to us. In other words, people (total strangers included) can find out more about us than we realise.

With today's powerful search engines and data analytics tools, it is fairly easy for anyone to build up the profile of someone else simply by associating pieces of information together (whether rightly or wrongly) using the person's name as a keyword.

The lesson is that individuals should not make public, in even a limited way, personal data about themselves that they do not want too many people to know. They could do so by using the "private" setting on Facebook, for example, or refrain from posting on social media altogether.

Take care when using social media – think before you post

Today, many prospective employers as well as recruiters use social media to gather information about job applicants. They look at what they do within their professional spheres. But they also look at what they do outside working hours.

It is of course very easy to post comments or personal opinions on social media platforms such as Facebook. Individuals have a tendency to post first, then think later. Little do they realise that their rantings and ravings online – or their descriptions of wild party behaviour and irresponsible pranks – may backfire on them when they become job-seekers later.

Prospective employers and recruiters might take these personal comments, opinions and behaviours into consideration when shortlisting candidates for the jobs at hand, even when they are well in the past and no longer at all relevant.

However, responsible prospective employers and recruiters should be careful not to piece together information about two or more individuals with the same name and perhaps other shared characteristics and come to the wrong conclusion. They should check with other sources as far as is practicable. For example, based on my LinkedIn profile, I could not possibly be an undergraduate currently; my LinkedIn photos and my namesake's Instagram photos don't match.

So, individuals beware if you don't want to be an open book online. Think before you post. Refrain now or regret later.

CHECKLIST OF GOOD PRACTICES

- As individuals:
  - we should not post too much personal information about ourselves online or on social media if we don't want other people to know too much about us, and
  - when sharing our personal information with people we know, we should use the "private" setting on Facebook, for example.
- As organisations, prospective employers and recruiters should be careful not to piece together information about two or more individuals with the same name and come to the wrong conclusion.

🔒 84 Take requests for personal data seriously – or else

All data protection laws grant individuals the right to access and correct their personal data in the possession or under the control of organisations. The time within which the organisation must respond to any such request varies from place to place, though it is typically now within the range of 20 to 40 days and set to reduce from 40 days to 30 days in Europe by 2018.

Will organisations really get into trouble if they fail to meet the regulatory deadlines to respond to or fulfil an individual's request for personal information? The short answer is "yes, definitely". And the data protection laws often provide significant penalties for such failures.

Here are a few examples.

Unacceptable delay by O2 in processing an access request

O2 is a telecommunications provider. An O2 customer asked for a copy of call records in respect of a mobile phone number from November 1999 to the date of the access request, which was in 2012. Under the relevant data protection law an organisation must respond to an access request by providing the requested personal data to the individual within 40 days of receiving the request. However, O2 took two months to reply to the request. The customer complained to the regulator.[1]

The regulator's investigations revealed that the delay was caused by the following:

[1] Data Protection Commissioner, Ireland, Case Study 2. https://www.dataprotection.ie/docs/Case-Studies-2012/1354.htm#2

- The telephone number used by O2 when conducting its initial search of its database contained an incorrect digit.
- More than two months after receiving the request, O2 requested a fee of €6.35 and did not commence processing the request until it received the fee.
- O2 admitted that, due to technical limitations, all such requests made to O2 could take up to ten weeks to process.

Therefore, even if the retrieval process had commenced as soon as the access request was received, the 40-day statutory timeframe would not likely have been met by O2, resulting in a failure by O2 to comply with the regulatory requirement.

The regulator required O2 to implement measures necessary for it to respond to access requests within the statutory timeframe.

Failure to respond to an access request

An individual made a request to a contracted service provider (CSP) for access to personal data in its possession. The CSP responded to the request after 24 days, explaining that it was seeking legal advice. When the complainant followed up with the CSP, 57 days after the initial request, the CSP said it was waiting for final legal advice and would respond after receiving it. The complainant lost patience when the request was not fulfilled 112 days after the initial request and filed a complaint with the regulator.[2]

The regulator expressed concern about the length of time taken to respond to the request. It questioned whether "obtaining legal advice" was a sufficient reason for delay. It found no reason to decline the request and issued a notice to the CSP requiring them to satisfy it by sending relevant personal data to the complainant.

Not taking a data access request seriously

An ex-employee made a data access request to their former organisation for a copy of their personal data relating to their employment. When they did not get a response after several months, they contacted the organisation, which said that the requested data was ready for dispatch.

---

[2] Office of the Victorian Privacy Commission, Australia: https://www.cpdp.vic.gov.au/images/content/pdf/privacy_case_notes/case_note_01_11.pdf

However, they were later informed that the requested data was already destroyed. The ex-employee complained to the regulator.[3]

When the regulator investigated the complaint, the organisation suddenly claimed to have discovered the requested personal data. At different times it gave varying reasons to justify its failure to comply with the access request.

While it might have taken more prescriptive action, the regulator formally warned the organisation and reminded it to comply with the relevant requirements of the data protection law when handling data access requests in future.

Excessive fee imposed for compliance with data access request

A woman had a colonoscopy at a private hospital. She complained about the presence of male non-medical staff in the operating room during the colonoscopy. Dissatisfied with the hospital's reply, the woman submitted a data access request to the hospital. She sought copies of "all data, including any recording, and including medical notes, concerning [her] consultation with Dr [X], colonoscopy and subsequent complaint".

The hospital gave the woman a copy of nine pages of her medical records and charged her a total fee of HK$3,250. She complained to the regulator[4] on the basis that the fee was excessive.

The regulator concluded that an organisation is allowed to charge only the costs that are "directly related to and necessary for" complying with a data access request. It said that any fee that exceeds the costs of compliance would be considered as excessive.[5] Because the hospital did not give a breakdown of the costs, the regulator in this case said that the hospital should have a proper indexing system for patients' medical records, and would not require an extensive search, resulting in unnecessary costs and time.

(Note: For data protection laws such as those in Singapore and Hong Kong that do not state a maximum fee and which recommend

---

[3] Office of the Privacy Commissioner for Personal Data, HK, Case No.: 2006C13 https://www.pcpd.org.hk/english/enforcement/case_notes/casenotes_2.php?id=2006C13&content_type=&content_nature=34&msg_id2=314
[4] Office of the Privacy Commissioner for Personal Data, HK, Case No.:2013C05 https://www.pcpd.org.hk/english/enforcement/case_notes/casenotes_2.php?id=2013C05&content_type=&content_nature=&msg_id2=417
[5] Note that in some data protection laws, the way fees for data access requests may be calculated are specified; also that they can be adjusted by the regulator, including before they are paid by an individual seeking access.

a reasonable fee for access requests, organisations should not make a profit by charging excessive fees. The general guide is that organisations should charge a fee that allows them to recover only the labour costs and actual out-of-pocket expenses involved in the process of complying with a data access request.)

Guidance for organisations

The above case studies demonstrate the importance of complying with the access requests made by individuals under the data protection law, whichever jurisdiction is involved. Organisations should adopt the good practices as laid out in the "Checklist of Good Practices".

CHECKLIST OF GOOD PRACTICES

Organisations should adopt the following practices when they receive requests from individuals to access and correct their personal data held by the organisations:

- Take the applicable statutory time period laws seriously.
- Authenticate the identity of the individual making the request to avoid disclosing personal data to the wrong person.
- Have policies and processes in place to quickly acknowledge the request and then to respond to it without undue delay.
- If the request falls within an exemption and your organisation decides to rely on that exemption, give written notice of the refusal and your organisation's reasons for it within the required time period.
- If there is a valid reason why your organisation must not comply with the request, give written notice of refusal and, if permitted by the data protection law, reasons for refusal within the required time period.
- If your organisation has technical difficulty retrieving the personal data within the stipulated timeline, put in place a plan to remedy the situation as soon as reasonably possible.
- Commence processing the request as soon as practical to ensure that there are no delays, even if the information is not released until any access fees are paid.

🔒 85 Uploading videos to social media may be fun to some but not to others

I'm sure many of us have witnessed this pervasive social phenomenon (if you are not already a participant of it) where people see something interesting, shoot a video of it and share it on social media. The subject matter can be anything, ranging from food to flora and fauna to funny antics. Each of these categories has its own band of followers, as indicated by the number of "Likes" on Facebook, for example. But what captures most people's attention are the funny antics that bring about lots of LOL (laughing out loud).

Funny antics to some but not to others

The funny antics can be of at least two types:

- those that are pre-planned and orchestrated, with some degree of free play to bring about unexpected funny sequences and
- those that catch people unawares, sometimes in their most embarrassing moments, and making fun of them at their expense.

In the first type of funny antics, someone can get hurt physically (for example, rolling down a hill in a beer barrel), but no one is hurt emotionally. It's all for the fun of it.

The second type isn't at all funny to the people – the victims – who are the butt of the joke. They may feel ridiculed or be hurt emotionally. People laugh at their clumsy fall down the escalator, their uncontrolled vomiting at the train station, or their wardrobe malfunction at a party. The victims consider that other people should respect their feelings and that they have no right to video them in those embarrassing situations and then upload the video to social media for the entertainment of thousands of total strangers.

How can the data protection law protect these "victims" since the videos are shot at public places and thus may be deemed as publicly available data? It may be argued that distress has been caused to the "victims", and they should have the recourse to not give consent to the "perpetrators" to post their videos. But there is no clear-cut answer. This is where moral values and ethics, sense of decency and propriety, and even anti-harassment laws, may have to be called into play. The providers of social media platforms could have a "take down" policy of posted content when requested by the "victims" themselves or their supporters to do so.

Insiders' unauthorised uploading of CCTV footage

Uploading "poor taste" videos indiscriminately to social media is not just confined to citizen journalists on the prowl. There have been occasions where some insiders in an organisation gain unauthorised access to the organisation's CCTV recordings, extract video footage of their colleagues who are caught in embarrassing situations and post it on social media. In such instances, the perpetrator(s) may be taken to task for unauthorised access to personal information and disclosing such information without the affected individual's consent.

CHECKLIST OF GOOD PRACTICES

- Organisations that host social media platforms should have a "take down" policy of posted content when requested to do so.
- Organisations should safeguard against insiders gaining unauthorised access to CCTV footage and uploading it to social media without consent.

86 Watch what you say about your employees or clients

How often have you heard people gossiping about others in a business or organisational context? They may be bosses and other employees gossiping about each other, for example, or salespersons, property agents or financial advisers gossiping about their clients.

Such gossiping happens everywhere – in public places such as cafés, buses and trains, in the office, as well as on social media. Did you know that your careless gossip or disclosures about others (even with good intent) can get you and your organisation into trouble under the data protection law?

Case study #1: Kindergarten headmistress reveals employee's divorce status

A teacher was unhappy that her headmistress disclosed her divorced status to colleagues at the kindergarten without her consent. The teacher complained to the regulator.[1]

The regulator reminded the headmistress that the organisation collected the teacher's personal data for human resource purposes related to her employment. The subsequent disclosure within the organisation or to anyone else was not directly related to the original collection purpose.

As a result, the headmistress had to apologise to the teacher and undertook not to further disclose her personal data in the future.

---

[1] Office of the Privacy Commissioner for Personal Data, HK, Case No.:2005A02, https://www.pcpd.org.hk/english/enforcement/case_notes/casenotes_2.php?id=2005A02&content_type=&content_nature=&msg_id2=239

Case Study #2: Property management company employee makes fun of resident

An unidentified individual made fun of a property owner in a poem. It was uploaded to an online chat room operated by residents of the condominium where the property owner lived. Unfortunately, the property owner soon discovered their name along with abbreviations of their flat and block number, which were commonly adopted and used by the management company. The property owner was displeased about being a subject of ridicule and lodged a complaint with the regulator.[2]

The regulator considered that the management company for the condominium was responsible for the poem being uploaded to the chat room because it was uploaded by one or more of its employees in the course of their employment (versus the upload being done by them in their personal or domestic capacity). The regulator reached this decision because:

- the poem was confirmed to have been uploaded through the computer located at the organisation's management office, the use of which was shared amongst its employees
- its employees confirmed that they would visit the website in question to check the latest comments from the residents which might be relevant to management matters
- its employees were aware that some senior officers of the organisation had been the target of attack in the website
- the complainant's name and address were personal data that could be easily obtained and known to its employees and
- a piece of paper containing the user ID and log-in password was stuck near the computer so that employees could easily share using it.

The regulator concluded that the organisation did not have in place sufficient monitoring, policies and guidelines to prevent its employees using personal data about property owners improperly. It directed the organisation to take remedial steps to protect property owners' personal data.

---

[2] Office of the Privacy Commissioner for Personal Data, HK, Case No.: 2008A01 https://www.pcpd.org.hk/english/enforcement/case_notes/casenotes_2.php?id=2008A01&content_type=&content_nature=&msg_id2=302

So what can we learn from the above case studies?

Watch what you say about another individual, whether or not it is with good intent, or if you share inappropriate personal data of others. As the saying goes, "Walls have ears", and the seven degrees of separation also applies. You will never know if someone spills the beans on you or the person whose personal data you disclosed without consent might discover it and this backfires on you. It will be a greater risk for you if you share personal data online as there are no "walls".

So often, I read comments from property agents, financial advisers and freelancers complaining about their clients on Facebook, supported by a number of "Likes". If employees can get fired with irresponsible comments, how much worse can it get for these business owners (or data controllers) when it comes to failing to comply with the data protection law?

As for organisations, the above case studies can also happen in your office and implicate your company. Ensure your staff are trained and understand their obligations under the data protection law. Your organisation will be held responsible for any breaches by your employees in the course of their employment. So ensure you have policies and guidelines in place and continue to monitor for potential data breaches, negligence or even mischief that may arise.

If your organisation uses chat rooms or social media, create an online usage and social media policy that limits what your employees can do, sharing only the data needed to provide the service or feature.

CHECKLIST OF GOOD PRACTICES

When disclosing personal information about other individuals, organisations and individuals should be aware of the boundaries they must not cross and take the following precautionary measures:

- Watch what you say (or write) about another individual, whether or not it is with good intent, or if you share inappropriate personal data of others. Their personal data needs to be protected from unauthorised disclosures.
- Ensure your employees are trained and understand their obligations under the data protection law.
- Develop and implement relevant policies if your organisation uses chat rooms or social media.

🔒 87 You leave behind more than your footprints and fingerprints

So, you have:

- trodden the corridors of power and history of the ancient monarchs, aristocrats, noblemen, the famous and the infamous
- traipsed about towns and villages in search of exotic local produce and indigenous handicrafts and
- trampled small creatures underfoot on sandy beaches and verdant mountain trails.

You feel satisfied that you now have the bragging rights to declare: "I've been there, done that!" You have left behind your footprints and fingerprints at the "must-go" places of the world.

But do you realise that when you travel overseas you leave behind more than your footprints and fingerprints? You actually leave behind a whole trail of "infoprints" – personal data about you. Here are a few examples of where your "infoprints" are being captured:

- at the immigration checkpoint when you enter a country
- when you book a tour or hotel accommodation overseas through a travel agency or web portal
- when you use a payment card to make purchases overseas and the transaction is not done electronically
- when you use the roaming feature of your mobile phone overseas

The immigration officer who checked your passport, the tour agent who took you to scenic attractions, the hotels you stayed in, the restaurants you dined at, the shops you patronised, and the telecommunications companies whose services you used, all have some of your personal data. Can you be assured that these organisations and individuals overseas would respect the confidentiality and privacy of your personal data and handle them appropriately and securely?

Transfer of personal data overseas

A number of jurisdictions around the world have data protection laws that place restrictions on organisations sending personal data across international borders.

However, those data protection laws do not apply if you book your tour or hotel accommodation directly with a tour agency or hotel overseas or through a web portal located overseas. In these instances, what can you do to have some assurance that your personal data will be handled appropriately and securely by the overseas tour agency, hotel or online service provider? Here are some tips:

- First, consider whether you will be providing personal data to an organisation that is located in a jurisdiction with a data protection law and whether that law is enforced by a responsible regulator.
- Next, check the published privacy policies of the overseas organisations, especially the consent clauses, your rights, the company's responsibilities and obligations – although a published privacy policy is no guarantee that the organisation actually acts in accordance with it.
- Finally, provide minimal personal data to the overseas organisation. If booking online, complete only those data fields that are compulsory (as indicated by asterisks) or use a different booking site if there are alternatives. If booking over the phone, challenge requests for personal data except where it is obviously necessary.

Vigilance is the order of the day

It is near impossible to wipe off every trace of your "infoprints" when you travel overseas. But you can minimise the risk of exposure by adopting a policy of self-vigilance. Here are some tips:

- Use web portals offered by reputable organisations when you make your overseas holiday or hotel bookings.
- Make payments online only if the website indicates that a reputable organisation has implemented a secure online payment mechanism – if you don't know about secure online payment mechanisms, the

banks or other organisations that issued the payment card you want to use will be able to tell you what to check before using your card.

■ As mentioned above, check the published privacy policies of organisations to which you may disclose your personal data.

■ Do not disclose your personal data or passport details unnecessarily (such as to sales outlets or sales people). If organisations seek to collect it, do not be shy about asking them the purpose for which they need it – or, to put it the other way around, keep the personal data that you disclose to the minimum.

■ Ensure that the salesperson handling your payment card does not make multiple imprints on paper payment slips or take snapshots of your card details in non-electronic transactions. (In some retail stores or restaurants, for example, the cashier's counter is located a distance away from the customers' area. The salesperson takes the customer's payment card to process the payment behind the counter. The customer should make sure that the salesperson is within sight.)

Remember, you do not want to leave behind more than your footprints and fingerprints when you return from your overseas trips or holidays.

CHECKLIST OF GOOD PRACTICES

Individuals planning and going for holidays overseas should take the following precautionary measures:

■ Only use web portals of reputable organisations when you book your holiday or hotel room overseas.

■ Make sure the reputable organisations have implemented secure online payment mechanisms. Check with your payment card issuer if you need more information about secure online payments.

■ Find out if the organisation is located in a jurisdiction that has a data protection law that is enforced and check their privacy policies before you disclose your personal data.

■ Do not disclose your personal data unnecessarily. Disclose just enough for the intended purpose. Choose alternatives if the organisation seems to be seeking personal data unnecessarily.

■ In non-electronic payment card transactions, ensure the salesperson handling your card does not make multiple imprints or take photos of your card details.

🔒 **88** Organisations disclosing personal data to third-parties – proper consent sought?

Almost all data protection laws in the world today require organisations to obtain consent from individuals before they can collect, use or disclose the individuals' personal data. But most jurisdictions don't prescribe how the consent clauses are to be worded, except for some guiding principles and guidelines. This is because different industry sectors, and even different organisations within the same sector, are so varied that it is well-nigh impossible to have standard consent clauses. The crafting of consent clauses is thus left to individual organisations.

So, are most organisations doing it properly in seeking consent from individuals in their consent clauses? I have come across a few horror stories of ambiguity in the wording of the consent clauses, especially where the individuals' personal data are to be disclosed to third-parties outside the organisation.

Update of club members' personal particulars

A country club, of which I'm a member, sent out a form to all its members to update their personal particulars. I filled in my membership number, full name, home address, telephone number, email address, national identification number, and bank account details (for the electronic transfer of funds to pay for the monthly subscription fees). So far so good. When I came to the end of the form I was alarmed by the small print that read:

> *I authorise [Name of Club] or its representatives to obtain any information from any source which it may require.*

The term "representatives" was so broad that it could refer to agents acting on behalf of the club, a separate entity of the club, or an outsourced vendor of the club membership system. This was tantamount to my giving the club a *carte blanche* to obtain any information from any source about me.

I sent an email to the membership department asking them to clarify who their "representatives" were, what additional "information" about me they would want to collect, and what these "sources" were. The membership department pointed me to the club's data protection policy, which was just as vague. Even the club's legal officer could not enlighten me further, as the club had only recently implemented their data protection policy. I came away with the feeling that the club had not thought through carefully the operational implications of their consent clause on their members. Worse, they could have simply "copied" the consent clause from another organisation without tailoring it to suit the unique operations of the club.

Registration of purchasers' personal particulars

I bought a new household appliance for my home. It came with a one-year warranty and exchange policy. The warranty could only be activated after I registered with the supplier the serial number, model and description of the appliance, plus my personal particulars. Filling in all these details was not a problem for me as I had done so umpteen times with other appliances and equipment I had bought in the past. What alarmed me was the consent clause in small print at the end of the warranty form, with two boxes for me to tick either "yes" or "no":

> *I disagree with [Name of Supplier] collecting, using and disclosing my personal data for the purposes of this warranty and for the repair or servicing of the registered appliance by [Name of Supplier] or any service centre.*

First of all, the text was phrased in the negative, so if I were not careful and ticked the "yes" box, I would end up with not granting the supplier permission to collect, use and disclose my personal data for the stated purpose. The warranty then would become null and void.

I felt uneasy ticking the "no" box to validate the warranty because it was too encompassing and unclear. I would have consented to the supplier collecting and using my personal data for the purpose of the warranty, but not to disclose it to any service centre without knowing what their relationship with the supplier was. The service centre could be part of the supplier's group of companies, a joint venture or a totally outsourced outfit (which could even be based overseas).

What the organisations should have done

As shown in the anecdotes above, organisations should craft consent clauses not merely to satisfy legal compliance with data protection laws. They should think through carefully the operational implications of their consent clauses on their customers or members. They should use clear and unambiguous language and avoid such vague and all-encompassing terms as "any". Where organisations provide choices for their customers or members, they must word the text such that it is not too all-encompassing. Some customers or members may consent to selective disclosure of their personal data but not to the whole consent clause. In such instances, organisations should consider splitting their consent clauses into parts to allow their customers or members to make selective choices.

When seeking consent from customers or members for disclosing their personal data to third-parties, organisations must not use vague terms like "representatives" or "associates", but be more explicit in stating their relationships with these third-parties. Examples of these third-parties could be entities within the same group of companies, joint ventures or partnerships, or external vendors and service providers. While it may be argued that entities within the same group of companies could be treated as one, most data protection laws view such intra-group data sharing as external disclosure, especially where each of the entities is a legal entity on its own.

If organisations intend to disclose their customers' or members' personal data to third-parties for a different purpose – sending of related marketing and promotional materials, for example – they should state it explicitly in the consent clause. And organisations should give their customers or members a choice to opt-in and not assume that they agree by default.

What should individuals do?

Individuals should familiarise themselves with their rights under the local data protection laws so that they can question organisations if the consent clauses are unclear or not specific enough. If in doubt, they should not give their consent so willingly to the organisations, especially where their personal data is to be disclosed to third-parties whose relationships with the primary organisations are not clear.

CHECKLIST OF GOOD PRACTICES

- When seeking individuals' consent for the disclosure of their personal data to third-parties, organisations should:
  - Consider the operational implications and not just legal compliance with data protection laws.
  - Refrain from using all-encompassing terms like "any", "representatives" or "associates".
  - Be specific about the relationships between the third-parties and the organisation.
  - Consider splitting the consent clause into parts to allow individuals to make selective choices.
  - Spell out any new purpose if it is different from the primary organisation's.
- Individuals should:
  - Familiarise themselves with their data protection rights so that they can question the organisations on their consent clauses.
  - Refrain from providing personal data when in doubt.

Final Thoughts

There you have it – 88 potential privacy breaches that can get organisations and individuals into trouble with the data protection law. These present risks to any organisation in terms of how personal data is collected, used, disclosed, stored or disposed of.

A fellow privacy professional asked us why we chose the number 88. "I take it 88 is a lucky number. Is that true? If true, is it a bad thing to associate a lucky number with a bad thing – a privacy breach?"

Maybe. But here is our take: how many times have we exclaimed how lucky we are when we narrowly avoided a misfortune or mishap? There is a sense of relief and we are thankful that nothing terrible happened. It is also not a coincidence that we finished this book at an auspicious time during the Lunar New Year period.

We hope that this book is your lucky guide. We have revealed many ways individuals and organisations can be blind-sided in the area of data protection and privacy: some of them are obvious – once mentioned. But they are easily overlooked in practice, especially when we are busy. For example, losing files by leaving them on a bus or in a café because you haven't figured out a way of carrying them around securely. Others are less obvious, such as knowing that there is a hard disk inside a multi-function device (that is, printer/scanner/fax/copier machine) and removing it before getting rid of the machine. Some are easy to build into everyday processes – for example, moving computer screens and CCTV monitors on reception desks and security counters so that passersby can't see personal data on them. Others require discipline and for all employees to play their part conscientiously.

For example, securely transferring confidential documents within an organisation or doing regular housekeeping to get rid of personal data that no longer needs to be retained.

By looking in the rear mirror of past cases and raising some of our own real-life experiences, we sincerely hope we have convinced you that you need a roadmap to your organisation's operational compliance with new or stricter data protection laws now in place or on the horizon. We hope that we have given you a clearer view of what to look out for.

What's next?

To recap, instead of looking at compliance with the data protection law from a perspective of privacy principles, use an information life cycle approach instead. A life cycle approach includes the privacy principles but makes it easy to look at them through an operational and therefore practical lens. It brings the privacy principles to life.

From our experience, many of our clients have attended data protection courses that cover the technicalities of the privacy principles. The courses give participants the "what" of the data protection law. But we constantly hear from our clients that they found it difficult to understand the legal terms used, let alone apply the principles to their daily work. The courses seem to use few if any examples and case studies of everyday business or operational scenarios to address the myriad of lingering questions and practical uncertainties to respond to "Now that I've finished this training course, what do I actually need to do?"

Metaphorically speaking, even those who have learned and understood the data protection law have only been given the "appetiser" of what must be done to comply with the law. We hope that this book provides the "main dish" of how to achieve operational compliance, beyond just legal compliance, and helps to fill competency gaps. And we hope this book whets your appetite for more, that it makes you keen to apply a worldwide standard and framework in your privacy programme and operations. For you, the International Association of Privacy Professionals (IAPP) provides two useful international certifications that provide data protection know-how – the Certified

Information Privacy Manager (CIPM) qualification for data protection officers and compliance managers. And the Certified Information Privacy Technologist (CIPT) qualification for application developers as well as infocomm or information security professionals. Both these useful certifications approach privacy from an information life cycle perspective and cover not just the legal aspects of data protection but also the practical operational aspects. More information about these courses and classroom training can be found on IAPP's website at www.iapp.org.

As a parting note, we would like to recommend what we fondly call the APSR (Assess, Protect, Sustain and Respond) approach to help further complement your efforts in achieving operational compliance. This a useful and practical privacy operational life cycle, first developed by IAPP and further enhanced by Straits Interactive, which adopts a risk-based approach to helping organisations get compliant and stay compliant. It is taught in the CIPM course.

The privacy operational life cycle

The first step in any organisation's data protection programme is to put in place its data protection committee. It may consist of stakeholders who head the processing and are owners of personal data within your organisation. It determines the scope of operations and the governance structure of your data protection programme.

Then you are ready to adopt the APSR operational life cycle.

First, you should "**Assess**" the possible risks relating to personal data in your business operations. You can do this by:

- taking a data inventory of all personal data in your care and
- documenting a data flow diagram of how personal data is collected, used, disclosed, stored and disposed within each department.

This should identify for you all the threats affecting each stage of the information life cycle and the organisation's vulnerabilities in meeting those threats – the so-called gap analysis.

In this book we have presented you with 88 potential privacy breaches that can happen to any organisation, many of which could be applicable to yours. In the following diagram, we have summarised 35 potential exposures to look out for:

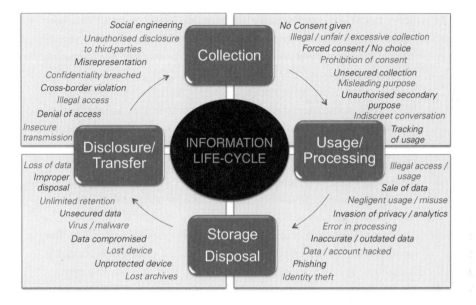

Next, identify:

- the privacy framework that applies to your organisation and that must therefore guide your privacy operations – that is, your local data protection law – and
- your organisation's regulatory risks, gaps and exposures – that is, do a data protection or privacy impact assessment[1].

The privacy impact assessment should also take into consideration the risks, gaps and exposures you have identified earlier. Once you have done the necessary activities, you are now ready for the next step.

In the "**Protect**" phase, you will need to address the risks, gaps and exposures identified in the data protection or privacy impact assessment. You do this by developing policies, guidelines and actions that need to be taken. In order to be effective, these should be a combination of administrative, physical and technical measures.

The checklists of good practices we have provided at the end of each chapter in this book will serve as a useful guide. Find the chapters that are relevant to your operations, but do take note that they have

---

[1] Refer to the diagram in the Introduction where we mapped the general data protection principles within the information life cycle for your convenience.

to be tailored to your organisation's unique circumstances. The most effective measures are those which are aligned with and embedded in the operating processes of your organisation so that there is employee ownership, responsibility and accountability.

Remember, the good practices and measures will need to be formally documented in your internal data protection and information security policies. In turn, your employment contracts should require employees to comply with all your internal policies, with disciplinary consequences if they fail to do so. With this combination, compliance with your internal policies can be enforced.

The "**Sustain**" phase is beyond the scope of this book. This involves monitoring, auditing and communications.

In our experience, many organisations stop at the Protect stage. The problem here is that the required policies and practices are quickly forgotten after the compliance project is over or after the privacy taskforce has met its objectives. Organisations, especially those new to data protection, hardly monitor any regulatory changes and metrics of whether the controls have been effectively implemented.

Because there are no continuing education and awareness programmes or even audits of the organisation's policies and practices, the organisation remains susceptible to the breaches we have identified in this book due to poor implementation and shallow awareness.

Finally, the "**Respond**" phase is to ensure that the organisation can effectively respond to complaints, inquiries, or requests about how personal data has been processed. In the worst-case scenario, there could be data or privacy breaches which require a formal breach response plan to be executed. If there are any such incidents, the organisation must investigate and prevent any further harm from happening. If there is a probe by the regulator, a critical factor is to demonstrate accountability and provide evidence that the organisation did everything possible to prevent the incident from happening.

For those organisations starting their compliance efforts from scratch or looking at improvements to make, a good accountability framework to consider is the Nymity Privacy Management Accountability Framework. (This is especially so if your organisation operates in multiple jurisdictions with data protection laws.) It sets out 13 high-level processes that describe how to implement a comprehensive data protection programme. Then it provides a number of proactive activities to choose from – use some or all of them – in terms of regulatory measures organisations should take to track and monitor compliance.

As can be seen, one cannot underestimate the amount of work needed to ensure operational compliance with the data protection law. That is why we at Straits Interactive have created an integrated software platform based on the APSR framework to assist our clients to manage and sustain their compliance efforts in the shortest time possible. We use this same platform to train and enable our clients, much to their appreciation, as it helps enhance automation, collaboration and productivity. Called Data Protection Management System (DPMS), a trial version of the software can be accessed at www.dataprotectionmgmt.com/book

At the end of the day, having a mature data protection and privacy management programme that supports operational compliance should help organisations justify investment in such a programme. It provides them with a competitive edge over competitors and increases client trust compared with competitors that have only a laissez-faire approach to their clients' privacy. Besides assurance, improved standards of information justify lower premiums in cyber-insurance – protection which every organisation should consider to manage its information security risk.

In conclusion, the following quote reflects the reality of data privacy today that all organisations and individuals covered by the data protection law should recognise:

> *When it comes to privacy and accountability, people always demand the former for themselves and the latter for everyone else.*[2]

---

[2] Quote from Glen David Brin, an American scientist and award-winning author of science fiction.

Acknowledgements

When we first proposed this book, the title was *50 Privacy Breaches*. By the time we completed the book, the number had grown to 88. By a stroke of good luck, we have been very fortunate to be at the right place at the right time to make this happen, being connected with privacy professionals, data protection officers, legal counsels and solution-providers, both locally and globally.

As consultants with Straits Interactive, our work in providing advisory services, audits, training and system implementation relating to data protection in Singapore, Malaysia and the region has also given us the opportunity to learn from our clients and course participants. In addition, by referring to case notes published by privacy commissions around the world, we have been able to write fairly comprehensive checklists to accompany each chapter. This was also helped by the informal consultations and discussions we had with officials and investigators from the data protection commissions in Singapore and Malaysia.

Hence, we wish to thank the following people and organisations for their contributions to our inspiration and knowledge, and for their help in creating this book:

- Staff and consultants with Straits Interactive, especially Alvin Toh, William Lim, Celine Chew, Angela Schooling, Wong Mei Kwan, Azhar Azib, Andrew Fam, Angeline Shepherdson and Benjamin Shepherdson
- Karen d'Almeida for the excellent book cover design

- Our legal advisors, Prof Abu Bakar, Prof Ang Peng Hwa, Dr Toh See Kiat
- International Association of Privacy Professionals for providing an excellent reference model of the Privacy Operational Life Cycle
- Personal Data Protection Commission, Singapore
- Personal Data Protection Department, Malaysia
- Duncan Brown, GM, Shred-It Pte Ltd, Singapore
- Terry McQuay, President and CEO of Nymity Inc.
- Melvin Neo and Justin Lau, our editors at Marshall Cavendish, who have been so patient and supportive of this book

Disclaimer

This book is intended to provide general information and tips on how to avoid operational data protection/privacy breaches in situations we have encountered personally. It does not constitute legal advice. If you would like information about specific circumstances or situations, you may contact us through the website of Straits Interactive Pte Ltd or Lyn Boxall LLC. Otherwise, you should consider obtaining legal advice from your regular legal advisers in your country.

About the Authors

Kevin Shepherdson, CIPM, CIPT, GRCP

As the CEO and co-founder of Straits Interactive Pte Ltd, Kevin Shepherdson provides and drives the vision, strategy and innovation of the company's Data Privacy & GRC (Governance, Risk Management & Compliance) offerings that build upon the foundation of enabling trusted businesses and responsible marketing. He is a Certified Information Privacy Manager (CIPM) and Privacy Technologist (CIPT), awarded by the International Association of Privacy Professionals (IAPP). In addition, he is co-chair of the IAPP Singapore KnowledgeNet chapter as well as an official trainer for IAPP's privacy as well as OCEG (Open Compliance & Ethics Group) GRC professional certification courses.

Kevin has consulted with more than 100 companies in the area of data protection and has trained a few thousand people on Singapore's and Malaysia's Personal Data Protection Act. He brings his experience in marketing and technology to Straits Interactive from Oracle, where he was head of demand generation, customer intelligence and the call centre for Asia-Pacific. Having worked with foreign multinational companies with strong data practices, Kevin is familiar with data privacy and protection laws in both the US and Europe. Prior to this, he was an award-winning marketing strategist at Sun Microsystems.

A veteran in the IT industry, Kevin has worked for a number of multinationals, including Creative Technology, Sun Microsystems and Oracle Corporation. Throughout his corporate career, Kevin was a multiple award-winner of both worldwide and Asia-Pacific employee excellence awards, including marketing excellence, market intelligence and technology innovation. He is a sought-after speaker for data privacy and protection issues in the ASEAN region.

Kevin holds a MSc (Internet & Media) degree from Nanyang Technological University and a Bachelor of Arts & Social Sciences from the National University of Singapore, and is a Certified GRC Professional as well as a certified Master Practitioner in Neuro-Linguistic Programming (NLP), Neuro-Semantics and Hypnotic Communication.

William Hioe, CIPM, CIPT

William Hioe is a senior consultant with Straits Interactive. He is a Certified Information Privacy Manager (CIPM) and Certified Information Privacy Technologist (CIPT). He has more than three decades of Information and Communications Technology (ICT) experience in the government and public sector. Currently, he is the managing director of Cynergie Consulting Pte Ltd, a company founded by him to offer consultancy and training services in strategic ICT planning, strategy development, policy formulation, enterprise architecting and process improvement. Prior to that he was senior director of strategic planning at the National Computer Board (NCB)/ Infocomm Development Authority of Singapore (IDA). Before that he was an assistant director in Systems & Computer Organisation at the Singapore Ministry of Defence.

During his career in the government and public sector, William has built up a wealth of knowledge and expertise in ICT planning, development, implementation and project management in such diverse areas as human resource management, financial management, logistics management, procurement management, decision support systems, wargaming, and command and control systems. At NCB/ IDA he was involved in the visioning, strategising and development of national-level ICT masterplans. He was also responsible for ICT policy research and formulation in such areas as secure e-transactions, digital signature, anti-spam, data governance, and data privacy and protection. With Cynergie Consulting, he has consulted with governments in South-East Asia in the areas of ICT masterplanning, visioning and strategy development.

William graduated with a B.Sc.(Engg) in electrical and electronics engineering from the University of London and a Masters in control engineering and operational research from the University of Cambridge. He is a certified enterprise architecture practitioner (TOGAF) from The Open Group.

Lyn Boxall, B.Com, LL.B (Melbourne), LL.M (Monash), GAICD, GRCP, GRCA, CIPM

Lyn Boxall is a lawyer with extensive private practice experience and international in-house experience. After 10 years as a lawyer in the banking and finance department of a prominent international law firm in Australia, Lyn moved in-house as Chief Legal Officer for GE Capital for Australia/New Zealand in 1996. This introduced her to privacy/data protection at a practical level, including as part of an international in-house team formed to embed the requirements of the 1995 EU Data Protection Directive into the company's global products and operations. She was also responsible for operational compliance, including from a data protection/privacy perspective, in GE Capital's very extensive call-centre operations in Australia.

Moving to Singapore in 2000, Lyn served as Regional General Counsel for Visa Asia Pacific for nine years, with responsibility for operational risk management and legal, regulatory and operational compliance with pan-regional scope. She left Visa after its global operations were centralised into the US and established Khardung Consulting, a corporate governance, compliance, and regulatory and risk consulting business. In March 2015, Lyn established Lyn Boxall LLC, practising Singapore law and specialising in data protection/privacy, information/cyber-security, payment systems, and governance, risk and compliance.

Lyn is an Advocate and Solicitor of The Supreme Court of Singapore, a Member of the New York Bar, a Solicitor of The High Court of England and Wales and a Barrister and Solicitor of The Supreme Court of Victoria and of the High Court of Australia.

Index